VOICES

INTERMEDIATE

CHIA SUAN CHONG AND LEWIS LANSFORD

National Geographic Learning

Australia · Brazil · Canada · Mexico · Singapore · United Kingdom · United States

National Geographic Learning,
a Cengage Company

Voices Intermediate Student's Book, 1st Edition
Chia Suan Chong and Lewis Lansford

Publisher: Rachael Gibbon

Commissioning Editor: Kayleigh Buller

Development Editor: Nicole Elliott

Director of Global Marketing: Ian Martin

Product Marketing Manager: Caitlin Thomas

Heads of Regional Marketing:

   Charlotte Ellis (Europe, Middle East and Africa)

   Irina Pereyra (Latin America)

   Justin Kaley (Asia)

   Joy MacFarland (US and Canada)

Production Manager: Daisy Sosa

Media Researcher: Leila Hishmeh

Art Director: Brenda Carmichael

Operations Support: Hayley Chwazik-Gee

Manufacturing Manager: Eyvett Davis

Composition: Composure

Audio Producer: New York Audio

Contributing writer: Billie Jago (Endmatter)

Advisors: Anna Blackmore, Bruna Caltabiano,
   Dale Coulter and Mike Sayer

For permission to use material from this text or product,
submit all requests online at **cengage.com/permissions**
Further permissions questions can be emailed to
permissionrequest@cengage.com

Student's Book with Online Practice and Student's eBook:
ISBN: 978-0-357-45867-9

Student's Book:
ISBN: 978-0-357-44319-4

National Geographic Learning
Cheriton House, North Way,
Andover, Hampshire, SP10 5BE
United Kingdom

Locate your local office at **international.cengage.com/region**

Visit National Geographic Learning online at **ELTNGL.com**
Visit our corporate website at **www.cengage.com**

Printed in Greece by Bakis SA
Print Number: 01 Print Year: 2021

Contents

3

Scope and sequence

		GRAMMAR	VOCABULARY	PRONUNCIATION
1 **Identity** *Pages 10–21*		present simple and present continuous; *used to* and *would*	character adjectives	understanding *-ing* endings; saying /ʊ/ and /uː/
2 **Success** *Pages 22–33*		present perfect and past simple; *have to, must, don't have to* and *mustn't*	work collocations	saying consonant groups (1): word endings; saying /ə/ and /ɜː/
3 **Working together** *Pages 34–45*		past tenses review; *make* and *let*	multi-word verbs	saying words spelled with *ear*; saying /aʊ/, /əʊ/ and /oʊ/
4 **Routines** *Pages 46–57*		zero and first conditionals; quantifiers	dependent prepositions	saying words beginning with /p/, /b/, /k/ and /g/; understanding connected speech
5 **Art** *Pages 58–69*		second conditional; *-ed* and *-ing* adjectives	feelings and how things make you feel	saying voiced and unvoiced final consonants; using sentence stress (1): stressing words for emphasis

READING	LISTENING	WRITING	COMMUNICATION SKILL	CRITICAL THINKING	USEFUL LANGUAGE
an article about online identities; previewing the text	people talking about their character in the past and present; understanding sequence: noticing time changes	an online self-introduction; proofreading before clicking 'post'	understanding different communication styles	evaluating arguments	talking about photographs; introducing yourself
an article about success; reading fluently: noticing chunks	a conversation about job interviews; summarizing: bullet points	a how-to article; planning: deciding what information to include	building trust	interpreting line graphs	talking about practice; building trust
an online discussion about competition in sport; identifying supporting examples	a news report about a team protecting animals; thinking about what you already know	an email of apology; structuring an email of apology	managing conflict	reflecting on ideas	talking about important people; managing conflict; dealing with your mistakes
an article about routines; finding meaning: using affixes	a conversation about building good habits; dealing with unknown words or phrases	a note about household routines; using headings	dealing with uncertainty	applying knowledge to a new situation	adapting to different ways of dealing with uncertainty; explaining how things work
an article about art; summarizing a text	explorers talking about art; understanding contrast (1): listening for contrast	an event description; writing an event description	dealing with intonation misunderstandings	analysing evidence: supporting quotations	dealing with intonation misunderstandings; describing an event

Scope and sequence

		GRAMMAR	VOCABULARY	PRONUNCIATION
6	**Where I'm from** *Pages 70–81*	present perfect continuous; describing movement	towns and cities	understanding weak auxiliary verbs; saying /l/ and /r/
7	**Balance** *Pages 82–93*	talking about the future; verb patterns with infinitive or *-ing*	money	using sentence stress (2): stressing important words; saying the letter *r*
8	**Essentials** *Pages 94–105*	defining and non-defining relative clauses; comparatives	food adjectives	understanding elision in words with *th*; saying /ɪ/ and /iː/
9	**Taking a break** *Pages 106–117*	third conditional; giving advice	holiday phrases	saying aspirated /p/, /t/ and /k/; saying consonant groups (2): inserting a short vowel
10	**The senses** *Pages 118–129*	passives; making predictions	technology and the senses	noticing challenging sounds; correcting pronunciation mistakes

READING	LISTENING	WRITING	COMMUNICATION SKILL	CRITICAL THINKING	USEFUL LANGUAGE
an article about a temporary city; recognizing synonyms	people sharing childhood stories; listening for signposts	a travel plan; describing steps in a plan	managing group conversations	interpreting bubble charts	managing group conversations; putting activities in time order
an advice column about time management; identifying supporting reasons	a podcast about money advice; identifying supporting information	a pros and cons essay; using an outline for a pros and cons essay	understanding ways of processing information	categorizing	talking to people with different ways of processing information; writing a pros and cons essay
an article about life on the International Space Station; recognizing ellipsis	people talking about different foods; activating vocabulary	a blog post about essential skills; choosing a topic for a blog post	giving and receiving feedback	personalizing	giving feedback; saying what's important
an article about time off from work; understanding contrast (2): reading for contrast	a conversation about holiday advice; listening for specific information	an email of complaint; how to write an email of complaint	dealing with unexpected behaviours	interpreting bar charts	considering unexpected behaviours; writing an email of complaint
an article about the senses; paraphrasing	people talking about future technology; collaborative listening	a description of a memory; showing instead of telling	listening to people's problems	interpreting a diagram	asking questions about famous buildings; asking questions when listening to people's problems; time expressions

Meet the explorers

ALISON WRIGHT

Lives: US
Job: I'm a photographer and writer. I've travelled to more than 150 countries and have published eleven books, including one about how I recovered after a terrible bus crash in Laos. I enjoy sharing my photographs and stories with travellers.
What did you want to do when you were younger? I got my first camera when I was ten and I wanted to be a photographer and writer ever since I was fifteen.
Find Alison: Unit 4

BRIAN BUMA

Lives: US
Job: I'm an ecology professor and author. I study changes to the planet – from wildfires to landslides to the movements of wildlife – in response to changing climates. I'm currently doing research into the effects of snow loss on forests around the world.
What do you do in your free time? Snowboard, mountain bike, build guitars
Find Brian: Unit 1

ALYEA PIERCE

Lives: US
Job: I'm a poet and educator who focuses on untold stories across the world. As an Afro-Caribbean female writer, I enjoy helping young people find their voices through creative writing and theatre.
Where is 'home'? Home for me is anywhere close to nature and art.
Find Alyea: Unit 5

FRANCISCO ESTRADA-BELLI

Lives: US
Job: I'm an archaeologist – this means I explore the history of an area by digging up what people left behind. I run an archaeological project in the Maya Biosphere Reserve in Guatemala. I've written about the Maya civilization and I'm also a research professor at Tulane University in New Orleans.
Describe yourself in three words: Archaeologist, explorer, father
Find Francisco: Unit 7

ANDREJ GAJIĆ

Lives: Bosnia
Job: I'm a shark research scientist – this means I work in the conservation of sharks and study the diseases caused by sea pollution in the Mediterranean Sea and other marine environments. I'm also a biology professor, author and underwater photographer.
What do you always take with you when you travel? Laptop (so I can work), camera, passport, notebook and chopsticks.
Find Andrej: Unit 4

GABBY SALAZAR

Lives: US
Job: I'm a conservation and wildlife photographer. Now, I'm also a doctoral student. I'm studying how environmental images and environmental education change how people feel about the environment and the actions they take to protect the environment.
Describe yourself in three words. Happy, curious, open
Find Gabby: Unit 9

GENA STEFFENS

Lives: Colombia
Job: I'm a photographer and writer. I'm currently living in the Colombian Amazon and am exploring the ways war and peace change the environment. I'm interested in new ways of telling visual stories, for example, by developing photographs on leaves.
Describe yourself in three words. Creative, independent, driven
Find Gena: Unit 6

MARY GAGEN

Lives: UK
Job: I'm a Professor of Geography and I work on climate change and forests. I study ancient woodlands around the world. I'm also passionate about science education and regularly run workshops to bring young people into a science lab.
What do you do in your free time? I live by the sea and most of my free time is spent in the water or hiking along the cliff paths.
Find Mary: Unit 8

REBECCA WOLFF

Lives: Canada
Job: I'm a researcher in the Andes of Peru and Ecuador. I look at the relationship between people, their environment, and how our environments can make us feel healthy or unhealthy.
How many languages do you speak? I speak English and Spanish fluently. I also speak a little bit of French, Hindi and Quechua.
Find Rebecca: Unit 3; Unit 7

NIRUPA RAO

Lives: India
Job: I'm a botanical illustrator, which means I draw and paint plants and trees. My recent work includes a project on the trees of south Indian rainforests and a children's book that helps young readers explore the wonderful world of plants.
What do you do to relax? Yoga, singing and playing the piano really help me relax.
Find Nirupa: Unit 5

RUBÉN SALGADO ESCUDERO

Lives: Mexico
Job: I'm a photographer. I've lived in and travelled to many different countries. In 2014, while I was living in Myanmar, I started my project Solar Portraits, showing the lives of people who have access to electricity for the first time through solar energy.
What advice would you give to someone who wants to explore the world? DO IT! You will never regret it.
Find Rubén: Unit 6; Unit 8

PABLO (POPI) BORBOROGLU

Lives: Argentina
Job: I'm a marine biologist and I specialize in penguins and marine conservation. I'm founder and president of the Global Penguin Society, an international conservation organization that protects the world's penguins through science, habitat protection on both land and sea, and education.
What's your fondest memory? Listening to my grandmother's stories about penguins when she visited them 100 years ago in Patagonia.
Find Pablo: Unit 2

TERESA CAREY

Lives: US
Job: I'm a science journalist and sailor. In 2008, I sailed the ocean on a small boat with only my cat for company. After many years as a professional sailor, I wanted to tell more science stories. I hope to inspire people to come together and create solutions.
What did you want to do when you were younger? What didn't I want to do?! I wanted to do everything!
Find Teresa: Unit 2

PRASENJEET YADAV

Lives: India
Job: I'm a biologist and photographer. I studied ecology, but realized early in my scientific career that my real interest was in storytelling. Now, I use my experience in research and my photography skills to communicate ecological and conservation issues to a wide audience.
What do you miss when you are away from home? My family, and of course, the delicious home-cooked food.
Find Prasenjeet: Unit 10

Hat designer Shilpa Chavan in her workshop, Mumbai, India.

Identity

GOALS

- Preview an article before reading
- Describe photos and different identities
- Practise using adjectives to describe character
- Understand sequence
- Understand different communication styles
- Write an online self-introduction

1 Work in pairs. Discuss the questions.

1 Look at the photo. Can you describe this place?
2 Can you describe the woman in the photo? What kind of person do you think she is?
3 How do you think she feels about her job? Why do you think this?

WATCH ▶

2 ▶ 1.1 Watch the video. Answer the questions.

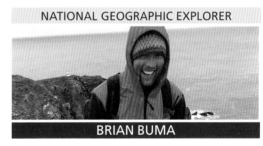

NATIONAL GEOGRAPHIC EXPLORER

BRIAN BUMA

1 What kind of person does Brian say he was as a child?
2 In what ways are things different for Brian now?

3 Make connections. Discuss the questions.

1 What kind of things did you enjoy doing when you were a child?
2 Do you still enjoy doing the same things now?
3 What did you do as a child that you would like to start doing again?

11

One true identity?

LESSON GOALS
• Preview an article before reading
• Understand an article about online identities
• Evaluate arguments

READING

1 Work in pairs. Discuss the questions.

1 Do you use social media?
2 Which social-media platforms do you use?
3 Do you use different platforms or different accounts for different purposes?

2 Match the words in bold (1–4) with the correct meanings (a–d).

1 Your online **profile** shows who you really are.
2 Having **multiple** profiles on one social network is a bit strange.
3 Most people have many different sides to their **personality**.
4 People may have a different **identity** in different social situations.

a your picture, information about you, etc.
b your character: the way you act and behave towards other people
c the qualities that make you what you are and make you different from other people
d many

3 Work in pairs. Do you agree or disagree with statements 1–4 in Exercise 2? Why?

4 Look at the Reading skill box. Preview the article on page 13 and answer the questions in the box.

READING SKILL
Previewing the text

Before you read, look at the whole text to get an idea of what it's about. Look at the title and any images. Read the first sentence of each paragraph. Ask:
• What's the main topic of the text?
• What do I know about this topic?
• What will I learn?

5 Read the article. Which three topics does it discuss?

a Social-media accounts and how people use them
b Problems with criminals stealing identities online
c Ways people show different sides of themselves to different audiences online
d Similarities between online and offline behaviour
e The dangers of spending too much time online

6 Complete the sentences with two words from the article.

1 Nicole Lee has a _____ on each of her social-media accounts.
2 danah boyd talks about someone who uses _____ online to connect with different audiences.
3 One Twitter user says that he leads different lives with his online contacts, friends and _____.
4 Mallory Johns shows different parts of _____ by using different social-media accounts.
5 The fact that we have different identities for different events shows that we have _____, which makes us amazing.

SPEAKING

7 Look at the Critical thinking skill box. In pairs, answer questions 1–3.

CRITICAL THINKING SKILL
Evaluating arguments

Writers often argue that their point of view is true or correct. However, sometimes people support their ideas with incorrect or false information, or don't support them at all. Think carefully about whether or not to believe what you're reading and whether you agree with the ideas. Ask:
• Is it a statement of fact or of opinion?
• Is the argument supported with evidence, such as:
  • specific examples or personal experiences?
  • data such as statistics or the results of scientific research?
  • expert opinions?
• Do you know of any evidence that goes against the argument?

1 What types of evidence does the article use?
2 Is Mark Zuckerberg's statement a fact or an opinion? How can you tell?
3 Which do you think makes a stronger argument – Mark Zuckerberg's quote or the article? Why?

One true online identity?

1 Technology writer Nicole Lee has five accounts on Twitter, two on Instagram and one on Facebook – and, she says, a different identity on each of them. She uses some of her accounts to focus on specific topics. Other accounts are a kind of joke, like one where she pretended to be tweeting for a hair salon, just to make people laugh.

5 Does having several different online identities make her a bit strange? Not according to author and social-media researcher danah boyd (who prefers her name to be written without capitals). According to boyd, for almost the whole history of the internet, people have had more than one online face. 'Different sites, different audiences, different purposes,' she says. 'I interviewed a young person last week 10 who was very clear about the need for multiple profiles,' boyd continues. This person used one social-media platform to share serious information about current events, another to share photographs with classmates, a third to communicate with 'everyone she's ever met' and text messages to chat to close friends and family. Each platform, it seems, showed a different side of her personality or a different part of 15 her life.

In her article *Having multiple online identities is more normal than you think*, Lee quotes an un-named Twitter user who strongly believes that most people have more than one identity, saying 'The life I lead in front of my family members is not the life I lead when I'm with my friends, which isn't the life I lead … online.' Lee's colleague 20 Mallory Johns also has different social-media accounts that show different sides of her personality. Some are more serious while others, such as an Instagram account that's just about French fries, are just for fun. She set it up, she says, because 'I thought my friends would get sick of all my food pics.'

How does our online behaviour compare with real life? With regard to identity, 25 the two worlds are similar. Each of us in some way becomes a different person depending on the situation we're in. At home, you might be a father, mother, son, daughter, brother or sister. At work, you become an engineer, manager or nurse – a very different identity with its own activities and responsibilities.

'Think of it this way,' says danah boyd. 'Would you invite everyone you've ever met 30 to your birthday party? To your office? To your wedding?' Different events include different groups of people and different identities. It shows that people are amazing because they have so many sides.

An alternative view

'You have one identity. The days of you having a different image for your work friends or co-workers and for the other people you know are probably coming to an end pretty quickly. Having two identities for yourself is an example of a lack of integrity*.'

– Mark Zuckerberg, founder and CEO of Facebook

*integrity = honesty

EXPLORE MORE!

Search online for 'how to build an online identity' for tips and ideas about creating and managing your online identity.

I'm teaching splitboarding

LESSON GOALS
- Understand descriptions of photos
- Practise the present simple and present continuous
- Notice different -ing endings
- Describe photos

READING AND GRAMMAR

1 Work in pairs. How many different identities do you have? Use these ideas or your own.

Occupation identities:
  worker, student, (name of your job), etc.

Relationship identities:
  father, mother, son, daughter, brother, sister, boyfriend, girlfriend, classmate, friend, etc.

Skill identities:
  musician, cook, English-speaker, problem-solver, runner, etc.

NATIONAL GEOGRAPHIC EXPLORER

2 Look at the photos of Brian Buma. What identity does each photo show?

3 Match the descriptions (1–3) with the photos (A–C) in Exercise 2.

1 I work as an ecologist, which means I study living things and the environment. In this photo, I'm working in South America on Cape Horn, the most southern island on the continent. We're working on this little island in very strong winds, walking through groups of penguins, and climbing mountains to study the forest. I'm finding where the southernmost tree in the world is located, and if the forest is growing, getting smaller, or not changing as the climate warms up.

2 Here, I'm splitboarding – a splitboard works like skis on the way up and like a snowboard on the way down. I taught snowboarding and splitboarding before I became a scientist and teacher. I taught students how to balance, how to use the equipment and how to get down the mountain safely while having fun. Here, I'm riding a splitboard with friends at Mt Baker, in Washington State in the US, after teaching for the day. That mountain is one of the snowiest places in the world. Nowadays, I splitboard as much as I can each winter in Colorado and Alaska.

3 I'm a parent of two children. In this photo, I'm teaching them how to fish, which is something we like to do for food. Here, I'm showing my older son the first fish he caught, a small salmon. This photo is from Juneau, Alaska, on a lake called 'Twin Lakes'. We're sitting on the edge of the lake in the rain, in our jackets, but it's still a lot of fun. He still catches many large fish – bigger than this one! And now, I'm teaching my sons to ski and race mountain bikes in the mountains of Colorado.

EXPLORE MORE!

Find out more about Brian's work. Search online for 'Brian Buma + National Geographic'.

4 Read the Grammar box. What's the difference between sentences a and b?

> **GRAMMAR** Present simple and present continuous
>
> Use the **present simple** to …
> - give background information and to describe people and places in a photo.
> *I **work** as an ecologist.*
> - talk about a permanent situation.
> *I'**m** a parent of two children.*
>
> Use the **present continuous** to …
> - describe what's happening in a photo.
> *Here, I'**m riding** a splitboard.*
> - talk about actions now or around now.
> *And now, I'**m teaching** my sons to ski.*
> - talk about changing situations.
> *The forest **is getting** smaller.*
>
> Use the present simple or the present continuous for action verbs. Don't use the present continuous for state verbs such as *be, like* and *know*.
> *These people are my students. ~~These people are being my students.~~*
>
> **Go to page 140 for the Grammar reference.**

a I'm teaching people to splitboard.
b I teach people to splitboard.

5 Choose the correct option to complete the sentences.

1 I *'m knowing / know* him. His name is Ed.
2 It was cold this morning, but the day *is getting / gets* warmer now.
3 In this photo, my cousin *is making / makes* dinner.
4 Be quiet. Yasmin *is talking / talks* on the phone.
5 They *'re having / have* two children.
6 *Are you / Are you being* ready to go?

6 Complete the photo descriptions.

I'll tell you about three of my identities. I
¹_____ (be) a runner, a manager and a mother. In this first photo, I ²_____ (run) in a 10k race in my home town. In this second photo of me at work, I ³_____ (give) a presentation. ⁴_____ (you / recognize) me in my business suit? This third photo shows me as a mother. I ⁵_____ (love) this photo. We ⁶_____ (celebrate) my son's third birthday with my parents. I ⁷_____ (not prefer) one identity to the others. I ⁸_____ (like) all of them.

PRONUNCIATION

7 🎧 **1.1** Look at the Clear voice box and listen to the examples. Notice how the *-ing* verb ending is pronounced.

> **CLEAR VOICE**
> **Understanding *-ing* endings**
>
> People pronounce words with *-ing* endings in several different ways. The standard pronunciation of *making* is /ˈmeɪkɪŋ/. However, it's also possible to hear people say /ˈmeɪkɪn/, /ˈmeɪkɪŋg/ and /ˈmeɪkɪŋk/. Being aware of these different pronunciations may help you understand a variety of accents.

8 🎧 **1.2** Listen and complete the sentences.

1 Here, my brothers are _____.
2 In this photo, we're _____.
3 I'm _____ in this photo.
4 My dad is _____.

9 Work in pairs. Practise saying the sentences in Exercise 8. How do you usually pronounce *-ing* endings?

SPEAKING

10 Work in pairs. Show three or four photos of yourself that represent your different identities. Talk about each identity. Use Exercises 3 and 6 as examples. Ask and answer questions. Use the Useful language to help you.

> **Useful language** Talking about photographs
>
> **Describing your own photograph**
> In this photo / Here, I'm … .
> This is me studying/singing/cooking.
> I really like … .
> This is my friend/dad/classmate.
>
> **Discussing another person's photograph**
> Who is … ?
> Why does this person look … ?
> This person looks like … .
> He/She seems to be …

I didn't use to be adventurous

LESSON GOALS

Describe people's character
Understand people talking about personal change
Talk about habits and situations in the past
Practise the sounds /ʊ/ and /uː/

Contestants on chairlifts during the first downhill mountain-biking tournament in Veduchi, Russia.

SPEAKING

1 Think of someone you know well. Write down three to five words to describe their personality. Compare with a partner.

VOCABULARY

2 Look at these adjectives that describe character. Find one word that describes you.

> academic adventurous ambitious competitive
> independent messy organized sensible shy sociable

3 🎧 1.3 Complete the sentences with the adjectives in Exercise 2. Use your dictionary if necessary. Then listen to check.

1 She isn't afraid to try new things. She's
  _____.
2 They want to be better than other people. They're
  _____.
3 I enjoy school work and studying. I'm
  _____.
4 He isn't tidy. He's _____.
5 You feel nervous talking to new people. You're
  _____.
6 We're neat and tidy. We're _____.
7 They really want to be successful. They're
  _____.
8 You usually think carefully before you make a decision. You're _____.
9 I'm happy working alone. I'm _____.
10 She loves talking to people. She's _____.

Go to page 135 for the Vocabulary reference.

LISTENING

4 Work in pairs. Answer the questions.

1 How would you describe yourself as a child?
  I was adventurous, but not with other people.
  I was shy.
2 What parts of your character haven't changed since you were a child?
  I'm still adventurous.
3 Have parts of your character changed or developed during your life?
  I used to be shy, but now I find it easier to meet new people.

5 🎧 1.4 Look at the Listening skill box. Listen and note what each speaker says about their character in the past, an important change and their character now.

LISTENING SKILL
Understanding sequence: noticing time changes

When you listen to someone explaining a series of events, to understand the order things happened in, pay attention to:
• verb tenses.
• verbs such as *used to*.
• time expressions such as *now, then* and *five years ago*.

1 Anna
  • character before: *not independent or academic*
  • important change: *left home*
  • character now: *independent and academic*

2 Erik
- character before: _____
- important change: _____
- character now: _____

3 Layla
- character before: _____
- important change: _____
- character now: _____

4 Wang-Wei
- character before: _____
- important change: _____
- character now: _____

5 Luisa
- character before: _____
- important change: _____
- character now: _____

6 Work in pairs. Answer the questions.
1 Which speaker is the most like you?
2 Which speaker is the least like you?

GRAMMAR

7 Read the Grammar box. Which sentence pairs (a–d) have the same meaning?

GRAMMAR *Used to* and *would*

Used to
Use *used to* and *didn't use to* to talk about past habits and situations that have changed.
I **used to** *live at home with my parents.*
I **didn't use to** *be independent.*

Would
Use *would* and *wouldn't* to talk about past habits that have changed.
I **would** *always leave the kitchen untidy.*
I **wouldn't** *do the washing up or put things away.*

Go to page 140 for the Grammar reference.

---

a *I used to live at home with my parents.* → I live at home with my parents now.
b *I didn't use to be independent.* → I'm independent now.
c *I would always leave the kitchen untidy.* → In the past, I always left the kitchen untidy.
d *I wouldn't do the washing up or put things away.* → I don't do the washing up or put things away.

8 Complete the conversation with the *used to* form of the verbs.
A: ¹_____ (you / do) a lot of sport when you were a kid?
B: Yes, I ²_____. I ³_____ (play) a lot of football. What about you?
A: No, I ⁴_____. I love football now, but I ⁵_____ (not like) it. I ⁶_____ (be) very shy and I never played team sports.

9 Circle *would/wouldn't* where you can use it. Cross out *would/wouldn't* where you can't use it.

When I was in high school, I ¹ *used to / ~~would~~* love playing the piano, and I ² *used to / would* practise for a couple of hours every day. I really loved it. I ³ *used to / would* play in music competitions and feel very competitive. I ⁴ *didn't use to / wouldn't* care about anything but music. I ⁵ *didn't use to / wouldn't* have a social life, although I'm very sociable now.

PRONUNCIATION AND SPEAKING

10 🎧 **1.5** Look at the Clear voice box. Listen and repeat.

CLEAR VOICE
Saying /ʊ/ and /uː/

/uː/ is a long sound. The lips are round and forward.
/uː/ f**oo**d, sch**oo**l, y**ou**

/ʊ/ is a short sound. The lips are less round and forward than for /uː/.
/ʊ/ w**ou**ld, c**oo**k, f**oo**tball

11 Make notes about four to six habits or situations in your past that have changed.
I used to be very competitive.
I didn't use to like cooking.
Every Saturday, I would play football.

12 Work in small groups. Talk about your past. Use your notes from Exercise 11 and ask and answer questions.
A: *I didn't use to like cooking.*
B: *Why not?*
A: *I didn't know how to cook. I would eat takeaway food for most meals.*
B: *When did you start cooking?*

EXPLORE MORE!

Search online for 'does character change over time' and find out more.

1D Understanding different communication styles

LESSON GOALS
* Learn about different communication styles
* Practise comparing your communication style with others
* Learn useful language to talk about usual behaviours

SPEAKING

1 Work in pairs. Have you ever spoken to someone who communicates in a very different way to you? How are they different? How does/did it make you feel?

My friend Nora likes to talk about her feelings about a topic, but I prefer to talk about the facts.

2 Read story A and answer questions 1–2.
1 What do you think are the differences between Lucia's and Yana's communication styles? Give reasons for your answers.
   a Who is the active communicator and who is passive?
   b Who prefers fast communication and who prefers slow communication?
2 How might Lucia and Yana feel about each other's communication style?

A There's never a moment of silence when Lucia is around. Her friends love inviting her to parties because she always tells interesting stories in entertaining ways. But Lucia's noticed that when she's alone with Yana, conversations often seem to come to a stop. For example, there was the time when Lucia told Yana about her bad shopping experience and Yana simply nodded. And when Lucia shared her story about how she lost her phone, Yana replied with a 'Hmmm …' This made Lucia feel uncomfortable and she started to avoid meeting up with Yana.

3 Read story B and answer questions 1–2.
1 What do you think are the differences between César's and Peter's communication styles? Give reasons for your answers.
   a Who is more direct?
   b Who is more competitive and who is more cooperative?
   c Who prefers more formal communication?
2 How might César and Peter feel about each other's communication style?

B César likes being a nice guy and when he asks for favours, he tries to do it in a way that won't create trouble for anyone. César doesn't like disagreeing with people. When he gives his opinions, he tries to do it gently and not force his opinions on others. So, when Peter first joined César's group of friends, César was surprised at how Peter would casually put his arm on César's shoulder and openly talk about his opinions on things. Also, whenever someone told a story, Peter always had a better story to tell. Peter was confident, but César wasn't sure if he was comfortable with the way Peter behaved.

4 Look at the six scales on page 19. Draw a circle (0) where you feel you naturally fall on each of these scales. Then compare your answers with a partner. Say how you think other people might feel about your communication style.

5 Think of someone you often have communication problems with. How would you describe their communication style? Mark X on each of the six scales. Share your answers with your partner.

MY VOICE ▶

6 ▶ 1.2 Watch the video about communication styles. In pairs, answer the questions.
1 What does the video say is the number one issue when communicating with people from different backgrounds and cultures?
2 What do we need to do before thinking about other people's communication styles?
3 Why might it be good to talk to people who have different communication styles from our own?
4 What might happen if a group of people all have passive and cooperative communication styles?
5 What can we do if our communication style is causing problems for us?

WHAT'S YOUR COMMUNICATION STYLE?

Emotional ◄——————————► Factual

Direct ◄——————————► Indirect

Fast ◄——————————► Slow

Competitive ◄——————————► Cooperative

Passive ◄——————————► Active

Formal ◄——————————► Informal

7 Work in pairs. Look at the Communication skill box. How can an understanding of your communication style help improve your communication? Can you give an example?

COMMUNICATION SKILL
Understanding different communication styles

When you meet someone who you have difficulty communicating with, try following these steps:

1 Think about your own communication style.
2 Think about their communication style.
3 Compare the two communication styles.
4 Consider the cause of the communication difficulty – is it because of the differences or similarities in styles? How do you feel about this?
5 Ask yourself: What can you do to improve communication between you both?

SPEAKING

8 OWN IT! Work in pairs. Look at your answers to Exercises 4 and 5. Compare your own communication style (*0*) with that of the person you have problems communicating with (*X*). Follow the steps in the Communication skill box.

9 Work in pairs. Look at situations 1 and 2. Are the people's communication styles similar or different? What advice would you give Toni and Ania?

1 Toni gets frustrated talking to Shanta. When he tells Shanta he's tired, she tells him she's more tired. When he tells Shanta about his problems, she says her problems are bigger. Toni doesn't think he's a competitive communicator, but he feels he becomes more competitive when he's with Shanta.

2 Bo likes talking to Ania, but Ania often thinks that Bo likes to create drama out of very small things. For example, when Bo thought his friend Thida was ignoring him, he got very emotional. Ania finds this so unnecessary and thinks that Bo needs to focus on the facts and the solutions.

I collect rare records

LESSON GOALS

• Learn how to introduce yourself online
• Practise proofreading your writing
• Write an online self-introduction

SPEAKING

1 Work in pairs. Answer the questions.

1 What do you love? Think of work, hobbies, entertainment, food, etc. Name three or four things.

I love playing football, watching old films and eating spicy food.

2 What activities do you do related to the things you love?

I often meet my friends to play football. I watch a lot of old films. I go out for Thai food almost every weekend.

3 Do you discuss your interests online, for example in groups on social media?

READING FOR WRITING

2 Look at the list of social-media groups (a–g). Then read Winson's and Aliya's self-introductions below. Which group (from a–g) is each writer introducing themselves to?

a An online community connecting people who love all kinds of sport

b A place to talk about clothes and clothing design

c An online meeting space for people who are learning English

d A group for people who love talking about films

e A reading club and online social space for talking about books

f A chat group for people who love music

g A group for online gamers

3 Which of the groups in Exercise 2 would you join? Are there any you would avoid joining?

4 Match each sentence in Winson's self-introduction (1–5) with a description (a–e) below.

a Says a little bit about his past

b Mentions what he's very interested in

c Talks about his other interests

d Talks about things he does now related to his main interest

e Explains a success or something good that happened

Winson K.
✧ Conversation starter • 15 hrs ago

¹I love fashion and helping people choose clothes that feel comfortable and look great. ²I'm a sales assistant at a small clothing store in Greenwich Village and I'm studying fashion design at City College. ³When I was a kid, I used to spend hours drawing clothing designs. ⁴Last year, one of my designs won City College's student fashion show. ⁵When I'm not working or drawing clothes designs, I ride my mountain bike, do yoga and continue my search for the world's best carrot cake.

👍❤8   3 Comments

👍 Like   ➦ Share

Aliya H.
★ Rising star • 13 hrs ago

I love listening to my favourite bands on vinyl. I listen to a record, read a book or magazine about vinyl or write reviews of them online nearly every day. I used to buy a lot of different bands on vinyl, but now I only buy and collect rare records. I recently bought a hard-to-find copy of The Beatles' *Yellow Submarine* online and was very excited about that. When I'm not working at my job in a bank or listening to my record collection, I enjoy spending time with my husband and kids and cooking.

👍❤6   4 Comments

👍 Like   ➦ Share

---

5 Complete the sentences with these expressions from Aliya's self-introduction.

I recently	love	nearly every day	used to	When I'm not

1 I _____ making food and learning new recipes.

2 I go cycling _____.

3 I _____ play the guitar for about two hours every day when I was in high school.

4 _____ won a photo competition and felt very happy.

5 _____ working, I enjoy going out with my friends.

6 Look at the Writing skill box. Then read sentences 1–5. Correct two errors in each sentence.

WRITING SKILL
Proofreading before clicking 'post'

We want our online posts to be as clear and correct as possible so that people understand our message and notice our ideas. Check your writing before you post it. Ask:

• Does each sentence begin with a capital letter?
• Have you used punctuation correctly?
• Are any words spelled incorrectly?
• Are the verb tenses and other points of grammar correct?
• Are any words missing?

1 I'm loving watching internationals football matches.
2 I'm an english student at a language scholl in Rio.
3 I not use to read book, but now I can't stop.
4 last year I won a new camera in a photo competition
5 When I'm not painting, enjoy swimming and listening music.

WRITING TASK

7 Think about the things you discussed in Exercises 1 and 3. Which group would you be interested in joining?

8 **WRITE** Write an online self-introduction for the group you chose in Exercise 7. Use Winson's and Aliya's self-introductions on page 20 as models. Use the Useful language to help you.

Useful language   Introducing yourself
I love …
I'm a … / I …
I used to …
Recently … / Last year …
When I'm not … , I …

9 Proofread your writing.

10 **CHECK** Use the checklist. The self-introduction …

☐ says what you love or are very interested in.
☐ explains what you do now.
☐ talks about your past.
☐ mentions a success.
☐ talks a little more about your life and other interests.

11 **REVIEW** Work in pairs. Read your partner's self-introduction. Does it include all of the items on the checklist?

12 Work in pairs. Recommend an online group for your partner to join, based on their profile. Use the ideas in Exercise 2 or think of your own.

Go to page 130 for the Reflect and review.

Artist MadC paints a 550m² wall alone in only seven days in Leipzig, Germany.

Success

GOALS

- Read fluently by noticing chunks in an article
- Talk about past actions with present consequences
- Practise describing jobs
- Summarize with bullet points while listening
- Learn ways to build trust
- Decide what information to include in a *how-to* article

1 Work in pairs. Discuss the questions.

1 Look at the photo. What success does it show?
2 Would a painting like this be popular where you live? Why? / Why not?
3 What feeling do you think the artist is trying to communicate? Do you think she's successful?

WATCH

2 ▶ 2.1 Watch the video. Answer the questions.

NATIONAL GEOGRAPHIC EXPLORERS

PABLO 'POPI' BORBOROGLU

TERESA CAREY

1 How did Popi feel about English at first?
2 What happened after he changed his mind?
3 What problem did Teresa have with her boat?
4 Who fixed the problem?

3 Make connections. Have you ever done something that you didn't like at first but then connected with?

23

2A
Success stories

LESSON GOALS
- Understand an article about success
- Practise noticing chunks
- Interpret a line graph

READING

1 Work in groups. Discuss the questions.

1 Think of some examples of successful people. What are they successful at?

2 What is 'success'?

2 Read the article on page 25 quickly. Number these topics 1–5 in the order that the article discusses them.

a A project showing photos of parents

b Rich people and happiness

c What we've learned about success

d Feelings of failure among top athletes

e Being successful by bringing up kids

3 Look at the Reading skill box and the sentences below. Match each chunk (1–8) with a common structure in the box.

READING SKILL
Reading fluently: noticing chunks

Chunks are groups of words that often appear together. Some common structures of chunks are:
- adjective *and* adjective: *rich and famous*
- adjective + noun: *silver medal*
- adverb + adjective/participle: *clearly disappointed*
- noun *and* noun: *men and women*
- preposition + noun phrase: *up to a point*
- verb + particle: *focus on*
- verb + noun phrase: *win a bronze medal*

With practice, you can begin to read chunks all at once rather than as separate words. This will make your reading more fluent.

Fu Yuanhui was [1]**in third place** and so she [2]**won a bronze medal**. She was [3]**obviously delighted** about being a [4]**bronze medallist**.

[5]**Mothers and fathers** may wonder what it means to be successful as a parent. More people are [6]**thinking about** traditional ideas of success.

Financial success may bring happiness, but only [7]**up to a point**. Research shows that [8]**rich and powerful** people report not being completely happy.

EXPLORE MORE!

4 Put these sentences (1–6) in the correct place in the article (a–f).

1 Which of the two athletes feels the most successful?

2 Being a parent is very challenging, but also one of life's great pleasures.

3 While you're thinking about what success means to you, let's take a look at some stories of success.

4 Perhaps that success isn't one thing and that it isn't final.

5 Bronze medallists think 'I didn't come in fourth place, so I got a medal' and feel happy.

6 This may mean we need to question the idea that more money will always lead to more happiness.

5 Look at the Critical thinking skill box and the line graph on page 25. Answer the questions in the box.

CRITICAL THINKING SKILL
Interpreting line graphs

A line graph shows how two pieces of information or data change together. Understanding what each part of the graph shows can help you understand the information more clearly. Ask:
- What values does it show on the left and along the bottom?
- How does one value change as the other changes?
- What does the graph show?

6 Answer these questions about the line graph.

1 How much do the least happy people earn?

2 Are more people happy in the group that earns $125,000 than the group that earns $75,000?

3 Are more people happy in the group that earns $50,000 than the group that earns $30,000?

SPEAKING

7 Work in pairs. Discuss the questions.

1 Is a silver-medal winner really a success if he or she doesn't feel like a success? Why? / Why not?

2 Is a stay-at-home parent as successful as a famous actor or an important businessperson?

3 Is it possible to be happy if you don't have a lot of money?

Search online for 'what is success'. What other ideas do people have?

SUCCESS STORIES

1 What does it mean to succeed? Is it proving that you're the best at what you do? Or simply doing something well enough and enjoying it? Or is it being rich and famous? a_____

5 ## Winning an Olympic medal

Who's the more successful athlete – the winner of the bronze medal or the silver-medal winner? The answer is obvious: silver, because second place is higher than third place. Here's
10 a different question: b_____

When Chinese swimmer Fu Yuanhui learned she'd won a bronze medal in the Rio Olympics in 2016, she was obviously delighted. 'I was that fast? I am so happy!' Images of her
15 reaction quickly spread across the internet. Something similar happened with photos of American gymnast McKayla Maroney's reaction to her silver medal in London in 2012 – but for a different reason: she was clearly
20 disappointed.

In fact, research at Cornell University found that in general, bronze-medal winners are happier than silver-medal winners. Why? According to psychologist Thomas Gilovich,
25 both medal winners focus on something that didn't happen. Silver medallists think 'I didn't get a gold medal' and feel unsuccessful.
c _____

Staying at home with the kids

30 A photo exhibition by Swedish photographer Johan Bävman has travelled to 25 countries and has got people thinking and talking about traditional roles for men and women, parenting nowadays and what it means to be a
35 success. Bävman's images of 45 'stay-at-home' dads aren't of smiling, happy families, but of real life: one father cleaning the floor with a baby on his back, another trying to comfort his crying daughter. Bävman, who is himself a
40 father, shows us that staying home with your kids – for both mothers and fathers – is one way to be successful. d _____

McKayla Maroney hides her silver medal while Fu Yuanhui happily shows her bronze.

Getting rich

A researcher at Harvard Business School studied the
45 connection between financial success and happiness. He talked to 2,000 rich and powerful people around the world and found that fewer than half of them felt completely satisfied with life. Almost all of them said they would need two or three times more money to feel completely happy.
50 Why do people who have a million dollars or more not feel completely successful? Probably because they know that there's someone who has even more money, according to experts. Another researcher discovered that financial success could bring happiness – but only up to a point
55 (see the graph below). e _____

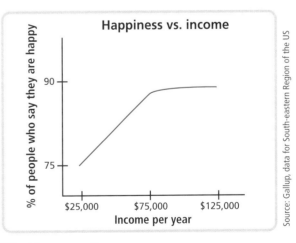

Happiness vs. income

Source: Gallup, data for South-eastern Region of the US

What is success?

We've looked at three faces of success in this article. What can we conclude? f _____ And also that the success you dream of may not feel like success
60 when you finally get it.

LESSON GOALS
- Understand people talking about success stories
- Practise the present perfect and past simple
- Practise saying consonant sounds together

Golfers practising in Tokyo, Japan.

LISTENING AND GRAMMAR

1 Work in pairs. Discuss the questions.

1 Author Cal Newport says that successful people are successful because they're experts at practising. What do you think makes successful people successful?

2 Have you ever done something difficult and eventually become successful at it? What was it? What did you do to become successful at it?

I took the driving test four times and failed. But I kept taking lessons and on my fifth try, I succeeded.

NATIONAL GEOGRAPHIC EXPLORERS

2 🎧 **2.1** Listen to Popi Borboroglu's and Teresa Carey's success stories. Answer the questions.

1 What skills does Popi talk about?
2 What skill does Teresa talk about?

3 🎧 **2.1** Listen again. Which of these sentences refer to Popi's experience (P) and which refer to Teresa's experience (T)?

1 I was a sea captain when I started my blog.
2 It was really hard because I was studying and working at the same time.
3 I studied to be a science writer.
4 I share what I've studied with people from around the world.

4 Read the Grammar box. Look at the bold verbs in sentences 1–2 from Teresa's story. Which sentence uses the present perfect and which uses the past simple? Why?

GRAMMAR Present perfect and past simple

Use the **present perfect** (*have* + past participle) to talk about:
- life experiences.

I've learned that writing is hard.

- something that started in the past and is continuing or still true in the present.

I've worked on penguin conservation for 31 years now.

- things that happened in the past but have a consequence in the present (or future).

I've put in thousands of hours studying … and now, I'm able to share my findings …

Use the **past simple** to tell a story about things that happened in the past.

I decided to study biology at university.
I went to school to study science journalism.

Go to page 141 for the Grammar reference.

1 **I've** always **wanted** to be a writer.
2 But, for years, I never **had** the courage to actually start writing.

5 Choose the correct option to complete the sentences.

1 Cooking is my passion. I *have always loved / always loved* cooking.

2 When I was a teenager, I *have cooked / cooked* with my parents every day.

3 I *have worked / worked* in restaurants in six different countries, so my dishes are quite international.

4 Since I *have become / became* a chef, I *have had / had* less time to cook at home.

5 I *have spent / spent* 3,000 hours cooking in my restaurant last year!

6 Work in pairs. Complete these present perfect sentences with what you think the consequence in the present might be.

1 My son's recently started taking swimming classes, so now …

My son's recently started taking swimming classes, so now he can enter a triathlon.

2 They've watched this musical more than fifteen times, so now …

3 She's taught the same class for three years, so now …

4 He hasn't driven his car for five years, so now …

5 We've played this video game hundreds of times, so now …

6 I've learned that anyone can do anything with practice, so now …

7 Complete the text with the past simple or the present perfect form of the verbs.

I ¹_____ (want) to learn to play the piano since I was twenty. I ²_____ (admire) pianists like Lang Lang for most of my life. I knew that Lang Lang ³_____ (start) playing the piano when he was three, and I ⁴_____ (be) afraid that twenty was too old to start. But then I ⁵_____ (read) a book by Malcolm Gladwell about how anyone can be an expert if they put in 10,000 hours of practice. So, I ⁶_____ (start) saving up for a piano and I ⁷_____ (buy) one last year. I ⁸_____ (take) fifty hours of lessons since then, and I ⁹_____ (become) quite good at playing. I ¹⁰_____ (spend) my savings on this, so now I really need to keep practising.

8 Work in pairs. Ask and answer these questions. Decide when to use the present perfect and past simple in your answers.

1 How long have you studied English for?

2 Have you ever taken any other English classes before this one? Where?

3 How often have you used English outside the classroom? When?

4 Have you ever watched a film in English? What film(s)?

5 What have you done to improve your English?

PRONUNCIATION AND SPEAKING

9 ⌂ 2.2 Look at the Clear voice box. Listen and repeat.

CLEAR VOICE
Saying consonant groups (1): word endings

When there is more than one consonant sound at the end of a word, it takes practice to learn to pronounce the consonant sounds together.
/ns/ si**nce**
/ks/ wee**ks**
/nθs/ mo**nths**

10 ⌂ 2.3 Try saying these words. How many consonant sounds are there at the end of the words? Listen to check and repeat.

1 last
2 difficult
3 skills
4 crisps

11 Work in groups. Take turns to talk about something you would like to be good at but haven't succeeded yet. The other people in the group should ask questions and make suggestions. Use the Useful language to help you.

Useful language Talking about practice

Asking questions
What do you want to improve?
What do you find difficult?
Do you have any related skills?
Can you (do any of this) already?
Have you (ever) tried … ?

Making suggestions
Why don't you … ?
I think you should …
You could try …

EXPLORE MORE!

Did famous people always succeed the first time? Search online for 'famous people who took a long time to become successful'.

You must be prepared

LESSON GOALS
- Understand a conversation about being successful at a job interview
- Practise using *have to, must, don't have to* and *mustn't*
- Learn collocations to talk about work
- Practise the sounds /ə/ and /ɜː/

SPEAKING

1 Work in pairs. Discuss the questions.

1 What do you think are the rules for success at job interviews?
2 How do you think these rules for success might be different depending on the type of job/company?

LISTENING

2 🎧 **2.4** Theo meets his friend Elisa to talk about a job interview he'll attend soon. Listen to their conversation. Which of these things does Elisa do?

a She warns Theo about the difficulties of working life.
b She teaches Theo how to take notes in job interviews.
c She helps Theo understand how to succeed at a job interview.

3 Look at the Listening skill box. How do you normally prefer to take notes?

LISTENING SKILL
Summarizing: bullet points

When you listen, sometimes you'll want to take notes to help you remember what you've heard. Bullet points are one way of doing this.

- Write down only the key information, use short forms and rephrase what you hear so you have less to write.
- Give clear headings to each set of bullet points, so you can immediately know what they are about.
- Remember to leave space between each bullet point so that you can add more information later.

4 🎧 **2.4** Listen again and complete the notes based on Elisa's advice.

Before the interview
- Spend time ¹_____ for the interview.
- Do some ²_____ on the company.
- Find out what ³_____ and skills are important for the job.
- Prepare a ⁴_____ that demonstrates those skills.
- Prepare some good questions to ask.

At the interview
- Don't ⁵_____. (It looks bad if they find out!)
- Dress ⁶_____. Make a good first impression.
- Don't be ⁷_____.

GRAMMAR

5 Read the Grammar box. In pairs, say what words you use for *have to / must, don't have to* and *mustn't* in your first language.

GRAMMAR   *Have to, must, don't have to* and *mustn't*

Use *have to* for general obligations and to show that something is necessary.
*I **have to** work shifts.*
Use *must* for obligations we have for ourselves.
*I **must** buy myself a new shirt.*
Use *don't have to* to show that something isn't necessary.
*You **don't have to** wear a suit.*
Use *mustn't* to show that something is not allowed or isn't a good idea.
*You **mustn't** lie in a job interview.*
Also use *have to* and *must* for strong recommendations.
*You **have to** do your research.*
*You **must** say that in your job interview.*

Go to page 141 for the Grammar reference.

6 Choose the correct option to complete the sentences.

1 In her new job, she *has to / must* wear a uniform.
2 When you start a new job, you *don't have to / mustn't* be afraid to ask questions.
3 If I want to be successful, I *don't have to / must* be willing to work hard.
4 You *don't have to / must* be best friends with everyone, but do build positive relationships.
5 With our last boss, we often *must / had to* stay late.
6 I *had to / didn't have to* manage anybody before, but now I have five people reporting to me.

VOCABULARY

7 ⌂ 2.5 Work in pairs. Complete the work collocations. Then listen to check.

apply for   call in   work (x2)   work for

1 _____ a company
2 _____ shifts
3 _____ sick
4 _____ part-time/full-time
5 _____ a job

do   go   meet   run   take on

6 _____ deadlines
7 _____ a company
8 _____ responsibilities
9 _____ overtime
10 _____ freelance

Go to page 135 for the Vocabulary reference.

8 In pairs, look at these statements. Discuss whether you agree or not and why.

1 It's better to work for a company than to go freelance.
2 If you do overtime, you should be paid for it. It doesn't matter what job it is.
3 People who need to call in sick shouldn't have to meet previously agreed deadlines.
4 People who work shifts should be paid more than people who work in nine-to-five jobs.
5 When you take on the responsibility of running a company, you're agreeing to working evenings and weekends.

PRONUNCIATION AND SPEAKING

9 ⌂ 2.6 Look at the Clear voice box. Listen and repeat.

CLEAR VOICE
Saying /ə/ and /ɜː/

These two sounds are very similar.
The /ə/ sound is made by relaxing your face and only opening your mouth a little.
/ə/ comp**a**ny

To make the /ɜː/ sound, make your lips into a half smile and make a longer version of the /ə/.
/ɜː/ w**o**rk

10 ⌂ 2.7 Work in pairs. Decide if these words have the /ə/ or the /ɜː/ sound. Listen to check and repeat.

answ**er**   ov**er**time   f**ir**st   id**ea**   s**er**vice   w**or**ld

/ə/	/ɜː/

11 Work in small groups. Write down three different jobs. Then answer these questions.

1 What do you think the rules for success are in each job?
2 How are the rules similar or different in the different workplaces?

2D
Building trust

LESSON GOALS
• Learn about the importance of building trust
• Learn different ways to build trust
• Practise building relationships in different situations

Trapeze artists practise at the Great Circus Bardum in Coacalco, Mexico.

SPEAKING

1 Work in small groups. Discuss the questions.

1 Think of someone you trust. What makes you trust them?

2 Now think of someone you don't trust. Why don't you trust them?

3 Do you think trust is important in all relationships? Why?

2 Read the paragraph. In pairs, answer questions 1–2.

> In order to be successful, we need to build successful relationships with the people around us. But how can we do that? In his bestselling book *7 Habits of Highly Effective People*, author Stephen R. Covey says, 'Trust is the glue of life. It's the most essential ingredient in effective communication.' He then goes on to say that trust is what holds all relationships together. So, why is trust so important? When we build trust, we're building relationships with the people around us. We're showing them that we're honest, reliable and have the ability to do the jobs we say we can do. Trust allows people to feel confident and safe and it enables them to open up. As the common saying goes, 'Without trust, we have nothing.'

1 What do you think the phrase 'trust is the glue of life' means?

2 How do people feel when they trust someone?

MY VOICE

3 ▶ 2.2 Watch the video about building trust. In pairs, answer the questions.

1 How many ways of building trust does the video talk about?

2 List three or more adjectives that the video uses to describe people we trust.

3 Name two ways we can show someone our abilities.

4 We can share personal stories to show that we are open about who we are. What other ways can we show that we're open and honest?

5 Give two examples of how we can show we're reliable.

4 Look at the Communication skill box. In pairs, say which of these five ways of trust building Zikri is using in situations 1–5 on page 31.

COMMUNICATION SKILL
Building trust

We build trust in different ways. We can do this by:
• showing our abilities.
• being open with information.
• showing that you trust the other person.
• finding things in common.
• Being reliable.

1

Zikri heard some people talking about his colleague Lay Hoon's work presentation. He calls Lay Hoon and tells her, 'There was some really positive feedback that I think you might like to hear.'

2

Zikri's neighbour is going on holiday and Zikri tells her, 'You can leave your cat with me. You know I'll look after her, like I did last time.'

3

Zikri is telling his new boss about his achievements in his previous job. He says, 'I led a team of people from five different countries. I enjoy working with people from different cultures.'

4

Zikri's friend Adam needs to borrow Zikri's car. He starts to explain to Zikri why he needs the car. Zikri says, 'Take the car. Don't worry about explaining. I trust you.'

5

Zikri's brother-in-law, Dani, tells Zikri that he used to work for a car company in Munich. Zikri says, 'Really? I used to work for a car company in Munich too!'

5 **Look at the Useful language box. Then complete the conversation between Zikri and Suda.**

Useful language Building trust

Showing our abilities
People often say I'm good at (fixing things).
I spend a lot of my time (practising the guitar).

Being open with information
Can I fill you in on what happened / you missed?
There's something I think you might like to hear.

Showing trust
It's OK. I trust you.
I know you can do it.

Finding things in common
I don't know if you (like football), but I …
Are you into (football)? Me too!

Being reliable
You can depend on me.
Leave it with me. I'll get it done.

Zikri: How was your weekend?

Suda: I stayed at home playing board games. Are you 1_____ board games?

Zikri: I love board games! I don't 2_____ if you know Dominion, but I used to play it at my friend's house. It's such a good game!

Suda: It's my favourite! I 3_____ a lot of my time playing it. You can borrow it if you like.

Zikri: Really? Thank you! But I think you 4_____ to know that we have two cats in our house. But I promise I won't let them near the game. You can 5_____ on me to look after it.

Suda: It's OK. I 6_____ you.

SPEAKING

6 **OWN IT!** Work in pairs. Choose two of the situations (1–4) and roleplay them. Use the tips in the Communication skill box and the Useful language to build trust with your partner.

1 You've just met each other at a party. You want the other person to like you.

2 You're doing a class project together. Student A, you know Student B is having a really busy time at work and you want to support them.

3 Yesterday, your English teacher gave the class some exam tips, but Student A wasn't in class. Student B, you don't have a good relationship with Student A, but you think this is a good chance to build up some trust.

4 Student A, your laptop has stopped working. Student B, you have experience of repairing laptops but need Student A to trust that you can do it.

7 Work in small groups. Discuss the questions.

1 How do you build relationships with the people around you? In what ways do you build trust with them?

2 Have you ever met someone who tried to build trust in a way that didn't feel comfortable to you? What happened? What do you think are the differences in the ways you build trust?

3 What's the difference between the trust you build with someone you've just met and the trust you have in someone you've known for years?

EXPLORE MORE!

What are some other ways to build trust in your relationships? Search online for 'building trust' and create your own top-five tips for building trust.

2E
Secrets of success

LESSON GOALS
- Decide what information to include in a *how-to* article
- Write a *how-to* article
- Peer review and discuss tips you've learned

How to take a great photo with your smartphone

The rule of thirds.

You've taken thousands of photo with your smartphone, but how many *great* photos have you taken? Make your next photo the best you've ever taken with these three tips:

 Follow the rule of thirds

People often put the main subject of the photo in the middle of the image. However, following the rule of thirds can make an image more balanced and pleasant to look at. Imagine lines dividing the image into nine equal parts. The viewer's eye naturally goes to the points where the lines cross. Try placing the main subject there.

 Take a few shots and choose the best one

Don't wait for the perfect moment and take one photo. To get one image of people with their eyes open and a nice smile, you usually have to take three to five. For photos of buildings or landscapes, try a few different camera positions. However, to avoid filling your phone with too many photos, you have to remember to delete the ones you don't want.

 Use filters

Most smartphones and many social media platforms have filters for photos. By touching a button, you can change the colour and light in an image to make it more interesting. Sometimes you have to try several different filters to find the perfect one for your photo. This simple trick can turn a good photo into a great one.

Good luck!

SPEAKING

1 Work in pairs. Discuss the questions.

1 Have you ever searched online for tips on how to do something? If so, what?

2 If you have found tips online, what format were they in – diagrams, written instructions, videos?

3 What devices do you use for taking photos – camera, phone, tablet?

4 Do you know any 'rules' or tips for taking good photos?

READING FOR WRITING

2 Read the *how-to* article on page 32 and answer the questions.

1 Match each topic (a–c) with a tip from the article (1–3).
   a Taking photos
   b Editing photos
   c Setting up photos

2 Have you ever used any of these techniques? If so, which ones?

3 Which tip do you think is the most useful? The least useful?

3 Think of a topic you'd like to write a *how-to* article about or choose one of these ideas.

How to …

• make a great cup of coffee

• give a great presentation

• get fit

• hang a picture

• be a good friend

• choose a pair of shoes

• have a perfect weekend

• pack for a holiday

4 Now think of five to eight possible tips for your topic.

How to take a great photo with your smartphone
Use natural light.
Follow the rule of thirds.
Make sure your battery is charged.
Take a few shots and choose the best one.
Use filters.
Hold your phone carefully when you take photos.

EXPLORE MORE!

Search online for 'how to' + something you'd like to learn how to do.

5 Look at the Writing skill box. Choose the best three ideas from your list in Exercise 4.

WRITING SKILL
Planning: deciding what information to include

For a *how-to* article, you may have a lot more than three ideas for tips. To choose the best three ideas to include, ask:

• Which ideas are the easiest to explain?

• Which are the most useful to readers?

• Which ideas can I add more detail to?

• Which are the least interesting? Cut these!

6 For each tip, make notes of information you want to include.

How to take a great photo with your smartphone
Follow the rule of thirds: don't put subject in centre; lines = nine equal parts; main subject at cross points.

Take a few shots and choose the best one: important for people; try different positions; delete bad photos.

Use filters: change colour and light; try a few options; makes a good photo great.

7 Look at the introduction to the article on page 32. Think of a question you can ask to introduce your own article.

WRITING TASK

8 **WRITE** Write a *how-to* article using your notes from Exercise 6. Use the article on page 32 as a model.

9 **CHECK** Use the checklist. The article …

☐ has a 'How to …' title that clearly explains what it's about.

☐ has a short introduction that asks a question and explains how readers will benefit.

☐ presents three tips.

☐ has a clear heading for each tip.

☐ has a paragraph for each tip that gives easy-to-follow instructions.

10 **REVIEW** Work in small groups. Read the articles by the other people in your group and answer the questions.

1 Have you ever used any of these techniques? Which ones? Did they work?

2 Which tip do you think is the most useful?

Go to page 130 for the Reflect and review.

Rescue workers and locals help a stranded whale in Mar del Plata, Argentina.

3

Working together

GOALS

- Identify supporting examples in an online forum
- Talk about an important relationship
- Think about what you already know before listening to a news report
- Talk about teamwork
- Learn about managing conflict
- Write an email of apology

1 Work in pairs. Discuss the questions.

1 Look at the photo. What are the people doing?

2 How does working together help them to achieve their goal?

WATCH ▶

2 ▶ 3.1 Watch the video. Answer the questions.

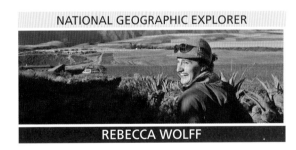

NATIONAL GEOGRAPHIC EXPLORER

REBECCA WOLFF

1 According to Rebecca, what is the challenge of teamwork?

2 What qualities does Rebecca say are important for everyone to get along?

3 Make connections. Do you have a memorable experience of working together with other people? Why was it memorable?

Do we need competition?

LESSON GOALS
- Understand an online discussion about competition in sport
- Identify supporting examples
- Reflect on the value of competition

READING

1 Work in pairs. Discuss the questions.

1 Which of these sports do you enjoy doing? Which do you enjoy watching?
- baseball
- basketball
- boxing
- car racing
- climbing
- cycling
- football
- gymnastics
- horse riding
- running
- skiing
- swimming

2 Do you compete in any sports?

3 Do you think competition is necessary in sport? Why? / Why not?

2 Read the question and replies on page 37 quickly. Who thinks competition is necessary in sport?

3 Read the question and replies again. Match each idea (1–7) with a writer.

1 You can enjoy doing sports without competing.

2 Competition helps improve the quality of a sport for people who don't compete.

3 I'm not sure about the definition of *sport*.

4 Sport without competition isn't interesting.

5 Having a winner is important.

6 A sport is an activity that includes exercising your body.

7 Working well in a team is an important part of many sports.

4 Look at the Reading skill box. Answer questions 1–5.

READING SKILL
Identifying supporting examples

Writers often use examples to support their ideas or to show that something is true. Words or phrases that signal examples include *for example*, *the best / an / another example is …* , *like* and *such as*, but not all examples are introduced with signal words.

1 What sports or events does Lisbet use as examples of competition?

2 How does she introduce each example?

3 What sports does Shen use as examples of not competing?

4 Does Shen use any special words to introduce his examples?

5 What sport does Adriana give as an example of teamwork?

5 Work in pairs. Answer the questions.

1 Whose reply – Lisbet's, Shen's or Adriana's – do you agree with the most?

2 What other examples can you think of that support their ideas?

3 Has your opinion about competition in sport changed since reading the article?

SPEAKING

6 Look at the Critical thinking skill box. In pairs, discuss questions 1–4.

CRITICAL THINKING SKILL
Reflecting on ideas

When we reflect, we think deeply about ideas and what's important or not important about them. We explore them from different angles and ask questions to understand what they mean to us as individuals and to society. When you reflect, ask:
- What does this idea mean to me personally?
- What opinions do I have about it?
- How does it connect with my personal experience?
- How can I apply the idea to other areas of life?
- How can the idea be applied in the wider world?

1 What does the word *competition* make you think of?

2 In what other areas of life do people compete?

3 Do you like competing? If so, in what areas?

4 Do you like people who enjoy competing?

EXPLORE MORE!

Search online for 'is competition good or bad' and find more opinions on this topic.

Formula One Mexico Grand Prix race in Mexico City, Mexico.

IS COMPETITION NECESSARY IN SPORT?

Jan K.

I've looked up *sport* in a few dictionaries, and they all say that it's a physical activity in which people or teams compete. But what about sports like running that people do for fun or fitness? Are those *not* sports because people don't compete, or are the dictionaries wrong?

▲ 5
▼ 0
💬 1

Replies:

Lisbet J.

Competition is at the heart of sport. For me, the best example is football. It's the most popular sport in the world. People in every country have a favourite team, watch matches on TV and go to live games. Without the winning and the losing, no one would care – there would be no point. Another example is the Olympics. They're all about competition and who gets the gold medal. Or what about Formula One racing? It's just incredible to watch car makers, drivers and support teams compete to be the fastest on the day. If people aren't competing, it isn't a sport, it's a hobby. And it's probably boring to watch.

▲ 5
▼ 0
💬 1

Shen F.

Sport has to include physical activity, but it doesn't have to include competition. I love winter sports – skiing, snowboarding, ice climbing. I never compete and I never want to, but I'm totally sure these are sports. Here's why: You have to make a physical effort to practise them and they require skill, training, special equipment and certain types of clothing. You can take lessons and improve in them. Of course, it's possible to compete in any of these sports, but it isn't necessary. Maybe Lisbet is talking about watching sports rather than actually doing them? Maybe competition makes a sport more interesting to watch, but it isn't necessary for participating in a sport and enjoying it.

 ▲ 5
 ▼ 0
💬 1

Adriana S.

For me, the most interesting sports have a mix of competition and people working together. In football, teamwork such as passing to move the ball around the field makes the game exciting. And as Lisbet says, the competition between the teams is also exciting. But competition is important even in sports where teams aren't fighting each other to win. Take winter sports, for example. Shen says he doesn't compete, but the equipment he uses, such as skis, has been developed and improved because people wanted to ski (or snowboard or climb) better and more safely – even if they were just competing with themselves to do their best. Developments in sports technology often come from people trying to do new things that no one has done before: better tricks, harder climbs, faster times. So, although Shen doesn't compete, he does benefit from others' competition.

 ▲ 5
▼ 0
💬 1

3B
He helped me reach my goals

LESSON GOALS
- Understand a story about an important relationship
- Practise saying words spelled with *ear*
- Talk about an important relationship

READING AND GRAMMAR

1 Work in pairs. Discuss the questions.

1 Think of a person who has helped you in life – a family member, friend, teacher, coach, etc. What did that person help you with?

2 Think of someone you've helped. What did you help that person with?

NATIONAL GEOGRAPHIC EXPLORER

2 Read Rebecca Wolff's story below about a person who helped her. Put the events from the story (a–e) in the correct order.

a Rebecca got to know Tad.

b Rebecca received financial support for her work.

c Rebecca started university.

d Rebecca keeps in touch with Tad.

e Tad gave Rebecca advice on research in Peru.

3 Match each description (1–3) with a sentence (a–c).

1 A main point of the story (past simple)

2 Background information (past continuous)

3 An event that happened before the main event in the story (past perfect)

a I was taking a class that he taught.

b He'd done a lot of research about the history of people in Canada.

c I first met Tad in my final year of university.

4 Read the Grammar box on page 39 and check your answers to Exercise 3.

I first met Tad in my final year of university. I was taking a class that he taught. He'd done a lot of research about the history of people in Canada, and his ideas were extremely interesting. I realized I could learn a lot from him, so I arranged to speak with him outside of class. From that meeting, he became an important teacher and guide to me. When I was doing research in Peru, we would meet every few weeks to discuss it. He gave me a lot of really valuable feedback and had lots of good ideas. He supported me on more projects after that and even helped me receive some money from National Geographic for my research. I completed my education a long time ago, but I still keep in touch with Tad. His ideas and advice helped me reach my goals – even when they sometimes seemed impossible.

Rebecca working in Peru.

GRAMMAR Past tenses review

Past simple

Use the past simple for completed events in the past and the main points in a story.

*I **realized** I could learn a lot from him.*

Past continuous

Use the past continuous (past simple *be* + *-ing* form) for events that were in progress at a specific time in the past and for background events.

*When I **was doing** research in Peru, we would meet every few weeks to discuss it.*

Past perfect simple

Use the past perfect simple (*had* + past participle) for events that happened before the main event in the past and to describe background events.

*He**'d done** a lot of research about the history of people in Canada.*

Go to page 142 for the Grammar reference.

5 Write sentences. Use the given verb tenses.

Past simple

1 Rebecca / not work / in Lima.
  Rebecca didn't work in Lima.

2 She / do / research in the Amazon.

Past continuous

3 National Geographic / support / her work.

4 She / study / health and climate.

Past perfect simple

5 I / not hear / about her work.

6 We / do / research about endangered animals.

6 Complete the story with the correct form of the verbs.

I first ¹_____ (meet) my friend Sara in 2002, while we ²_____ (study) at the same university in Valencia, Spain. She's a bit older than me, so she ³_____ (be) there for a year by the time I ⁴_____ (arrive). Both of us ⁵_____ (do) the Earth Sciences course and often ⁶_____ (see) each other on campus. Before I went to university, I ⁷_____ (worry) that I was going to spend all of my time studying and have no time for fun. I ⁸_____ (learn) from Sara to work hard then have fun. We often ⁹_____ (study) together and went dancing afterwards – it was great!

PRONUNCIATION AND SPEAKING

7 🎵 **3.1** Look at the Clear voice box. Listen and repeat.

CLEAR VOICE
Saying words spelled with *ear*

There are two main ways to pronounce *ear* in a word.

When you say /ɪə/, like in h**ear**, your mouth is in a small smile for the /ɪ/ that is then relaxed for the /ə/. Sometimes, people also pronounce the *r*.

h**ear** /hɪə/, /hɪər/

When you say /ɜː/, as in h**ear**d, your lips, tongue and jaw are relaxed. Sometimes, people also pronounce the *r*.

h**ear**d /hɜːd/, /hɜːrd/

8 🎵 **3.2** Work in pairs. Tick (✓) the sound of *ear* in the words. Then listen to check and repeat.

	/ɪə(r)/	/ɜː(r)/
1 **ear**ly	☐	☐
2 y**ear**	☐	☐
3 l**ear**n	☐	☐
4 d**ear**	☐	☐
5 f**ear**	☐	☐
6 **ear**th	☐	☐

9 You're going to tell a story about when you first met an important person in your life. Think about the questions and make notes.

1 What is the background to the story? What were you doing at the time?

2 What are the main events? What happened when you met?

3 What important things had happened before the main events?

10 Work in pairs. Take turns to tell your story from Exercise 9. Use the Useful language to help you.

Useful language Talking about important people

I have/had a friend/coach/teacher named …
We first met about … years ago.
Before we met, …
One of my earliest memories of him/her is …
I learned about … from him/her.
He/She taught me how to …

3C
Part of the team

LESSON GOALS
- Understand a news report about a team protecting animals
- Practise thinking about what you already know
- Practise the sounds /aʊ/, /əʊ/ and /oʊ/
- Talk about teamwork

SPEAKING

1 Work in pairs. Discuss the questions.

1 What groups or teams are you part of?

2 What are the advantages of working in a team to solve a problem?

VOCABULARY

2 ∩ **3.3** Choose the correct word to complete the multi-word verbs in the text. Then listen to check.

> **The Ocean Cleanup**
>
> At the age of 16, Dutch inventor Boyan Slat [1] **consisted / came** up with a way of collecting plastic in the ocean and the following year he gave a TED Talk about it. One year after that, he started an organization called The Ocean Cleanup to [2] **belong / deal** with the problem of plastics in the world's seas. People who had seen his TED Talk online were ready to [3] **sign / carry** up to the project. When there were problems with the equipment, the team didn't [4] **give / work** up but instead [5] **came / kept** on making improvements and welcoming new members. The team soon [6] **consisted / signed** of more than ninety scientists and engineers to [7] **keep / carry** out research and make clean-up trips. People who work for The Ocean Cleanup are proud to [8] **belong / deal** to an organization that's [9] **working / giving** on one of the world's biggest problems.

Go to page 136 for the Vocabulary reference.

3 Work in pairs. Discuss the questions.

1 What clubs, teams or organizations did you belong to when you were a child?

2 If you could sign up to a class or a club to learn any new skill, what would you choose?

3 If you could create a 'dream team' for any activity, who would it consist of?

4 If you could organize a team to come up with a solution to deal with one problem in the world, what problem would you choose to work on?

LISTENING

4 Look at the Listening skill box. Then look at the images and the text in the news report on page 41. In pairs, discuss questions 1–3.

LISTENING SKILL
Thinking about what you already know

Before you listen to a talk, think about the topic. This may help you begin to think about words that you might know related to the topic and may also help you predict some of the ideas that you will hear. This can help you understand the listening. Before you listen, ask:

- What do I know about the topic?
- What will I probably learn about it?

1 What animals live in South Africa?

2 Why do some people want to stop others from hunting endangered animals?

3 How can we protect endangered animals from hunters?

5 ∩ **3.4** Listen to the news report. Choose the correct words to complete the sentences.

1 The Black Mambas *fight with / look for* hunters.

2 When they find someone who may be a criminal, they *call for help / arrest them*.

3 Their training helped develop their *survival / computer* skills.

4 The Black Mambas teach children about the importance of *rules / elephants, lions and rhinos*.

5 When they first signed up, the women mainly wanted *a job / to help their community*.

6 Work in pairs. Tell each other as much information as you can remember from the report.

GRAMMAR

7 Read the sentences. Which one is about *allowing* something to happen? Which one is about *causing* something to happen?

1 They **make** vehicles stop so they can search them.

2 Usually there's no problem and they **let** the vehicle pass.

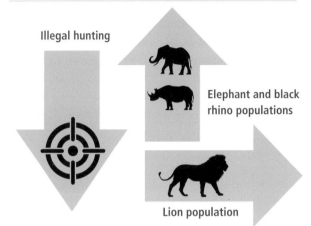

Nkateko Letti from The Black Mambas works with a student at Maseke Primary School near Kruger National Park in South Africa.

The Black Mambas

The Black Mambas are a female-led team working to stop illegal hunting in South Africa's Kruger National Park. In this report, we look at how they do it.

Good news from South Africa

Illegal hunting

Elephant and black rhino populations

Lion population

8 Read the Grammar box. Check your answers to Exercise 7.

> **GRAMMAR** *Make* and *let*
>
> Use *make* to mean *cause*.
> *The simple fact that the Black Mambas are watching **makes** a lot of hunters stay away.*
> Use *let* to mean *allow*.
> *They don't **let** hunters move freely in the park.*
>
> **Go to page 142 for the Grammar reference.**

9 Complete the sentences with the correct form of *make* or *let*.

1 The organizers of the Black Mambas _____ new members do three months of training before they can start work.

2 When France did badly in the 2010 World Cup in South Africa, the French Football Federation _____ them fly home in economy class.

3 All space agencies _____ their astronauts pass a test in both English and Russian before they _____ them join the team on the International Space Station.

4 When business was slow in 2020, a hotel in Tokyo, Japan _____ guests stay for free if they wrote about the hotel on social media and posted a photo.

EXPLORE MORE!

PRONUNCIATION AND SPEAKING

10 🎧 **3.5** Look at the Clear voice box. Listen and repeat

> **CLEAR VOICE**
> **Saying /aʊ/, /əʊ/ and /oʊ/**
>
>
>
> /aʊ/, /əʊ/ and /oʊ/ are long sounds that combine two different vowel sounds.
> /aʊ/ pr**ou**d, t**ow**n
> /əʊ/ l**o**cal, al**o**ne
> /oʊ/ is sometimes used instead of /əʊ/ for the same words.
> /oʊ/ l**o**cal, al**o**ne

11 Work in pairs. Discuss the questions.

1 What work have you done with a team that you feel proud of?
   I feel proud of the cars I help build at my job.

2 What local problem in your town has been or could be solved with teamwork?
   One local problem in my town is rubbish beside the roads. Often, volunteer groups clean it up.

3 What tasks are difficult to do alone but easier in a team?
   Working alone, it's difficult to prepare meals. It's easier with a few people working together.

Find out more about other groups. Search online for 'groups working to save endangered animals'.

3D
Managing conflict

LESSON GOALS
- Learn about ways of managing conflict
- Reflect on our preferred ways of managing conflict
- Practise adapting how you manage conflict

SPEAKING

1 A conflict is a difference in opinion, a disagreement or an argument. Work in pairs. Discuss the questions.

1 Do you think it's possible for people to work together without conflict? Why? / Why not?

2 How do you feel about conflict? How do you normally deal with it?

2 Do the quiz about dealing with conflict on page 43. Then compare your answers with a partner.

3 Work in pairs. Check your results on page 154. Do you agree with them? Why? / Why not?

MY VOICE ▶

4 ▶ 3.2 Watch the video about managing conflict. In pairs, answer the questions.

1 How does Paulo deal with conflict in the five different scenarios?

2 What are the pros and cons of each approach?

3 What would you do if you were Paulo? Why?

5 Look at the Communication skill box. In pairs, complete tips 1–5 with the words below.

COMMUNICATION SKILL
Managing conflict

Many of us have a preferred way of dealing with conflict. However, the way we respond to conflict should depend on the situation. So, take time to consider the situation and decide on the best way of dealing with that conflict.

Avoid   Compromise   Force   Give in   Work together

1 _____ when the issue is small, when it's not the right time or place to talk, or when it's better to wait until everyone's calmer.

2 _____ when there's no time for longer discussions or when you need a quick way to lower the negative feelings.

3 _____ when you've realized you're wrong, when the issue is more important to them than to you, or when the relationship is very important to you.

4 _____ when you need everyone to commit to a solution, or when you need to build a long-term relationship.

5 _____ when you need to stand up for yourself, when you've tried other ways and they haven't worked, or you need a quick solution.

6 OWN IT! Work in pairs and look at these situations. Which way(s) of managing conflict do you think would be the most suitable? Why?

1 Your team mate doesn't like your design of the team t-shirt. She is critical but has no suggestions. The printing company closes soon.

2 Your best friend Siti is upset that you forgot her birthday again. She never forgets yours.

3 Your brother is unhappy that you've booked a beach holiday with friends instead of going on a family holiday. Your brother loves the beach.

4 Your new colleague Mike is complaining angrily because your boss called him Mickey. You don't understand why this is such a big deal.

5 Every time you try to speak, Gabi interrupts and finishes your sentence. It annoys you a lot, but Gabi is a good friend and you like her.

7 Look at the Useful language box. Do you use any of these phrases when dealing with conflict in your first language?

Useful language   Managing conflict

Giving in
You're probably right.
I'm happy to do it your way.

Avoiding
I'd prefer not to talk about this now.
I'll leave it to you to decide.

Forcing
Let me tell you how this has made me feel.
This is what I think we should do …

Compromising
If I do (this), can you do (that)?
I'm happy to agree on (this) if you can do (that).

Working together
I'd like to hear your side of things.
What do you think is the best way forward?

QUIZ

Young capra ibex fighting in The Alps, France.

1 After discussing for fifteen minutes, you and your friends are getting annoyed because you can't all agree on where to go. You want to watch the new Bong Joon Ho film, Milena wants burgers from the American diner and Renata wants everyone to come to her house for pizza. What do you do?

a You say you're happy to go anywhere and let them decide.

b You say you're actually going to go home.

c Together with Milena and Renata, you find a cinema that serves burgers and pizzas.

d You tell them about the amazing film and why tonight's the only night you can watch this film together.

e You agree to go to Renata's house for snacks, then the American diner for dessert, and a late-night screening of a different film at the cinema.

2 You are upset with your team mate Linda because she hasn't done her share of the work. You talk to Linda about this and she starts to shout angrily. What do you do?

a You say sorry for upsetting her and you're happy to pick up any work she can't do

b You walk away because you don't want to get into an argument about this.

c You ask Linda questions about why she wasn't able to do the work and try and find a solution together.

d You tell Linda that she's creating problems for the team and that it is you who should be angry.

e You tell her what she's done so far is great and offer to do half of her work if she does the other half.

3 You share a room with Jialing. She's messy and you're tidy. One day, you find her mess on your side of the room. What do you do?

a When she talks about it, you tell her, 'It's OK. I don't mind.'

b You don't say anything about it and keep your feelings to yourself.

c You talk about the situation with her and find a way that works for both of you.

d You tell her that it's not healthy to live in such a mess and talk about how she needs to change.

e Although you don't like living in a messy room, you tell her you're happy if she keeps the mess to her side of the room.

SPEAKING

8 Look at the situations in Exercise 6 again. With a partner, choose three situations and roleplay them. Use the Useful language to deal with the conflict.

9 Work in small groups. Think of a time when you, or someone you know, experienced a conflict. Discuss the questions.

1 How did you/they deal with the conflict? How could you/they deal with it differently?

2 What is your preferred way of managing conflicts? Which approach makes you feel uncomfortable? Why?

3 How can you improve the way you manage conflicts?

EXPLORE MORE!

How might these five conflict-management styles be represented as a graph? Search online for 'Thomas Kilmann + conflict instrument graph'.

3E
I'm so sorry

LESSON GOALS
- Learn to structure an email of apology
- Practise useful language for apologizing
- Write an email of apology

SPEAKING

1 Work in pairs. Discuss the questions.
1 When and why do people apologize?
2 When might an email of apology be better than a text message or a voicemail?
3 Why might some people prefer to write an email of apology than speak to them in person?

READING FOR WRITING

2 Read the email and answer the questions.
1 Why is Danay apologizing?
2 What was the impact of Danay's mistake?
3 Why did Danay make this mistake?
4 What has Danay done to ensure it doesn't happen again?

New Message

To: Petra.85@Zak.com

From: Danay.VNG@VangAndNoy.com

Subject: I'm so sorry!

Dear Petra,

I'm writing to apologize for not sending out all the invites for our club meeting and only sending them to the players. I'm sorry to be the cause of the delayed training schedule.

The reason was that I had two sets of email addresses – one for the players and one for the coaches. I sent the meeting invites to the players and I was going to send them to the coaches when I had to take an urgent phone call and I simply forgot about sending the rest of the invites.

I've now created one mailing list for everyone in the club – players and coaches – so in the future, I'll make sure this doesn't happen again.

If there's anything else you'd like me to do, please let me know.

Best wishes,

Danay

---

3 Look at the Writing skill box. In pairs, find examples of 1–4 in Danay's email.

WRITING SKILL
Structuring an email of apology

When writing an email of apology, you should:
1 Say that you're writing to apologize.
2 Admit the mistake you've made.
3 Explain what happened and the reason for your mistake.
4 Say what you've done or what you're going to do to correct the mistake.

---

4 Look at the Useful language box. In pairs, consider situations 1–3 and replace the words in brackets with words that suit each situation.

Useful language Dealing with your mistakes

Apologizing and admitting fault
I'm so sorry I (didn't send out the meeting invites).
I must apologize for (not sending out the meeting invites).
I can imagine you must be very (upset/angry/annoyed) about (the meeting).
It was my fault/mistake.
I didn't mean to (make you upset / upset you).

Saying what you're going to do about the mistake
In future, I'll ensure that I (pay more attention).
In the future, I'll make sure I (get it right).
I'd like to make it up to you by (organizing the next meeting).
Will you let me (organize the next meeting) to make up for my (careless/terrible) mistake?

1 You told everyone on your team that you created the design for the new company logo and forgot to mention that your colleague Aigul helped you do it.
2 Your team member Vani asked you for some important information, but you emailed that information to Artur by mistake.
3 You lost your phone three days ago and didn't call your dentist to cancel your appointment.

Gingerbread hearts on sale at a market in Germany.

WRITING TASK

5 WRITE Write an email of apology. Choose an option (a, b or c). Use the model email on page 44 and the Useful language to help you.

a The deadline for your assignment was five days ago. You've only just finished your assignment and you want to hand it in to your teacher. Write her an email to apologize.

b You booked the wrong flight for a business trip and had to buy a new flight at the airport. This mistake cost the company some money. Write an email to your manager apologizing and explaining why.

c Think of something that you want to apologize to your friend or family member about. Write an email to say you're sorry.

6 CHECK Use the checklist. The email …

☐ uses appropriate greetings at the start and at the end.

☐ starts by saying that you're writing to apologize.

☐ admits the mistake you made.

☐ explains what happened and gives the reason for the mistake.

☐ says what you're going to do about this.

☐ uses paragraphs to clearly organize the different points.

7 REVIEW Work in pairs. Read your partner's email. Imagine you've received this email. Give your partner feedback on their apology.

1 What did they do well?

2 Has it improved the situation for you? Why? / Why not?

3 What could they improve?

Go to page 131 for the Reflect and review.

People enjoy a coffee in Florence, Italy.

4

Routines

GOALS

- Understand new vocabulary in an article using affixes
- Describe routines when greeting people
- Deal with unknown words while listening
- Practise using phrases with dependent prepositions
- Deal with uncertainty
- Write about household routines

1 Work in pairs. Discuss the questions.

1 Look at the photo. Who or what do you think the customer in white is?
2 How are cafés in your town similar or different?
3 What do you usually order in a café?

WATCH ▶

2 ▶ 4.1 Watch the video. Answer the questions.

NATIONAL GEOGRAPHIC EXPLORERS

ALISON WRIGHT   **ANDREJ GAJIĆ**

1 What activities does Alison do every day?
2 What activity does she do with friends?
3 How does Andrej start the day?
4 What does he do besides work?

3 Make connections. Discuss the questions.

1 Yoga, running and walking are important to Alison. Andrej loves music and spending time in nature. Do you do any of these activities?
2 Alison and Andrej meet friends for coffee or dinner. What do you usually do with your friends?

The power of daily routines

LESSON GOALS
- Understand an article about routines
- Deal with new vocabulary using affixes
- Apply knowledge to a new situation

READING

1 Work in pairs. Discuss the questions.

1 Do you have a routine you follow every day, or do you do things differently each day?

2 Do you enjoy having a routine or do you find it boring?

2 Read the title of the article on page 49. In pairs, discuss these questions.

1 How can a routine help you get through the day?

2 What do you think is meant by 'the right routine'?

3 Read the article quickly. Were any of your ideas from Exercise 2 mentioned?

4 Read the article again. Match the beginnings of the sentences (1–5) with the endings (a–e).

1 In an emergency situation, a routine may

2 For artists, a routine can

3 For working people, rushing through their morning routines may

4 In business, workers who choose their own routine

5 A personally chosen routine can

a lead to success.

b block creative thought.

c work longer hours.

d save lives.

e make you feel happier.

5 Look at the Reading skill box. Underline one affix in each bold word (1–8) in the article.

READING SKILL
Finding meaning: using affixes

Affixes are groups of letters added to the beginning or end of a word to change its meaning. When you read a new word, look to see if it has a prefix such as *re-* or *un-* or a suffix such as *-ment*, *-ive*, *-ity*, *-al* or *-ful*. Then look for the word that the affix is attached to. Ask:

- Do I know the root word?
- Does the affix change the part of speech?
- Does the affix change the meaning?

6 Write the part of speech – N (noun), A (adjective) or V (verb) – for each word.

1 encouragement

2 helpful

3 survival

4 creativity

5 creative

6 unnecessary

7 laziness

8 rethink

7 Look again at the words in Exercise 6. In pairs, answer these questions.

1 Which three suffixes change a verb to a noun?

2 Which two suffixes change a verb to an adjective?

3 Which two suffixes changes an adjective to a noun?

4 Which prefix means *not*?

5 Which prefix means *do again*?

SPEAKING

8 Look at the Critical thinking skill box. In pairs, discuss situations 1–3.

CRITICAL THINKING SKILL
Applying knowledge to a new situation

Information is a collection of facts and ideas. Knowledge is the understanding that allows you to use this information in different situations. When you apply knowledge to a new situation, ask:

- What have I learned about this topic?
- How does that knowledge apply to the new situation?

1 Students in school
- What does a typical school routine include?
- Do you think this routine improves creativity or reduces it? Why?

2 A bored office worker
- What types of work might be boring for office workers?
- What kind of routine could they create to make work less boring?

3 A person working alone from home
- What problems could arise because of a lack of routine?
- What sort of routine might help improve the quality of their work?

EXPLORE MORE!

Search online for 'positive morning routines' for more ideas on the best way to start the day.

Getting through the day

How the right routine can make your life better

People do their morning exercise in Shanghai, China.

1 What does the word *routine* make you think of? For many of us, it may be an image of doing the same thing day after day – the boredom of repeating the same actions over and over again. However, the reality is that
5 a carefully planned routine can support mental health, improve creativity and increase the quality of your work.

A routine can also bring a sense of order to daily life and provide a sense of place and purpose – we know where we are and what we have to do next. In 2010, 33 miners
10 were trapped in a mine in Chile after part of the roof fell in. When they realized there was no way out, team leader Luis Urzúa set up a work and eating schedule for them. Experts agreed that Urzúa's [1]**encouragement** to keep to a routine was a key factor in keeping the miners
15 alive and well until their rescue – 69 days later.

But routines aren't just [2]**helpful** for [3]**survival**. Artists from painter Joan Miró to author Adele Parks have said that a work routine is the key to [4]**creativity** and success. If you don't have to think constantly about
20 what to do every day, your mind is free to think about big ideas.

However, when developing a routine, it's important to set up the right sort of routine. Researchers in the US concluded that people who wake up to an alarm, quickly
25 shower and eat and then rush off to work are missing out on the best [5]**creative** thinking time of the day.

Science journalist Anne Murphy Paul writes that the best approach is to 'set the alarm a few minutes early and lie awake in bed, following our thoughts where they
30 lead'. This gives your mind time and space to be creative when you aren't thinking about anything else or rushing to the next thing.

It would be [6]**unnecessary**, though, for all of us to have the same routine – especially in the workplace. Simon
35 Slade, CEO of a digital marketing training company in New Zealand, says that his employees 'have complete control over their personal schedules'. He judges his employees not on the time they put in, but on the work they produce. 'This means the input of hours and how
40 an employee organizes them doesn't really matter to me, as long as they are continuing to improve and producing excellent work.' You might think this encourages [7]**laziness**, but researchers in Germany found that workers who set their own schedule actually work more
45 hours than those whose routine is set by the company.

While some routines may lead to boredom, a carefully – and personally – chosen one not only allows space for creativity and increases productivity, it can also increase comfort and happiness. So, ask yourself: is my
50 daily routine working for me? If not, it may be time to [8]**rethink** it.

If they shake my hand …

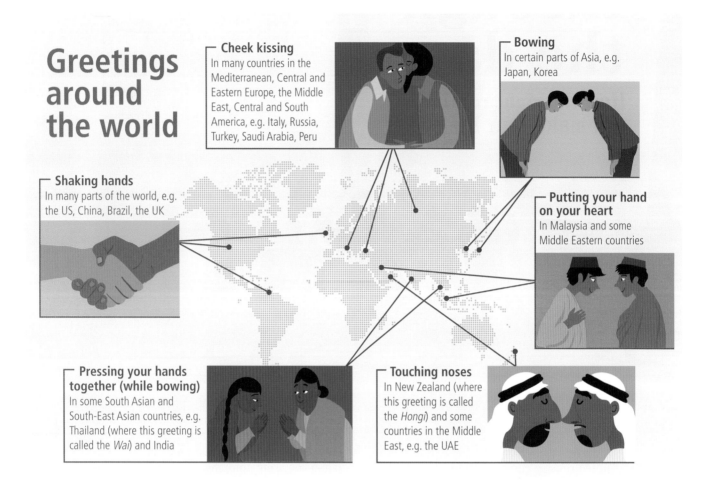

Greetings around the world

Cheek kissing
In many countries in the Mediterranean, Central and Eastern Europe, the Middle East, Central and South America, e.g. Italy, Russia, Turkey, Saudi Arabia, Peru

Bowing
In certain parts of Asia, e.g. Japan, Korea

Shaking hands
In many parts of the world, e.g. the US, China, Brazil, the UK

Putting your hand on your heart
In Malaysia and some Middle Eastern countries

Pressing your hands together (while bowing)
In some South Asian and South-East Asian countries, e.g. Thailand (where this greeting is called the *Wai*) and India

Touching noses
In New Zealand (where this greeting is called the *Hongi*) and some countries in the Middle East, e.g. the UAE

LISTENING AND GRAMMAR

1 Work in pairs. Discuss the questions.

1 How do you usually greet …
- people you've just met?
- a family member or a friend?
- someone in school / at work?

2 What does your greeting depend on, e.g. age/gender/context?

3 Have you ever had to greet someone in a different way than is usual for you? What happened?

2 Work in pairs. Look at the infographic above and answer these questions.

1 Which of these greetings have you experienced? Where did you experience them?

2 Which ones would you be less comfortable with? Why?

NATIONAL GEOGRAPHIC EXPLORERS

3 🎧 4.1 Listen to Alison Wright and Andrej Gajić talking about how they greet people. When do they greet someone in the following ways?

Alison
1 shakes hands
2 gives a kiss on each cheek
3 says 'Namaste'
4 greets without touching

Andrej
5 kisses someone on the cheek
6 shakes hands and high-fives
7 hugs another man

4 Read the Grammar box. Work in pairs. What's the difference between the zero conditional and the first conditional?

GRAMMAR Zero and first conditionals

Use the zero conditional (*if/when* + present, + present) to talk about something that is generally true.
*If I'm in the US, I usually **shake** hands.*
Use the first conditional (*if* + present, + *will* + infinitive) to talk about a possible future situation.
*If I **see** my colleague later today, I'**ll shake** his hand again.*
You can also use alternatives to *if* in conditional sentences.
As soon as *I see my friends and family, I hug them.*
*Usually when I greet people, I hug them, **unless** I feel they don't want to hug me.*

Go to page 143 for the Grammar reference.

5 Complete the sentences with the present simple or *will* + infinitive.
1 If you go to Malaysia, it's possible you _____ (see) people greeting each other with their hands on their hearts.
2 When Irish people greet each other, they usually _____ (not touch) noses.
3 When I go to Japan next month, if someone _____ (bow) to me, I'll do the same.
4 I always _____ (shake) my father's hand unless I've already seen him that day.
5 If my mother wants a hug, I _____ (give) her one.

6 Work in pairs. Choose the correct option to complete the sentences about the cheek-kiss greeting.
1 In France, people often greet each other with two or more kisses, *unless / in case* you're in Brittany's Finistère region, where they only give one kiss.
2 Most people don't kiss with their lips *as long as / in case* they are ill. They just lightly touch cheeks and make the kissing sound with their lips.
3 Some people will put their hands on the other person's shoulders *unless / as soon as* they come in for a cheek kiss.

4 A hug can go with the kiss *as long as / as soon as* the person is a close friend.
5 In Ecuador and Portugal, men don't usually give other men cheek kisses, *unless / as long as* they are family members.
6 In some countries, the cheek kiss is an informal greeting. So, you shouldn't immediately go for a cheek kiss *as soon as / unless* you're introduced to your boss.

PRONUNCIATION AND SPEAKING

7 🎧 4.2 Look at the Clear voice box. Listen and repeat.

CLEAR VOICE
Saying words beginning with /p/, /b/, /k/ and /g/

When you say /p/ and /k/ there is no voice from the throat and air comes out of your mouth.
/p/ **p**ut, **p**ress
/k/ **k**iss, **c**ase
When you say /b/ and /g/, there is voice from the throat, but less air comes from your mouth.
/b/ **b**ow, **b**oss
/g/ **g**ive, **g**reet

---

8 Complete these sentences so that they are true for you. Compare your answers with a partner. Ask questions for more information.
1 When I meet someone, I _____ unless _____.
2 When I meet lots of new people, I often _____.
3 If someone tries to do the *Hongi* with me, I _____.
4 As soon as I see _____, I _____.
5 I'm happy to give cheek kisses as long as _____.
6 Some people in my country choose a low-contact greeting like the _____ in case _____.
7 If someone greets me in a way that makes me uncomfortable, I _____.
8 My advice to a visitor to my country is to greet people by _____.

EXPLORE MORE!

What's a fist bump? Or an air kiss? Search online for 'greetings around the world'.

Get plenty of fresh air!

LESSON GOALS
- Understand a conversation about building good habits
- Learn to use quantifiers like *too much/many, a tiny bit, enough*
- Practise phrases with dependent prepositions
- Understand connected speech

SPEAKING

1 Work in pairs. Discuss the questions.

1 Do you have any good or bad habits? What are they?

2 Have you ever tried developing a good habit or breaking a bad habit? How did you do it?

LISTENING

2 🎧 4.3 Listen to Kit, Yulia and Thiago's conversation. Then in pairs, answer the questions.

1 What are some changes Kit has made to his life?

2 What habit does Yulia want to break?

3 What does Kit suggest doing to stay motivated? How does he do this?

3 🎧 4.4 Look at the Listening skill box. Then listen to the extracts from Kit, Yulia and Thiago's conversation and answer questions 1–4.

LISTENING SKILL
Dealing with unknown words or phrases

When we hear a word or phrase we don't understand, the context – the sentences and words around it – can give us clues about the unknown word.

The context might tell us …

- what part of speech the word is. (Is it a verb, a noun, an adjective?)
- what category the word belongs to. (Is it a part of a car? A type of food?)
- if the word/phrase is only part of an example or part of a main point.
- the meaning of the word/phrase.

1 What phrase explains the meaning of *staying indoors*?

2 What part of speech is *workouts* and what does it mean?

3 What example does Kit give of how he *committed to doing this*?

4 What does *cutting down* mean?

GRAMMAR

4 Read the Grammar box. What's the difference between the two things in 1–3?

GRAMMAR Quantifiers

Use quantifiers to talk about amounts:

- *not … enough* means *less than what is needed.*
*I wasn't getting **enough** sleep.*
- *too little* means something is not enough.
*Half a teaspoon is **too little**.*
- *too much/many* means that something is more than you need.
*I was … staying indoors **too much** … spending **too many** hours sitting at my desk.*
- *so much/many* means *really a lot.*
*I drink **so much** tea when I'm working.*
- *a lot of, lots of* and *plenty of* mean a large amount of something.
*That's **a lot of** sugar. I drink **lots of** coffee. You're getting **plenty of** fresh air.*
- *a (tiny/little) bit of* means a small amount of something.
*I now put only **a tiny bit of** sugar in my tea.*

Go to page 143 for the Grammar reference.

1 *too many* and *too much*

2 *too much* and *so much*

3 *a lot of* and *lots of*

5 Work in pairs. Choose the correct option to complete the sentences. Which sentences do you agree with?

1 There are *so many / too many* books I want to read and I'd love to read a little every night.

2 Drinking *too much / too many* coffee can keep me awake at night, so I only drink one cup a day.

3 I work from home and just don't get *too many / enough* exercise.

4 I want to spend *too much / a little bit of* time alone every day.

5 I'll have *plenty of / not enough* time to save money when I'm older, so I prefer to spend my money now.

6 I'd like to stop being late all the time. I've got into *so many / lots of* trouble for being late for things.

A man cycles in Powys, UK.

VOCABULARY

6 🎧 **4.5** Complete the sentences with the correct preposition. Some prepositions can be used more than once. Then listen to check.

---
about   in   of   on   to   with
---

1 I'm so **fed up** _____ my messy room.
2 I'm **worried** _____ my health.
3 I often **feel guilty** _____ missing my tennis class.
4 I **spend** all my **time** _____ my work.
5 After I do exercise, I always **feel proud** _____ myself.
6 I like to **reward myself** _____ new shoes for my hard work.
7 He **committed** _____ reading a book every week.
8 Do you **believe** _____ setting goals?
9 They are so **enthusiastic** _____ starting their vegan cooking classes.
10 I really **look forward** _____ feeling healthier.

Go to page 136 for the Vocabulary reference.

7 Make sentences that are true for you with the phrases from Exercise 6.

I'm fed up with not getting enough sleep.

PRONUNCIATION

8 🎧 **4.6** Look at the Clear voice box and listen to the examples. Notice how the words are joined together.

CLEAR VOICE
Understanding connected speech

Sometimes when people speak, they join words together. This often happens when a consonant sound at the end of one word is followed by a vowel at the beginning of the next word.

a lot of

lots of

not enough

9 🎧 **4.7** Listen to these phrases from Exercise 6 and mark the connected speech.

1 fed up with my messy room
2 worried about my health
3 spend time on my work
4 feel proud of myself
5 believe in setting goals

SPEAKING

10 Work in small groups. Answer the questions.

1 What do you need plenty of to be happy?
2 What don't you get enough of?
3 How do you reward yourself when you've done something well?

4D
Dealing with uncertainty

LESSON GOALS
- Reflect on how much we avoid uncertainty
- Learn about different levels of uncertainty avoidance
- Practise adapting to different levels of certainty

SPEAKING

1 Work in pairs. Answer the questions and say how you felt.

1 Think of the last time you gave someone instructions. How did you make sure that they knew what to do?
   a You gave them a general idea of what to do.
   b You gave them step-by-step instructions.
   c You asked them to repeat the instructions back to you.
   d You watched and corrected them while they did the task.

2 Think about the last time you met up with a group of friends. How much did you know about the plan beforehand?
   a I knew exactly where we were going and what we were going to do.
   b I knew what we wanted to do and where we wanted to go but not in much detail.
   c I knew what we wanted to do, but we didn't really make a plan.
   d What plan?

2 Read the story about Carolina and answer questions 1–4.

Carolina likes routines and likes to plan everything carefully in advance. Every Tuesday, she spends the evening at her parents' house. Every Thursday, she meets her friends for coffee and every Friday, she stays at home and makes pizza. Having some control over what's going to happen makes her feel safe. Then one day, Carolina meets Akos. Akos never plans things in advance, is always late and prefers to be flexible. He likes to make decisions based on how he's feeling that day and thinks that eating pizza every Friday is limiting his freedom. When Carolina tries to make plans to meet for coffee in advance, Akos sounds interested, but he never gives her definite answers. His behaviour really annoys Carolina.

1 The word *uncertainty* refers to a feeling of not knowing for sure what's going to happen. Who do you think prefers to avoid uncertainty? Carolina or Akos?
2 Who do you relate more to? Carolina or Akos?
3 What do you think Carolina might say about Akos?
4 What do you think Akos might say about Carolina?

3 Work in pairs. Decide if these statements are made by someone who prefers to avoid uncertainty (A) or someone who doesn't mind uncertainty (DM).

1 'I feel uncomfortable with new things and unknown situations.'
2 'I don't know the future and I can't control it. And that's OK.'
3 'Situations change, so I prefer to make decisions as things happen.'
4 'We should stick to what we know works well.'

MY VOICE ▶

4 ▶ 4.2 Watch the video about avoiding uncertainty. Work in pairs. What does the video say about these topics?

1 People who avoid uncertainty and routines
2 People who don't mind uncertainty and the future
3 How people who avoid uncertainty might feel about people who don't mind uncertainty
4 How people who don't mind uncertainty might feel about people who avoid uncertainty

1 You go to your favourite restaurant one evening with your best friend Ana and she is shocked to see that they have changed their menu. She can't find any dishes she's familiar with and she suggests going to a different restaurant. You get annoyed with her for being inflexible.

2 You have an important exam in two weeks and according to the study timetable you've written, you have to study four chapters of the book today. Your friend Zoltán calls you to watch a film with him at the cinema; the film is only showing for two more days. You tell him about your study plan, but Zoltán says you need to relax and stop stressing about the exam.

3 Your mother drives for 40 minutes to go to the supermarket twice a week. You're trying to persuade her to shop for groceries online because it would be more convenient and would save her time. Your mother has never shopped online before. She thinks that online shopping is risky and she isn't keen.

5 Look at the Communication skill box. In pairs, think about Carolina's story in Exercise 2. What advice could you give Carolina? What advice could you give Akos?

COMMUNICATION SKILL
Dealing with uncertainty

The people we meet might respond differently to uncertainty from us. Consider seeing things from their point of view and adapting a little.

With people who don't mind uncertainty, …

• remember we can learn a lot from the unknown and the unfamiliar.
• allow for flexibility.
• show you understand the importance of action and change.

With people who avoid uncertainty, …

• offer details when making decisions.
• provide a context with background information.
• show you understand the importance of structure and plans.

SPEAKING

6 **OWN IT!** Work in pairs. Who prefers to avoid uncertainty more in situations 1–3 above? What would you do in each of the situations?

I'd say to Ana that it might be interesting to try one of the new dishes …

7 Look at the Useful language box. Which of these phrases can you use when dealing with someone who avoids uncertainty? Which of them can you use when dealing with someone who doesn't mind uncertainty?

Useful language Adapting to different ways of dealing with uncertainty

Showing flexibility
For me, either way is fine.
Let me know what you're comfortable with.

Providing context
The reason I do it this way is …
Let me explain why (I'm doing this).

Showing that you understand the importance of something
I understand that (structure/flexibility) is important / means a lot to you.
I can see why you (spend time on planning).

8 Work in pairs. Roleplay the situations in Exercise 6. Take turns to be the person who avoids uncertainty and together, decide what you're going to do. Use the Communication skill box and the Useful language to help you.

9 Work in small groups. Discuss the questions.
1 How much do you avoid uncertainty? On the line below, mark where you think you normally are and say why.
2 Do you know someone who has a very different response to uncertainty from you?

Don't mind uncertainty	Avoid uncertainty
1 ←————————————→ 10	

EXPLORE MORE!

Is our preference for avoiding uncertainty connected to our culture? Search online for 'culture + uncertainty avoidance'.

While we're away

LESSON GOALS

Use headings to organize a note
Learn useful phrases to explain how things work
Write a note about household routines

Hello! We're so glad you can stay in the flat while we're away. Here are a few notes about our household routines that may be useful:

1 _____

If you need to wash any clothes, you can use the coin-operated washing machine in the downstairs laundry room. There's some washing powder and a few coins in the kitchen in case you need some change. Everyone in the building shares the laundry room, so move your things from the washer to the dryer as soon as you can.

2 _____

Rubbish collection is on Monday morning and recycling is on Thursday, so remember to take out the bins the night before.

3 _____

If you want to watch TV, you need to use two remotes. First, use the larger one to turn on the cable and then the smaller one to turn on the TV. You can use the menu button on the larger remote to choose what you want to watch and control the volume with the smaller one.

4 _____

You can see that we have a few plants. The big one in the living room needs plenty of water every two days. There's a watering can nearby. Give the big plant one full can on Mondays, Wednesdays and Fridays. The smaller plants just need a little water once a week, on Wednesdays.

5 _____

If you have any problems, you can talk to the next-door neighbours – Jürgen and Pablo. They're nice guys and will be happy to help if you need anything.

Have fun!

SPEAKING

1 Work in pairs. Discuss the questions about your household routines.

1 What's the routine for rubbish and recycling collection? Are they picked up on a certain day each week or month?

2 How does your family/household take care of the laundry?

3 Do you have any plants or pets at home that need looking after?

READING FOR WRITING

2 Read the note on the right. Answer the questions.

1 Where are the washer and dryer?

2 What two things are necessary to use these?

3 When should the rubbish and recycling bins be put out?

4 Which remote can you use to turn the TV volume up or down?

5 What does the guest need to take care of in the flat?

6 Who should the guest talk to if they lose the key to the flat?

3 Look at the Writing skill box. Think of a heading for each section in the note (1–5).

WRITING SKILL
Using headings

In a note with useful information, headings help the reader see quickly and clearly what information is in the text and make it easy to find the information again later. Headings can usually be very short: one to three words.

4 Imagine someone is going to stay in your home while you are away. Choose three to five of the following things to tell them about or think of your own ideas.

- Looking after a pet
- Using the WiFi
- Doing laundry
- Using the TV or music system
- Taking care of rubbish and recycling
- Looking after the plants or garden
- Collecting the mail
- Using a shared public space

- Using the computer
- Important information about the kitchen
- What to do if there is a problem

5 Look at the Useful language box. Underline the sentences in the note that use these expressions.

> **Useful language**   Explaining how things work
>
> If you need to … , you can …
> If you want to … , you need to …
> If you have any problems, you can …
> There's … in case …
> Remember to …

6 Write sentences about the topics you selected in Exercise 4. Use the expressions in the Useful language box.

If you need to use the WiFi, you can log on to the HOME *network with the password that's on the back of the black internet box.*

If you want to use the dishwasher, you need to put in a dishwasher tablet.

If you have any problems, you can call me on my mobile.

WRITING TASK

7 **WRITE** Write a note for a house guest about your household routines. Write about your own house or flat, or imagine one. Use the note on page 56 as a model, and your sentences from Exercise 6.

8 **CHECK** Use the checklist. The note …

☐ greets the house guest.

☐ has three to five useful pieces of information.

☐ uses headings to organize the information.

☐ provides step-by-step instructions.

☐ says what to do in case you have problems.

9 **REVIEW** Work in pairs. Read your partner's note. Imagine you're the house guest. Answer these questions.

1 Does the note clearly explain what you need to do? Why? / Why not?

2 Are there any other details you'd like to know?

3 Is there any information you think is unnecessary?

Go to page 131 for the Reflect and review.

Professional singers perform
*The Mile-Long Opera: A
Biography of 7 O'Clock*, in
New York City, US.

5

Art

GOALS

- Analyse quotations in an article
- Talk about images and unlikely or imaginary situations
- Describe a piece of art
- Learn about how intonation can affect what we understand
- Write a description of an event

1 Work in pairs. Discuss the questions.

1 Look at the photo. What kind of art do you see?
2 What are the people doing?
3 What story do you think they're trying to tell?

WATCH ▶

2 ▶ 5.1 Watch the video. Answer the questions.

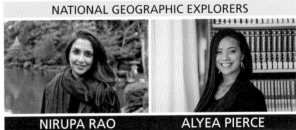

NATIONAL GEOGRAPHIC EXPLORERS

NIRUPA RAO   **ALYEA PIERCE**

1 According to Nirupa, why do people create art?
2 What examples of art does Nirupa give?
3 According to Alyea, what can art allow us to do?
4 Alyea talks about two paintings. What do the paintings show?

3 Make connections. Discuss the questions.

1 In your opinion, why do people create art?
2 Give an example of a piece of art you like. Why do you like it?
3 Do you think art is important? Why?

LESSON GOALS
• Understand an article about art
• Practise summarizing an article
• Analyse quotations

READING

1 Work in groups. Discuss the questions.
1 What are some famous examples of art?
2 What famous artists can you name?
3 Do you know of any artists in your own city or country? What kind of art do they make?

2 Read the article on page 61. Work in pairs and answer the questions.
1 Does it mention any of the examples of art you thought of in Exercise 1?
2 What is the writer saying about pop music, video games, street painting and comics?
3 Do you agree or disagree with what the writer says? Why?

3 Look at the Reading skill box. Choose which two sentences (a–e) are the main points of the article. Then combine the two sentences to create a summary of the article.

READING SKILL
Summarizing a text

After you read a text, it can be helpful to write a one- or two-sentence summary. This can help you better remember the main points.

a Pop music, which includes many different styles of song, is usually popular with young people first.
b Pop music, video games, street painting and comics are art if they are beautiful and make people feel emotion.
c Video games are popular all over the world and allow people to discover the world.
d Good art requires skill to create and usually communicates some kind of message or idea that people can understand.
e In Buenos Aires, building owners sometimes ask artists to paint pictures on the walls to make an area more beautiful.

4 Work in pairs. Do you think pop music, video games, street painting or comics are art? Why? / Why not?

5 Look at the Critical thinking skill box. Then answer questions 1–5.

CRITICAL THINKING SKILL
Analysing evidence: supporting quotations

Writers sometimes directly quote other people. This can show that the author isn't the only person who thinks in a certain way. When using a quotation, writers say whose words they're quoting and put the quoted words inside quotation marks. When you read a quotation in a text, ask:
• Who originally said the words?
• Is there a reason why that person was chosen – are they an expert, for example?
• Do the quotations support the author's ideas?

1 Underline the quoted words in the article.
2 Circle the person or book that the quotations come from.
3 Which two quotations define the word *art*?
4 Which two quotations report facts about how and why one type of art is made?
5 Do you think all of the quotations support the author's ideas? Why? / Why not?

SPEAKING

6 Work in small groups. Discuss the questions.
1 Which of the following quotations do you agree with? Why?
a 'Good business is the best art.' – Andy Warhol
b 'Great artists need great clients.' – I.M. Pei
c 'Gardening is the art that uses flowers and plants as paint, and the soil and sky as canvas.' – Elizabeth Murray
d 'Football is an art, like dancing is an art – but only when it's well done does it become an art.' – Arsène Wenger
e 'Hairdressing is an occupation and art form that dates back thousands of years.' – Queen B
2 Answer the final question of the article: Where do you see art?

EXPLORE MORE!

Search online for 'what is art' and see what other ideas you can find.

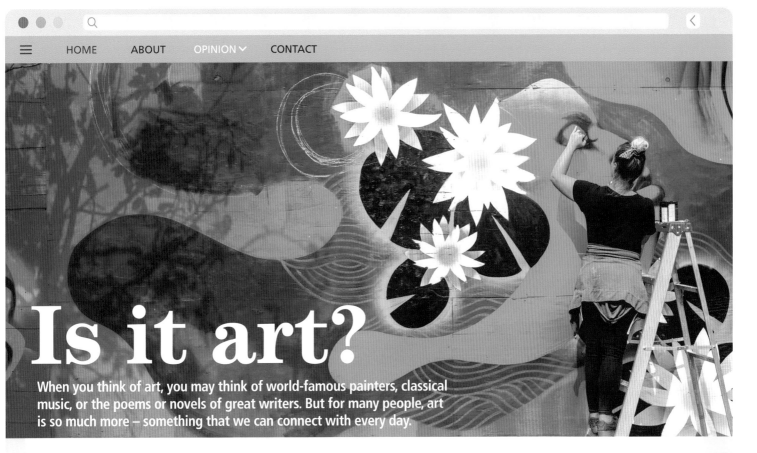

Is it art?

When you think of art, you may think of world-famous painters, classical music, or the poems or novels of great writers. But for many people, art is so much more – something that we can connect with every day.

Pop music

1 Pop (short for *popular*) is music that usually first becomes popular with young people and often has a strong beat and a simple tune. It's also, according to music writer Paul McGuinness, 'the world's most
5 important art form'. The Oxford Dictionary says that works of art are 'appreciated primarily for their beauty or emotional power' – and pop music can definitely have those, at least sometimes. Of course, not all pop music is art. But when good pop music
10 speaks to our emotions and our sense of what it means to be human, or communicates some kind of message, then it's art.

Video games

When it comes to entertainment, video games such as *The Legend of Zelda* are hugely popular around
15 the world. But are they art? Gaming expert Chris Melissinos believes that video games may be one of the most important art forms in the history of the world. Why? They allow players to make a deep connection with an artistic experience. 'If you can
20 observe the work of another and find in it personal connection, then art has been achieved,' he says. 'Video games are a natural evolution of what we've always done: play – to discover our world, discover each other, and discover ourselves.'

Street painting

25 In many cities, painting or writing on a building or in a public place without permission is a crime. But not in all cities. According to writer Emily Baillie, in Buenos Aires, Argentina it isn't a crime: 'All the artist needs is permission from the building owner.' In fact, building owners often ask
30 street artists to paint in order 'to add something interesting to their bare walls'. Marton Otonelo, speaking for the local government, says that street art in Buenos Aires is 'part of the city'. Other cities such as Zürich, Switzerland have areas of the city where street painting is not only legal, it's actually
35 encouraged. But this doesn't mean that anything anyone paints or writes on a city wall is art. Good street art requires skill to create, can make a city more beautiful and can be enjoyed by the people who live there.

Comics

From Japanese manga to the globally famous *Avengers*
40 series, stories told with pictures are popular around the world. They're sometimes called comics, though many of them deal with serious ideas. They may be called graphic novels, though some popular ones tell true stories. Artist Darran Anderson points out that comics are often read and
45 thrown away, but that doesn't mean they aren't art. They also help us to 'understand a place and time and those who lived there. Manga doesn't need to be high art. Manga is manga.'

Now what do you think of when you think of art? If you look around, you can see that art is all around us – from songs
50 on the radio to video games, street paintings and maybe even an old magazine in the dustbin. Where do you see art?

If I had five more years ...

LESSON GOALS
- Learn about two famous images
- Practise using the second conditional
- Talk about possibilities in the future

World-famous images that stand the test of time

Katsushika Hokusai

Before he died at the age of 89, the last words of artist Katsushika Hokusai were 'If I had five more years, I could become a true artist.' Though he was popular in Japan at the time, his work wasn't world famous, and he clearly felt that he had more to learn. In fact, in many countries Hokusai still isn't a famous artist, but you've probably seen his most famous print *The Great Wave* in an advertisement, an art museum or as an emoji on your smartphone. He created the image between 1830 and 1832, when he was around 70 years old. Hokusai would be amazed at its global popularity if he were alive today.

Frida Kahlo

If Mexican painter Frida Kahlo hadn't been in a road accident in 1925, she might not have become an artist. She began painting because she was bored lying in bed with her injuries, unable to move easily. Some of her most famous images show her own face. 'I paint myself,' said Kahlo, 'because I am so often alone and because I am the subject I know best.' She had pain for the rest of her life, which may be one reason why her art communicates strength and deep emotion. By the time of her death in 1954, at the age of 47, she was world famous. Her work has become increasingly popular since then. If you went on a world tour now, you'd see Kahlo's self-portraits on t-shirts, mugs, handbags and other items. Kahlo's work explores the ideas of living your dreams and being strong even when life is hard.

Frida Kahlo souvenir notebooks for sale in Playa del Carmen, Mexico.

The Great Wave by Katsushika Hokusai.

READING AND GRAMMAR

1 Work in pairs. Look at the two images on page 62. Answer the questions.

1 What do the images show?
2 Have you ever seen these images or similar ones?
3 Why do you think they're popular?

2 Read the article on page 62. Tick (✓) who sentences 1–6 are true for.

	Hokusai	Kahlo
Which artist …		
1 spoke about wanting to get better at making art?	☐	☐
2 produced one image that is very famous?	☐	☐
3 has a famous face?	☐	☐
4 lived to an old age?	☐	☐
5 was well-known in many countries while alive?	☐	☐
6 created something that people today still enjoy?	☐	☐

3 Work in pairs. Discuss the questions.

1 Which of the two images do you prefer? Why?
2 Do you know any other world-famous images?

4 Read sentences a–b. Answer questions 1–3.

a If you named the most important artists of the twentieth century, Mexico's Frida Kahlo *would* almost certainly be on the list.
b You would see her face everywhere *if* you went looking for her work today.

1 What verb form follows *if*?
2 What verb form is used after *would*?
3 When is a comma used?

5 Read the Grammar box. Then put the words in 1–5 in the correct order.

GRAMMAR Second conditional

Use the second conditional (*if* + past simple, *would/could* + infinitive) to talk about imagined situations in the present or future.
*Hokusai **would be** amazed **if** he **were** alive today. (= imagined present situation)*
***If** I **had** five more years, I **could become** a true artist. (= imagined future situation)*

Go to page 144 for the Grammar reference.

---

1 you / If / painted / like Kahlo, / be / you'd / famous
2 wouldn't / I / him / if / saw / I / Hokusai / recognize
3 Frida Kahlo / her face / on handbags today, / If / saw / surprised / be / she'd
4 them / were / If / go to see / we / Hokusai's prints / in the museum, / could
5 if / paint / I / like Kahlo / tried / couldn't / I

6 Make second conditional sentences. Use one expression from A and one from B.

A
If I go to Mexico City
You can buy a Frida Kahlo painting
If you become a great painter
You can watch Hokusai paint
If I have a lot of money
B
I won't spend it on art
if you travel to the past
I will visit the Kahlo museum
you will be famous
if you have millions of dollars

If I went to Mexico City, I would visit the Kahlo museum.

SPEAKING

7 For each topic, write a sentence that's true for you.

1 Develop a talent (for art or something else)
If I could develop a talent, I'd choose playing jazz piano.
2 Meet a famous artist (painter, writer, musician or other artist from any time period)
3 Travel to any city (to visit museums, see art, listen to music, etc.)
4 Share one thing (a song, a work of art, a food, a festival, a word, an idea, etc.) from my own country with the world
5 Go back in time (to any point in history) for one day

8 Work in small groups. Take turns to talk about your ideas in Exercise 7. Ask and answer follow-up questions.

A: If I could develop a talent, I'd choose playing jazz piano.
B: Oh, that's interesting. Why jazz piano?
A: I love listening to jazz.

EXPLORE MORE!

Search online for 'The Great Wave + images' and see how many different versions of the image you can find.

Street art at the Kochi-Muziris Biennale 2018 in Kochi, India. Photo by Nirupa Rao.

SPEAKING

1 Work in small groups. Discuss the questions.
 1 Do you ever go to live performance events like concerts/gigs, street festivals or the theatre?
 2 What's the most memorable performance you've ever seen?

LISTENING AND GRAMMAR

NATIONAL GEOGRAPHIC EXPLORERS

2 🎧 5.1 Listen to Nirupa Rao talking about art. What things does she talk about? Choose the correct words to complete these notes.
 1 Music she has *listened to / performed / written*
 2 *Cartoons / Photography / Paintings* – especially pictures of people
 3 A film that she *enjoyed / didn't see / didn't like*

3 🎧 5.2 Now listen to Alyea Pierce talking about the same topic. Answer the questions.
 1 What type of performance did she go to?
 2 How did it make her feel?
 3 What type of art isn't interesting to her?
 4 What did she see that someone made?
 5 What did the person use to make it?

4 🎧 5.3 Look at the Listening skill box. Then listen to five extracts from Nirupa and Alyea. Which contrast expression from the box does each extract include?

LISTENING SKILL
Understanding contrast (1): listening for contrast

Speakers use certain words and phrases to indicate a contrast between ideas. Common contrast expressions include *although*, *but*, *despite the fact that*, *however* and *though*. When you listen for contrast, ask:
- Did the speaker use a contrast expression?
- What two things or ideas are they contrasting?

5 🎧 5.3 Listen again. What ideas do Nirupa and Alyea contrast?

6 Read these quotes and complete sentences 1–2. Then read the Grammar box to check.

Nirupa: 'If I see them all together in a museum, I must admit that I feel a little bored.'

Alyea: 'For me, no artwork is boring.'

 1 We use words ending in _____ to describe things.
 2 We use words ending in _____ to describe our feelings about things.

> **GRAMMAR**   *-ed* and *-ing* adjectives
>
> An *-ed* adjective describes how someone feels.
> *I feel **excited** by contemporary African dance.*
> An *-ing* adjective describes the thing that causes a feeling.
> *It was incredibly **exciting** every time we made that final sound!*

Go to page 144 for the Grammar reference.

7 Complete the adjectives with *-ed* or *-ing* endings.

1 Which do you feel more excit_____ by: sports, art or science?

2 Have you ever left the cinema because you thought a film was bor_____?

3 Do you think learning about the lives and influences of artists is interest_____?

4 Have you ever felt amaz_____ by a piece of art?

5 Would you be interest_____ in learning to sing a song in another language?

6 What's the most amaz_____ building you've visited?

8 Work in pairs. Ask and answer the questions in Exercise 7.

VOCABULARY

9 Choose the correct words to complete the sentences.

1 I'm **confused**. I *don't understand / love* the story.

2 The new album was **disappointing**. We expected it to be *bad / good*, but it wasn't.

3 You felt **inspired**. The art made you want to *create something / go to sleep*.

4 She was **relaxed** listening to the music. She *sat and listened quietly / got up and danced*.

5 The painting was **shocking**. We *expected / didn't expect* it to look like that.

6 His poetry is **annoying**. I *hate / love* the way he uses language.

7 The drawings were **embarrassing**. I *put them on the wall / threw them away*.

8 I felt **frightened** by the film. I prefer *funny / scary* films.

10 🔊 **5.4** Complete the texts about works of art. Then listen to check.

confusing   disappointed   boring

I was ¹_____ by *2001: A Space Odyssey*. It's supposed to be a great film, but it's ²_____ – I really didn't understand what was happening, especially at the end. There are a lot of very long scenes where no one speaks and that makes it ³_____ because nothing happens.

inspiring   relaxing   shocked

I love Astrud Gilberto singing *The Girl From Ipanema*. Her voice is ⁴_____ – it makes me feel calm. It's ⁵_____, because she sings in English, not her first language – Brazilian Portuguese. I'd like to do that! She felt a bit ⁶_____ when she suddenly became world famous because of that song.

annoyed   embarrassed   frightening

At the Salvador Dalí museum, I was ⁷_____ with people taking selfies in front of paintings – it stopped me enjoying the art. Dalí's paintings are serious and some are a bit ⁸_____ – like a bad dream. I would feel ⁹_____ to photograph myself in front of a piece of art – I would feel silly.

Go to page 137 for the Vocabulary reference.

PRONUNCIATION AND SPEAKING

11 🔊 **5.5** Look at the Clear voice box. Listen and repeat.

CLEAR VOICE
Saying voiced and unvoiced final consonants

For voiced consonants such as /b/, /d/, /g/, /z/, /m/, /n/, and /v/, your throat vibrates.
*jo**b**, amaze**d**, bi**g**, lesson**s**, museu**m**, stole**n**, gi**v**e*

For unvoiced consonants such as /p/, /t/, /k/,/s/, /ʃ/, and /f/, your throat doesn't vibrate.
*ra**p**, shock**ed**, shoc**k**, ticket**s**, fini**sh**, photogra**ph***

12 Work in pairs. Talk about situations 1–5. Use *-ed* and *-ing* adjectives.

1 You watch a horror film.
Horror films are supposed to be frightening, but I usually don't feel frightened. They're sometimes just silly. So, I probably wouldn't feel frightened. I'd feel entertained.

2 You're watching a ballet on television.

3 A concert you have tickets for is cancelled.

4 As a gift, someone pays for you to have painting lessons.

5 You hear that the famous *Mona Lisa* painting has been stolen from the Louvre museum in Paris.

Understanding intonation

LESSON GOALS
- Think about the ways we use intonation to communicate
- Learn about how we might use intonation differently
- Learn to stress words for emphasis
- Practise dealing with misunderstandings due to intonation issues

SPEAKING

1 Look at the infographic below. In pairs, discuss the questions.

1 What do you think the phrase 'it's not what you say, it's how you say it' means?
2 Can you think of a time when someone misunderstood what you meant to say? Why do you think that was?
3 When we talk about intonation, what different things are we talking about?
4 Do you think people around the world use their voice in the same way? What kind of differences might there be?

2 Work in pairs. What are some different ways you might say these sentences? How does each of these ways send a different message about how you feel?

1 'Good morning.'   3 'This painting is very interesting.'
2 'Art is fun.'   4 'Well, I'm not really into poetry.'

3 🎧 5.6 Listen to the sentences from Exercise 2 being said in two different ways. How do you think the speakers are feeling in examples a and b?

MY VOICE

4 ▶ 5.2 Watch the video about intonation. Which of these sentences summarizes what the video says?

a We need to realize that people with different first languages and cultures might use intonation differently.
b If more people spoke with rising intonation on the last word, there would be fewer misunderstandings.
c People need to use polite intonation patterns when disagreeing.

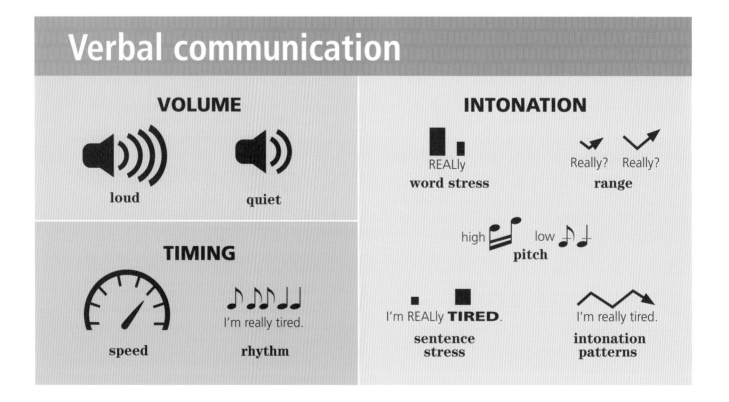

Verbal communication

VOLUME
loud   quiet

TIMING
speed   rhythm
I'm really tired.

INTONATION
REALly
word stress

Really? Really?
range

high low
pitch

I'm REALly **TIRED**.
sentence stress

I'm really tired.
intonation patterns

5 ▶ 5.2 Watch the video again. Answer the questions.

1 The way Chia says 'Good morning!' might sound cheerful to some people. But how might it sound to others?
2 Why was the gallery owner annoyed with Liping?
3 Why do intonation misunderstandings happen?

6 Work in pairs and sit back-to-back. Take turns to say phrases 1–3 in a way that expresses feelings a or b. Can your partner guess how you feel just from your intonation?

1 'Well, I think you're wrong.'
   a I feel sorry I have to tell you this.
   b I really don't like you.
2 'I've made a huge mistake.'
   a I'm so upset and sorry that I've done this.
   b I'm not at all sorry about it, so will you please stop talking about it?
3 'Can you lend me some money?'
   a I'm asking because you borrowed from me last week and never paid me back.
   b I feel really embarrassed because I don't usually borrow money from people.

7 Work in pairs. Look at the Communication skill box. Do you think being aware of how intonation can be used differently in different cultures can help avoid misunderstandings?

COMMUNICATION SKILL
Dealing with intonation misunderstandings

Sometimes, when people have different intonation to what you usually hear, it can surprise or confuse you.

If you're confused by someone's intonation
Ask yourself: *What impression (e.g. rude, bored) are they giving me and what's giving me that impression?* If the reason is their intonation, you could …
• ask yourself what else intonation could mean.
• ask them to clarify what they mean.

If someone misunderstands your intonation
Find out what it is they misunderstood – was it your words, your body language or your intonation? If the reason is your intonation, you could …
• have a conversation about what you really mean.
• explain how intonation is different in your first language.

PRONUNCIATION AND SPEAKING

8 ♫ 5.7 Look at the Clear Voice box. Listen and repeat.

CLEAR VOICE
Using sentence stress (1): stressing words for emphasis

When we put stress on a word, the intonation changes. This makes us notice that word. This can happen when we're trying to emphasize the word, correct what someone is saying, or contrast the word with something else.
She prefers rap to jazz. – not anyone else
She prefers rap to jazz. – but not necessarily to other types of music
She prefers rap to jazz. – she likes rap more than jazz

9 **OWN IT!** Work in pairs and look at situations 1–3 below. What intonation do you think caused the misunderstanding?

1 Nasia wants to go to the new exhibition at the museum and she asks her friend Lee if he's been yet. Lee replies simply with 'No, I haven't.' Nasia thinks Lee isn't interested and asks Yury instead.
2 Ed's housemate Jo has been working at the kitchen table and Ed wants to make dinner. So he says, 'Could you tidy up here?' Jo looks at him in shock and silently starts to tidy up her mess.
3 There's a stranger sitting in the office and Ayan isn't sure who he is. So Ayan asks Paul, 'He's the new client?' Paul replies, 'Yeah, I know.'

10 Work in pairs. Roleplay the situations in Exercise 9. Use the Communication skill box and the Useful language to help you.

Useful language Dealing with intonation misunderstandings

Checking what someone's intonation means
I'm sorry, but what did you mean by that?
I'm not sure if I understood you correctly, but are you (upset) with me?
When you said … did you mean you were (pleased)?

When someone misunderstands you
Sorry, I didn't mean it that way.
I'm afraid you might have misunderstood me.
I didn't mean to be/sound (rude) at all.
I'm sorry, maybe it came across the wrong way.

LESSON GOALS
- Practise describing the programme of an event
- Learn useful language to encourage people to come to an event
- Write a description of an event

SPEAKING

1 Work in pairs and discuss the questions.

1 Have you ever been to an art gallery? What kind of events or activities did you see there?

2 Do you often find out about events online, e.g. on social media? What kind of events are they? What kind of events are you interested in?

READING FOR WRITING

2 Read the event description on the right and answer the questions.

1 What kind of event is it and where will it take place?

2 When will it take place?

3 What is this event description trying to get the reader to do?

4 Do you have to pay for entry?

5 Where do you think you might see an event description like this one?

3 Read the event description again. Then complete the programme.

Programme	
7 p.m.	A quick ¹_____ of five rooms
8 p.m.	Performance by a local light ²_____
8:30 p.m.	Food and ³_____
9 p.m.	'Light and Music' ⁴_____
9:45 p.m.	Light show in ⁵_____ of the building

Lights On!
An evening of light and art

If you love light art and can't get enough of it … or if you've never experienced light art and want to be amazed … then join us on Tuesday 9th August at 7 p.m. for an evening of beautiful lights.

Lights On! is a celebration of light art. Enjoy the magic and experience different ways light is used to make art. Come and be lost in the fascinating worlds that light and shadow can create.

We start the evening with a quick tour around the gallery. Here, you will walk through five rooms with seven light-art exhibitions. At 8 p.m., we have a performance by a local light artist, followed by some food and drinks. After that, there'll be a talk on light and music. The evening ends with a stunning light show in front of the building.

Tickets are free but limited, so register now before they're all gone!

Donations to the gallery are welcomed but not necessary.

We look forward to seeing you there.

4 Read the event description again and answer these questions. Then look at the Writing skill box to check.

1 When is the imperative used?

2 When is the present tense used? Why do you think the writer chooses to use the present tense more than the future *will*?

WRITING SKILL
Writing an event description

When you write an event description, use these tips to encourage people to come:

- Say who the event is for.
- Use imperatives to encourage the reader to come and give reasons why.
- Make any necessary information clear, e.g. what the event is about, where and when it takes place and how much it costs.
- When describing the programme, keep your sentences short and simple. You can use the present simple or the future *will,* but the present simple creates a feeling of closeness to the event – like it's happening immediately.

5 Look at the Useful language box. Then in pairs, look at the event below and use the Useful language to answer questions 1–4.

Useful language   Describing an event

When, where and the price
The event is / will be held (at the museum) on the (4th May).
Join us (on Good Street) on the (4th May).
Tickets are (free / €20 per person).

Giving details about the programme
Your (day/evening) starts with (a tour).
We then have (a performance by an artist).
This is followed by (a talk).
The event ends with (a light show).

Encouraging people to attend
Come and experience (the magic of light).
Enjoy (the gorgeous art).
Learn / Find out more about (light art).

> **Event**: 10km charity run + lunch
>
> **Place**: Bushy Park
>
> **Date and time:** This Saturday at 9 a.m.
>
> **Price to join:** $20
>
> **Why go?** Charity, fresh air, exercise, delicious food

1 When and where will it happen?
2 What's the programme?
3 How much do I have to pay to join?
4 What are some reasons to go?

WRITING TASK

6 **WRITE** Write a description of an event. Use the Useful language to help you. Choose an option (a or b).

a You're helping your local museum tell people about an art workshop that they're organizing. It's an art workshop for beginners and costs €5 to attend. Art materials will be provided.

> **Programme**
>
> 7 p.m.   Talk about art by director of the local museum
> 7:45 p.m. Drinks and snacks
> 8 p.m.   Drawing lesson
> 9:30 p.m. Painting lesson

b Write a description for your own event. Include the following information in your description:
- What the event is and who it's for.
- The time, date, place and cost of entry.
- What the programme consists of.
- Why people should come.

7 **CHECK** Use the checklist. The event description …

☐ says what event it is.

☐ says who should come.

☐ gives clear information about when and where the event takes place, and how much it costs.

☐ clearly describes the programme.

☐ uses imperatives to encourage people to come.

8 **REVIEW** Work in pairs. Read your partner's event description. Answer the questions.

1 How many of the points in the checklist does it include?
2 What interests you about the event? Why?
3 Is there any more information you'd like to know about the event?

Go to page 132 for the Reflect and review.

People walk with umbrellas in the rain in Shanghai, China.

6

Where I'm from

GOALS

- Interpret a bubble chart in an article
- Talk about moving to a new place
- Practise describing a neighbourhood
- Listen for signposts in a story
- Manage group conversations
- Write a travel plan

1 Work in pairs. Discuss the questions.

1 Look at the photo. What things in the photo would you also see where you live?
2 Is there anything you'd never see where you live?

WATCH ▶

2 ▶ 6.1 Watch the video. Answer the questions.

NATIONAL GEOGRAPHIC EXPLORERS

GENA STEFFENS

RUBÉN SALGADO ESCUDERO

1 What sort of place did Gena grow up in – a small town or a large city?
2 What does Rubén love doing in Madrid?
3 What does Gena love that's near her apartment?
4 What does Rubén love about Mexico City?

3 Make connections. Discuss the questions.

1 Is your home town more like Gena's or Rubén's?
2 What do you love about the place you live in now?
3 Is there anything you don't like about the place you live in now?

6A
City life

LESSON GOALS
- Understand an article about a temporary city
- Recognize synonyms
- Interpret a bubble chart

READING

1 Work in pairs. Discuss the questions.

1 What's the biggest city you've ever visited or lived in?
2 What do cities need to provide for the people living there?

2 Read the article on page 73 quickly. Which of your ideas from Exercise 1 does it mention?

3 Look at the Reading skill box. Find synonyms in the article for the words in bold (1–4).

READING SKILL
Recognizing synonyms

A synonym is a word that has the same meaning as another word. Writers use them to avoid repeating the same words and to make their writing richer and more interesting. It's often possible to guess the meaning of unknown synonyms from the words around them.

For example, in these sentences, we can guess that *urban area* refers to the same idea as *city* and is therefore a synonym.

*Creating the **city** requires more than a year of planning and preparation. Like any **urban area**, the Prayagraj Mela has its own government …*

1 metropolis – _____
2 celebration – _____
3 gathering – _____
4 medical centre – _____

4 Read the article again. Choose the correct answer (a–c).

1 How many people were in Kumbh Mela tent city on its most crowded day in 2019?
   a 120 million
   b 30 million
   c more than the population of Tokyo

2 What is an important part of every Kumbh Mela festival?
   a listening to music
   b dancing
   c cleaning yourself

3 What did two people make an announcement about?
   a lost people and things
   b the schedule of performances
   c warnings about traffic

4 What did the organizers provide in 2019?
   a free food
   b a tent for every visitor
   c medical help

5 Which group of people was the largest in 2019?
   a police officers
   b cleaners
   c healthcare professionals

5 Look at the Critical thinking skill box and the bubble chart on page 73. Answer the questions in the box.

CRITICAL THINKING SKILL
Interpreting bubble charts

A bubble chart is a simple way of comparing the size of numbers. Understanding what each bubble represents can help you understand the information more clearly. Ask:

- What information does it show? What do the numbers mean?
- What relationship does it show between the pieces of information?
- Why is a bubble chart a useful way to show this information?

6 Work in pairs. Look at the bubble chart again. How big would a bubble be representing the population of the city or town where you live?

SPEAKING

7 Work in groups. Discuss the questions.
1 What fact about Kumbh Mela is the most surprising to you?
2 Have you ever been to a large gathering such as a festival or a conference? What was it like?
3 What other large gatherings do you know about, either in your own city or country, or around the world?

EXPLORE MORE!

Choose a country and search online to find out the population of three cities from that country. How big would the bubbles be if you added them to the bubble chart on page 73?

The world's second largest city?

¹ About 120 million people visited Kumbh Mela tent city over 49 days in 2019. There were 30 million there on the busiest day – not quite as many people as live in Tokyo, but more than every other city in the world. What makes
⁵ this more amazing is that this ¹**metropolis** is temporary.

Every three years, a city of tents appears as part of the ²**celebration** of Kumbh Mela at one of four places in India: Haridwar, Ujjain, Nashik or Prayagraj. The festival is believed to be the largest single ³**gathering**
¹⁰ in the world. One of the main activities is washing in the water of India's great rivers: the Ganges, the Shipra, the Jamuna or the Sarasvati, depending on the location of the meeting. There are also musical performances, dancing and a great variety of food to try.

¹⁵ Throughout the day and night, announcements over the speaker system reveal the human drama of life in the tent city. 'Whoever has taken my trousers, that were drying on my car,' a voice says, 'at least return the car keys from the pocket. You can keep the trousers.' And
²⁰ 'It is Babu speaking. I have lost my wallet and brother. Please come here the moment you hear this.'

Creating the city requires more than a year of planning and preparation. Like any urban area, the Prayagraj Mela has its own government – the Prayagraj Mela Authority –
²⁵ set up in 2017 to make sure that people's basic needs are met. Here's what they provided in 2019:

- 122,000 toilets
- 20,000 rubbish bins
- 300 kilometres of roads
³⁰ - 524 buses
- more than 4,200 luxury tents
- more than 1,500 rickshaws (small taxis)

People coming for short stays usually bring their own meals, but the authorities supplied basic foods that visitors could buy at 160 'fair price' shops. Five temporary buildings in the city held more than 7,300
³⁵ tonnes of flour – that's more than the weight of 1,800 elephants! In addition, they set up 160 stations to provide clean drinking water.

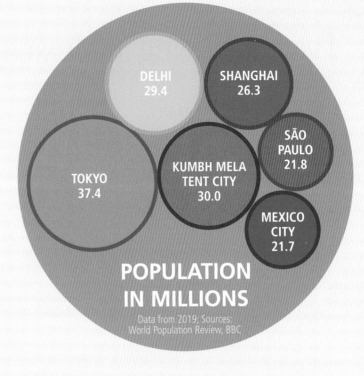

DELHI 29.4
SHANGHAI 26.3
SÃO PAULO 21.8
TOKYO 37.4
KUMBH MELA TENT CITY 30.0
MEXICO CITY 21.7

POPULATION IN MILLIONS

Data from 2019; Sources: World Population Review, BBC

Like any big city, Kumbh Mela has a healthcare system. In 2019, this included a central ⁴**medical centre** with
⁴⁰ 100 beds as well as ten smaller clinics. There were 86 ambulances, 9 river ambulances and 1 air ambulance. On busy days, a staff of 193 doctors and more than 1,500 other healthcare professionals treated 10,000 people.

Kumbh Mela also has a police department. In 2019, more
⁴⁵ than 30,000 police officers operated 40 police stations, directed traffic and worked to keep people safe. They watched the crowds with 1,000 CCTV cameras and, if necessary, guided people away from areas that were becoming too crowded.

⁵⁰ And there were cleaners – 22,000 of them – to keep the city tidy.

Dr Ashok Kumar Paliwal, head of the health and family welfare team at the festival's hospital, appears to feel that the word 'city' may not be enough to describe
⁵⁵ Kumbh Mela. 'It's an ambitious project,' he says, searching for a bigger word than 'city'. 'What we are creating here is a country.'

6B
I've been living in Mexico

LESSON GOAL
- Understand people talking about living in different countries
- Practise using the present perfect continuous
- Practise understanding weak auxiliary verbs

LISTENING AND GRAMMAR

1 Work in pairs. Discuss the questions.

1 Do you know anyone who doesn't live in the town/city they were born in? Where were they born? Where do they live now?

2 Why do you think people might move to a different town/city?

NATIONAL GEOGRAPHIC EXPLORERS

2 🎧 6.1 Listen to Rubén Salgado Escudero talking about moving countries. Answer the questions.

1 Where was he born? Where did he move to?
2 What are some things he learned there?
3 How often does he go home for a visit?

3 🎧 6.2 Now listen to Gena Steffens talking about moving countries. Answer the questions.

1 Where does she live now? When did she move there?
2 What does she love about moving to a new place?
3 What are some difficult things about moving to a new place?

4 Read the Grammar box. Change the example sentences to the present perfect simple. In pairs, say how this change affects the meaning.

> **GRAMMAR** Present perfect continuous
>
> Use the present perfect continuous (*have/has been* + *-ing* form):
> - to talk about an action/event that started in the past and has continued or repeated until now and might still be happening.
> *I've been travelling* back to visit once a year.
> - to focus on the duration of an activity.
> *I've been living* in Mexico for more than three years now.
> - to focus on the action/situation in a recently completed action.
> *I've been practising* and I've learned many new words and sayings.

Go to page 145 for the Grammar reference.

5 Complete the sentences with the present perfect continuous of the verbs.

1 I _____ (live) in this city for two years and I think I'll probably carry on living here for at least five more years.

2 I _____ (learn) to cook now that I don't have my parents cooking for me.

3 I _____ (try) to move my things from my parents' house since I moved out, but there are still lots of my things in their house.

4 My family _____ (ask) me to visit them more often.

5 I _____ (make) many new friends since I've moved here.

6 Look at the infographic on page 75. Choose the correct option or tick (✔) where both are possible.

1 There *has been / has been being* an increase in the percentage of people living in cities since 1950.

2 More people *have chosen / have been choosing* to live in cities. In 2018, more than half of the world's population were living in cities.

3 The majority of people living in Dubai *have moved / have been moving* there from abroad.

4 People from different countries *have migrated / have been migrating* to cities like Dubai and Sydney.

7 Work in pairs. What else can you say about the information presented in the infographic? Write three sentences describing what you see.

8 Use the words (1–4) to make sentences that are true for you. Use the present perfect continuous or present perfect simple.

1 think about moving
   I've been thinking about moving to a different country since I graduated.

2 study English … since

3 consider learning a new language

4 live alone / with my parents / with friends … for

MIGRATION

International migration over the years

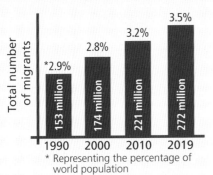

Total number of migrants

- *2.9% — 153 million — 1990
- 2.8% — 174 million — 2000
- 3.2% — 221 million — 2010
- 3.5% — 272 million — 2019

* Representing the percentage of world population

Percentage of world population living in cities

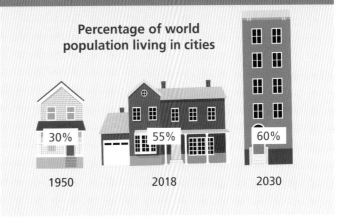

- 30% — 1950
- 55% — 2018
- 60% — 2030

Cities with the highest percentages of foreign-born population
Data from 2015

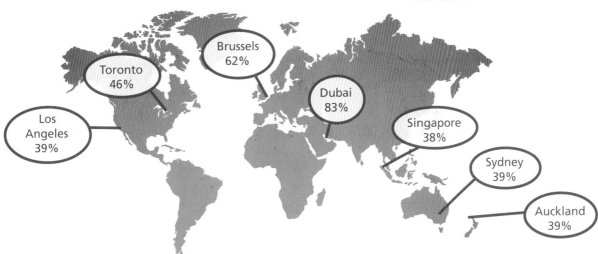

- Toronto 46%
- Brussels 62%
- Dubai 83%
- Singapore 38%
- Los Angeles 39%
- Sydney 39%
- Auckland 39%

PRONUNCIATION

9 🎧 6.3 Look at the Clear voice box and listen to the examples. Notice the weak forms of *have/has* and *been*.

CLEAR VOICE
Understanding weak auxiliary verbs

Some people often weaken auxiliary verbs and it can be difficult to hear the present perfect continuous when words are weakened and shortened:

- *have* and *has* are often pronounced with a schwa, as /(h)əv/ and /(h)əs/.
- *been* is often shortened from /biːn/ to /bɪn/.

*How long **have** you **been** living here?*

*She **has been** cooking spicy food for me.*

EXPLORE MORE!

How long have people been migrating to other countries? Find out more by searching online for 'history of migration'.

10 🎧 6.4 Work in pairs. How might these sentences be pronounced with weak forms? Listen to check.

1 It has been increasing every year.
2 People have been coming from different countries.
3 I have been learning the local language.
4 You have been thinking about this.

SPEAKING

11 Work in small groups. Discuss the questions.

1 Do you prefer to live in a city or in the countryside? Why?
2 With more people working from home now, will they be able to live wherever they want? What are some advantages and disadvantages of that?

6C
I lived in a suburb

LESSON GOAL
- Describe different neighbourhoods
- Listen for signposts in stories
- Describe movement
- Practise the sounds /l/ and /r/

SPEAKING

1 Work in small groups. Talk about the area that you grew up in.

- Where did you live?
- What kind of buildings were there?
- What kind of places did you go to?

VOCABULARY

2 🎧 **6.5** Work in pairs. Complete the sentences with these words. Then listen to check.

---
chain stores   district   harbour   hostels
monument   neighbourhood   office blocks
shopping mall   stalls   suburbs
---

1 We like spending our weekends at the _____ because there are shops, restaurants and a cinema all under one roof.

2 There are _____ in the city centre for backpackers and travellers who don't want to pay lots of money for a hotel.

3 Many people who work in Tokyo don't live in central Tokyo. They live in the _____ – areas outside a city with lots of houses for people to live in.

4 When we travel, we often see the same _____ that are in our city selling the same clothes – it's a bit boring.

5 The entertainment _____ is often quiet during the day, but it comes alive in the evening.

6 There's a farmers' market in the town square every Saturday and you can buy fresh fruit from the market _____ there.

7 There is a huge _____ in the city centre to the first president of our country.

8 I like walking to the _____ and watching the boats and ships there.

9 The people in my _____ are very friendly.

10 The _____ are very quiet at night because everyone goes home after work.

Go to page 137 for the Vocabulary reference.

LISTENING

3 🎧 **6.6** Listen to Leonora and Yongsheng sharing childhood stories. Are these sentences a part of Leonora's story (L) or Yongsheng's story (Y)?

1 He/She lived in a suburb.
2 He/She lived near a market.
3 He/She was walking to his/her friend's house.
4 He/She was on his/her bicycle.
5 He/She went across the road.
6 He/She climbed up a tree.
7 He/She thought he/she saw some wild animals.
8 He/She thought an animal was following him/her.

4 Look at the Listening skill box. In pairs, think of other signposts you can use when telling a story.

LISTENING SKILL
Listening for signposts

When someone is telling a story, they might use certain words or phrases that can help you follow the story. For example:

Once / There was once → This is the start of my story.

One day / One evening / The next day → This helps you follow the order of what happened.

Well, … → I'm going to start a long turn, so listen carefully.

Anyway, … → I'd like to stop talking about this and go back to what I was saying before.

5 🎧 **6.6** Listen again. In pairs, match the signposts that Leonora and Yongsheng use (1–5) with the meanings (a–e).

1 ***It's a funny story, actually.***
2 ***Well,*** *I used to live in a …*
3 ***Anyway,*** *I climbed up a tree.*
4 ***At that time,*** *I didn't know this.*
5 ***So,*** *there was this cute cat.*

a Let's stop talking about the other topic and get back to the story.
b But of course, I know this now.
c I've just explained about the cat.
d Are you ready to hear this? Here we go …
e I'd like to tell you this story and I'd like you to be interested in it.

Colourful houses in Cape Town, South Africa.

GRAMMAR AND PRONUNCIATION

6 Read the Grammar box and the paragraph below. Underline the descriptions of movement.

GRAMMAR Describing movement

Use a verb of movement + adverb to describe the way someone or something is moving.
I **climbed** down really **quietly**.
Use a verb of movement + preposition to describe the direction of movement.
I **jumped over** the fence.
I **went through** a tunnel.
Use a verb of movement + adverb + preposition to describe both the manner and the direction of movement.
I **walked** very **quickly towards** my friend's house.

Go to page 145 for the Grammar reference.

Once, I was walking along the main road when I thought I saw my schoolfriend in front of me. I ran towards her, waved excitedly at her and then gave her a big hug. But it wasn't my friend at all! I turned around quickly and walked away from the confused girl. I was so embarrassed, but my friend thought it was very funny when I told her about it.

7 Choose the correct option to complete the sentences.
1 Drive *slowly / gently* away from the train station *to / towards* the shopping mall and you'll see my house.
2 To get to my school, walk *across / through* the market and then cross *over / along* the road.

3 I often cycle *by / towards* a main road and there are lots of cars driving very *quickly / quietly*.
4 There was no bridge, so we couldn't go *across to / away from* the other side.

8 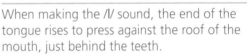 Look at the Clear voice box. Listen and repeat.

CLEAR VOICE
Saying /l/ and /r/

When making the /l/ sound, the end of the tongue rises to press against the roof of the mouth, just behind the teeth.
/l/ actua**ll**y, fo**ll**ow, a**l**ong
When making the /r/ sound, the end of the tongue is down and the mid/back part of the tongue rises.
/r/ dist**r**ict, ac**r**oss, **fr**om

---

9 Work in pairs. Take turns to say one of the two words (1–6). Guess which word your partner is saying.
1 lane/rain   4 berry/belly
2 light/right   5 grass/glass
3 correct/collect   6 arrive/alive

SPEAKING

10 Work in pairs. Think of a journey you used to take when you were a child. Describe the journey to your partner.
I used to walk to my friend's house. I'd walk down my street and then go around the corner …

EXPLORE MORE!

Sometimes, finding out about other people's childhood stories might remind you of your own interesting ones. Search online for 'best childhood memories'. Which of these remind you of your favourite memories?

6D Managing group conversations

LESSON GOAL
• Talk about difficulties in group conversations
• Learn ways to manage group conversations
• Practise dealing with group conversations

People chatting in the streets of Ho Chi Minh City, Vietnam.

SPEAKING

1 Work in pairs. Have you ever been in a group conversation where you felt like you couldn't follow the conversation? Answer the questions.

1 Who was in that conversation and what were they talking about?
2 Why do you think you felt like you couldn't follow the conversation?
3 What did you do when this happened?

2 Work in pairs. Read the story about Natalia and answer questions 1–4.

Natalia has been meeting up with Killian every week to practise chatting in English. She finds it easy to understand Killian's English and really enjoys their conversations. She told him that she'd love to know more people she could speak English with. So one day, Killian introduced her to his English friends. Natalia was very excited, but she soon started feeling lost during their conversations. When they were speaking about the television programmes they watched and the snacks they ate when they were children, Natalia found it hard to follow what they were saying and believed it was because her grammar and her vocabulary weren't good enough. She became less confident about her English and was very quiet during these conversations.

1 Why did Natalia feel lost during the group conversations?
2 What did she think was the reason for this?
3 Why do you think Natalia was able to understand so much during her conversations with Killian but not during her conversations with his friends?
4 Have you ever lost confidence in your English like Natalia? What happened?

MY VOICE ▶

3 ▶ 6.2 Watch the video about group conversations. Complete the notes.

Why group conversations can be difficult

1 Everyone is _____ about something that you know _____ about.
2 There are more _____, more _____ and more people talking at the _____ time.
3 Everyone in the group is _____ in their own way.
4 It feels like there are more people _____ us.

4 ▶ `6.2` Watch again. Are these sentences true (T) or false (F)?

1 If you spoke excellent English, you'd have no problems understanding group conversations.
2 It's easier to control the direction of a group conversation than a one-to-one conversation.
3 If you're unfamiliar with a topic, you should ask questions and help others notice that you don't understand what they're saying.
4 It can be easier to hide and say nothing in a group conversation than compete for the chance to speak.
5 The different communication styles and different relationships people have with each other can make group conversations hard to understand.

5 Look at the Communication skill box. Which of the four issues in Exercise 3 can each of these tips solve?

COMMUNICATION SKILL
Managing group conversations

- Listen and watch. Learn the rules of the group.
- Ask questions when you don't understand. Help them to notice that you're not following the conversation.
- Plan what you want to say and wait for the right moment. If you can't find the right moment, try to link what they're saying to what you want to talk about.
- Remember: Group conversations can be very difficult for many different reasons. If you can't follow the conversation, the issue might not be your language skills.

6 `6.8` Work in pairs. Listen to Natalia describing four situations (A–D) that are making her feel uncomfortable. Answer the questions.

1 What's making these group conversations difficult for Natalia?
2 What advice could you give Natalia in each situation?

7 `6.8` Work in pairs. Look at the Useful language box and listen to situations A and B again. Which of these phrases could Natalia use in these situations?

Useful language Managing group conversations

Showing you're not familiar with the topic
What's (Blue Peter)? Sorry, I don't know what that is.
Can I get you to explain (smart technology) a bit more? I'm afraid I'm a bit lost.
Who's (Tymon) and what's their relationship to (Hilmi)? Are they friends of yours?

Linking to a topic familiar to you
This reminds me of …
On the topic of (favourite childhood games), have you heard of (hopscotch)?
Earlier you were talking about (technology) and I just wanted to say that …
That's interesting. I've also heard that …

Involving quieter members of the group
Was it the same for you?
What about you?
What do you think? Do you agree?
I really want to hear what (Hilmi) thinks about this.

SPEAKING

8 **OWN IT!** Work in groups of four. Roleplay situations 1–3, taking turns to be 'you'. Use the Communication skill and Useful language to deal with the situations.

1 Everyone is talking about a popular place in town that they all know. You are the only person who doesn't know what they're talking about.
2 Everyone is talking about their favourite food. They're speaking quickly and there's a lot of interruption in the group. You really want to tell them about your favourite food.
3 Everyone is talking about the people in their family except one quiet member of your group. You notice this and try to include that person.

9 Work in small groups. Discuss the questions.

1 Which of these do you prefer when talking in your first language and why?
   a one-to-one conversations
   b talking in small groups
   c talking in large groups
2 Do you feel the same when talking in English?
3 What have you learned in this lesson that might improve how you manage group conversations?

You're coming to my home town!

LESSON GOAL

• Describe steps in a plan
• Put activities in time order
• Write a suggested travel plan

SPEAKING

1 Work in pairs. If you had one day to spend in an unfamiliar city, how would you plan what to do? What are some advantages and disadvantages of these options (a–f)?

a look online for information about what to do there
b read a guidebook
c ask friends who've been there on holiday
d ask friends who've lived there
e ask someone in the travel industry
f not plan anything in advance – I love an adventure

READING FOR WRITING

2 Read the travel plan on the right and answer the questions.

1 How long will Jana be in Málaga for?
2 Why doesn't Manuel take Jana to those places himself?
3 Is Manuel's one-day tour of Málaga a tour you might like to do? What would you enjoy? What would you do differently?

3 In pairs, look at these activities (a–e). In what order does Manuel suggest Jana do them?

a Go to the Roman Theatre
b Go to a restaurant at the port
c Go to a café on Calle Alcazabilla
d Go to the Picasso museum
e Go to Malagueta beach

4 Look at the Writing skill box. How many signposts can you find in Manuel's suggested travel plan?

WRITING SKILL
Describing steps in a plan

When writing a plan, it is important to clearly show the order of events.

By using signposts such as *to start, after that* and *while*, we can make the order of the plan clearer to the reader.

Put each new point or new activity in a new paragraph so that the plan is easy to read.

Hi Jana,

I'm so pleased to hear that you're going to be in my home town! I haven't been living in Málaga for the last three years, but I'll try my best to suggest a one-day tour.

To start your day, try to get to the city centre at about 9 a.m. for some churros (Spanish doughnuts) and a hot chocolate or a coffee.

After that, take a nice long walk around the streets of the old town. On the way there, you'll see street performers along Calle Marqués de Larios. There are many old buildings and monuments in the old town that you'll love. You must see the Roman Theatre. It's the oldest historic monument in Málaga and has some great views, so you won't want to miss it.

At this point, you might be tired, so stop in one of the cafés on Calle Alcazabilla.

Málaga is a city rich with art and culture. So while you're there, you must go to at least one of the many museums. There's the Carmen Thyssen Museum, the Revello de Toro Museum and many more. But the one I'd recommend is the Picasso Málaga Museum. It has 285 of Picasso's works and I think you'll like it there.

Lunchtime is usually between 2 and 4 p.m. in Spain. For lunch, I would go to a *chiringuito* (a small bar selling tapas) on Malagueta beach for some sardines and fried fish. After lunch, enjoy the sunshine and take a nap on the beach or have a swim.

Later in the evening, you can have dinner at one of the many restaurants at the port. And then you can end the day enjoying a drink on one of the many roof terraces in Málaga and taking in the amazing night views.

There are so many things to do in Málaga, but if I had only a day, these are the things I would do. It's a pity I don't live there anymore or I'd love to show you around.

I hope you enjoy your trip and do let me know what you think of Málaga!

Take care,

Manuel

People walking along Calle Marqués de Larios, Málaga, Spain.

5 Look at the Useful language box. In pairs, answer questions 1–5.

> **Useful language** Putting activities in time order
>
> To start your day, (have churros in a café).
> After that, (take a long walk …).
> Then, (walk towards the Roman Theatre).
> At this point, (you might be tired).
> While you're there, (you must go to …).
> Next, (go to the Roman Theatre).
> Later in the (evening), (you can have dinner …).
> You can end the day (enjoying a drink).

Which of these phrases can you use …

1 at the beginning of your suggested travel plan?
2 to signal the next activity?
3 to signal an activity you should do at the same time as another activity?
4 to signal the time of the day to do an activity?
5 to suggest the last activity in the plan?

WRITING TASK

6 A friend has asked you to suggest a one-day tour of your town/city. Make notes for 1–2. You can write about the town/city you live in or a town/city you used to live in.

1 What places and activities would you like to suggest? Try to include at least four ideas.
2 Then put the places and activities in order using signposting language from the Writing skill box.

7 **WRITE** Using your notes from Exercise 6, write your suggested travel plan.

8 **CHECK** Use the checklist. Your travel plan …

☐ describes at least four places to visit.

☐ includes signposting language to signal the first activity in the plan.

☐ uses signposting language to clarify the order of the activities.

☐ has a new paragraph for each activity.

☐ clearly signals the last activity in the plan.

9 **REVIEW** Work in pairs. Read your partner's travel plan. Would you like to do these things? Does the order of the activities make sense? Is there anything you'd change?

Go to page 132 for the Reflect and review.

A professional highliner walks between
two cliffs above Rio de Janeiro, Brazil.

7

Balance

GOALS

- Identify supporting reasons in an advice column
- Talk about the future
- Talk about managing money
- Identify supporting information in a podcast
- Deal with different ways of processing information
- Write a pros and cons essay

1 Work in pairs. Discuss the questions.

1 Look at the photo. Where is the person in the photo?
2 What is he doing? How do you think he feels?

WATCH ▶

2 ▶ 7.1 Watch the video. Answer the questions.

NATIONAL GEOGRAPHIC EXPLORERS

FRANCISCO ESTRADA-BELLI   **REBECCA WOLFF**

1 Why do Francisco and Rebecca feel it can be hard to achieve balance in their lives?
2 What do they do to try and achieve that balance?
3 Why does Rebecca think it's important to create time for yourself?

3 Make connections. Discuss the questions.

1 In what areas of your life do you try to achieve a balance?
2 How do you try to achieve this balance?
3 Do you have any tips for achieving balance you can share?

Balancing time

LESSON GOALS
- Understand an advice column about time management
- Identify supporting reasons
- Categorize ideas

READING

1 Work in pairs. Answer the questions.

1 What are some of your jobs or responsibilities at home, at work, in your studies, etc.?
   I have to tidy up, answer emails, …

2 What are some things you like doing for fun?
   I like going out with friends, listening to music, …

3 Do you have enough time to do everything on both lists? If not, how much extra time would you like in one week?

2 Read the advice column on page 85. Number these topics in the order they appear in the text.

a The best way to plan the things you need to do

b How to deal with things that make it hard for us to concentrate

c How much time you should work before resting and how long you should rest

d Problems that result from not working efficiently

3 Look at the Reading skill box. Then read the advice column again and answer questions 1–4.

READING SKILL
Identifying supporting reasons

Writers often support their ideas with reasons – explanations of why something is true or correct. Identifying reasons helps you better understand the relationship between ideas. Words or phrases that signal reasons include *the reason, one of the reasons, because (of)* and *since*. The reason may appear before or after the action or effect.

1 Why does the person with the time-management problem take work home?

2 Why should you stand up and move around when you take a microbreak?

3 Why does a to-do list reduce stress?

4 For what reason may we lose up to forty per cent of our productive time?

SPEAKING

4 Look at the Critical thinking skill box. Put the ideas (a–i) into the best category (1–3).

CRITICAL THINKING SKILL
Categorizing

Categories are useful for seeing the connections between ideas. They can help us understand ideas better, organize them in our minds, and remember them more clearly.

We can categorize ideas by thinking about how they're useful or important. For example, it may be easier to remember nine tips for managing our time if we break them down into three categories:

1 Tips for organization
2 Tips for managing stress and tiredness
3 Tips for focusing your attention

This helps us notice not only the idea itself, but the reason it might be useful or important.

a Don't work late into the night.
b Find a quiet place to work.
c Take microbreaks frequently.
d Decide which tasks are the most important.
e Switch off your phone and put it away.
f Get plenty of sleep.
g Schedule a time to do work.
h Do one task at a time.
i Write a specific to-do list.

5 Work in pairs. Can you add any tips of your own to any of the categories in Exercise 4?

6 Work in pairs. Discuss the questions. Give reasons for your answers.

1 Which of the tips in Exercise 4 do you already follow?
   Since I'm a teacher, I schedule all of my work. Classes happen at a certain time.

2 Are there any you don't follow?
   At work, I can't find a quiet place to work because my desk is in a noisy office, and I have to be there.

EXPLORE MORE!

Search online for 'how to work smarter' and find more ideas.

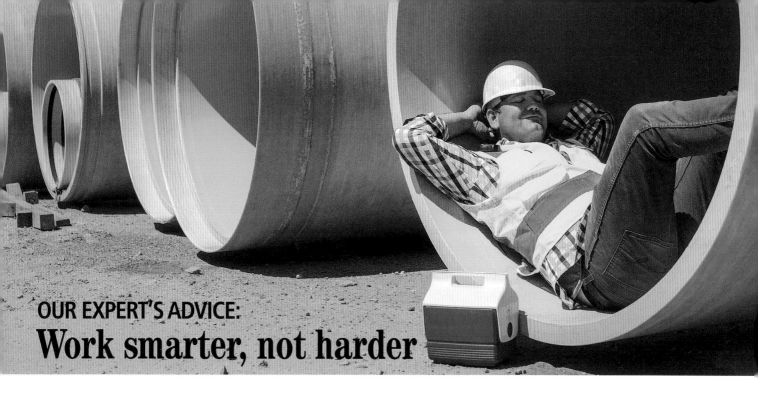

OUR EXPERT'S ADVICE:
Work smarter, not harder

The problem I like my desk job in a busy office, but sometimes there aren't enough hours in the work day! Since I often don't finish tasks by home time, I take work home. Too often I don't see friends or spend time with my partner because I have to work. I think I would have more free time if I could find a way to work more efficiently. Do you have any practical suggestions?

Our expert replies This seems to be a pretty common problem these days and work–life balance is so important. I can't give you more hours in a day, but I can make three practical suggestions that may help you do more in less time.

1 Try taking microbreaks

When you stop work for a minute or two to say hello to a colleague or just to rest your brain, you're taking a 'microbreak'. Research in Germany showed that a five-minute break every half hour reduced stress levels. On top of that, researchers in the US and Singapore found that social microbreaks helped to increase workers' happiness. They also discovered that workers who were normally bored at work became more motivated and did their job better after taking a social microbreak. How long should you work between breaks? Exactly 52 minutes, according to another study.

Because the most effective microbreaks include a change in your body position, if you've been sitting, you should stand up and move around to give both your mind and your body a change. But even a simple action such as looking out of the window can leave you more relaxed and better able to concentrate.

2 Keep a 'to-do' list – and follow it

A to-do list is powerful for three reasons. First, it reduces stress because it helps you see what's important (and what's not). Second, it gives you a plan for what to do and in what order. Third, it shows what you've achieved at the end of the day – which makes you feel good. When you make a list, be specific about what you want to do and break large tasks down into smaller steps. Instead of 'presentation', for example, write 'finish preparing presentation slides'. Be realistic about what you can do in a day and don't put too many or too few items on the list. Finally, make sure your to-do list includes breaks.

3 Focus!

The average person checks their smartphone 58 times per day – thirty times during work hours – and research shows that just having a smartphone on your desk reduces your ability to concentrate. If the phone is switched on, we can lose up to forty per cent of our productive time because of the constant *pings* announcing new text messages, emails or 'Likes' on social media. So, if you don't already, put your phone on 'silent'. Letting yourself think about just one thing will allow you to work better and faster.

Leaving work at the office isn't always easy, but by using a few tricks to work smarter, you can get more done in your working hours and have more time to enjoy relaxing with friends and family.

85

It's going to be a lot of fun

LESSON GOALS
* Understand people talking about their future plans
* Talk about the future
* Notice the main stress in sentences

LISTENING AND GRAMMAR

1 Work in pairs. Discuss the questions.

1 Which leisure activities do you find the most relaxing?

2 Is there a special place you like to go to take a break – a certain café, a park, the beach?

NATIONAL GEOGRAPHIC EXPLORERS

2 🎧 **7.1** Listen to Francisco Estrada-Belli talking about his plans. Answer the questions.

1 When is Francisco going to Guatemala?
2 Who is he going with?
3 What are they going to do there?
4 Why is the trip important?

3 🎧 **7.2** Listen to Rebecca Wolff talking about her plans for getting away from work. Choose the correct option to complete the sentences.

1 Rebecca is planning to go camping *a few times* / *for a few months.*
2 First, she plans to sleep in *her car* / *a tent.*
3 She *hopes to see* / *wants to avoid* bears.
4 When she goes to a lake, she plans to *drive* / *walk.*
5 She's also looking forward to *the scenery* / *swimming in the lake.*

4 Work in pairs. Discuss the questions.

1 Would you like to take a trip like the one Francisco is planning? Why? / Why not?
2 Would you like to take a car-camping or backpacking trip like Rebecca's?

5 Read sentences a–c. Then answer questions 1–4.

a 'I'm doing a backpacking trip with friends.'
b 'The views are going to be amazing at the top!'
c 'Most of the camping I do at that time will be in my car.'

1 When are Rebecca's camping trips: in the past, the present or the future?
2 Which sentence talks about an arrangement?
3 Which sentence is about a plan to do something at a specific time?
4 Which sentence is a prediction?

Francisco and his son on a scuba-diving trip off the Maya coast, Mexico.

Rebecca drinking her morning coffee on a camping trip in Garibaldi Provincial Park, Canada.

6 Read the Grammar box. Choose the best options to complete the conversation.

> **GRAMMAR** Talking about the future
>
> Use *be going to* + infinitive to talk about:
> • future plans and intentions.
> *We're going to go scuba diving.*
> • predictions.
> *It's going to be a lot of fun.*
> Use the present continuous to talk about future arrangements.
> *In the next few months, I'm taking a few camping trips.*
> Use *will* + infinitive for facts in the future, predictions, instant decisions and promises.
> *The trail will be very steep.* (fact in the future)
> *It will probably be rainy.* (prediction)
> *I'll give you an example.* (instant decision)
> *I've promised myself that I'll plan time away from work.* (promise)
>
> Go to page 146 for the Grammar reference.

A: Are you free tonight?
B: ¹*I'm working / I'll work* until six, but then I'm free. Why?
A: ²*I'm going to / I'll* go on a scuba-diving holiday in a few weeks and I'd like some advice.
B: Sure! ³*I'll / I'm going to* be happy to help. ⁴*I'll come / I'm coming* over after work.
A: ⁵*I'll be / I'm being* at the gym until about six, so how about after seven?
B: OK. ⁶*We'll both need / We're both needing* to eat, so let's meet for pizza.
A: Great idea. The usual place?
B: Perfect. I promise ⁷*I'm not going to be / I won't be* late like last time!

7 Complete the sentences. Use one verb with *going to* and one verb in the present continuous.

1 David _____ (take) three days off next week because the next few months _____ (be) busy at work.
2 Sylvia _____ (start) her Czech course in Brno in July and she _____ (need) a place to stay.
3 I _____ (bring) my friend Lia hiking with us on Saturday. You _____ (like) her.
4 It _____ (not / rain) next week, so we _____ (go) camping.

EXPLORE MORE!

Search online for 'plans with friends + ideas'. Which ideas have you tried? Which would you like to try?

PRONUNCIATION AND SPEAKING

8 🎧 **7.3** Look at the Clear voice box. Listen and repeat.

> **CLEAR VOICE**
> **Using sentence stress (2): stressing important words**
>
> When we talk about the future, the words *will* and *going to* usually aren't stressed. The stressed words are usually the most important ideas in the sentence. Usually, the final word takes the main stress:
> *I'm going to take an <u>examination</u>.*
> *New cars will be <u>electric</u>.*
> Stress may also fall on important information at the start of the sentence:
> *<u>Tomorrow</u>, I'm going to <u>rest</u>.*
> However, if you want to make the meaning of a statement clearer, you might stress a different word.
> *I'm not <u>giving</u> the examination. I'm <u>taking</u> it.*

9 🎧 **7.4** Work in pairs. Look at these sentences and underline the words you think will be stressed. Practise saying the sentences. Then listen to check.

1 Next week, we'll celebrate my friend's birthday.
2 Next month, I'm going to be busy.
3 We'll meet at a café.
4 I'm going to take the IELTS exam.
5 When are you leaving?
6 We're going to travel.

10 Read the questions. Make notes.

1 What are some of your future plans and intentions?
   Take IELTS exam
2 What arrangements do you have in the next few weeks?
   Meet friends tonight
3 What are some facts about your future?
   My birthday – October
4 What predictions can you make for the next year? The next five years? The next twenty years?
   2040 – all new cars electric

11 Work in pairs. Talk about your notes in Exercise 10. Ask questions for more information.

A: I'm going to take the IELTS exam.
B: When are you going to do that?
A: Next month.

7C
A balanced budget

LESSON GOALS
• Talk about money
• Practise saying the letter *r*
• Identify supporting information in a podcast
• Practise verb patterns with infinitive or *-ing*

SPEAKING

1 Work in small groups. Read the quotations about money. What do they mean? Do you agree with them?

> 'No, not rich. I am a poor man with money, which is not the same thing.' – *Gabriel García Márquez*

> 'Friends and good manners will carry you where money won't go.' – *Margaret Walker*

VOCABULARY AND PRONUNCIATION

2 🔊 **7.5** Read the advice. Match the words in bold (1 10) with the definitions (a–j). Then listen to check.

> Money can cause a lot of worry, but simple ¹**financial** planning can help reduce worry. Here's one simple idea: If you don't have a ²**budget**, make one. This is a list of money you earn, such as the ³**salary** you get, and the money you spend, including living ⁴**expenses** like your rent or ⁵**mortgage** payments, bills, food, and money you pay back on a ⁶**loan** for a car or other expensive item. It also includes ⁷**luxuries** such as meals out or trips to the cinema. Keeping a record of how much you earn and spend makes it easy to see where you ⁸**waste** money. It can also help you decide how much money you can ⁹**afford** to save each month. If you saved just $10 each month, it could easily ¹⁰**be worth** $1,500 after ten years.

a money you receive for work
b related to money
c things you don't need that give you pleasure
d a plan that shows how much money you expect to earn and spend over a period of time
e use more than you need
f money you spend for a particular purpose
g have a value in money
h have enough money for something
i money you've borrowed from a bank
j an agreement with the bank to lend you money to buy a house or flat

Go to page 138 for the Vocabulary reference.

3 🔊 **7.6** Look at the Clear voice box. Listen and repeat. How do you usually say the words *afford* and *earn* – with or without the /r/ sound?

CLEAR VOICE
Saying the letter *r*

Some people say /r/ in words only when there is a vowel sound after it, either in the same word or the next word. In other words, they don't say the /r/.
no /r/ sound: *afford* /əˈfɔːd/, *earn* /ɜːn/
with /r/ sound: *afford* /əˈfɔrd/, *earn* /ɜrn/
Research shows that it can be easier to understand a person's accent if they usually say /r/.

4 🔊 **7.7** Listen and repeat both ways of saying each word.
1 numbe**r**   3 wo**r**th   5 mo**r**tgage
2 ca**r**   4 c**r**edit ca**r**d

LISTENING

5 🔊 **7.8** Listen to the podcast about money. Number the topics (a–c) in the order you hear them.
a How to create a budget
b The 50–30–20 rule
c Borrowing and credit cards

6 🔊 **7.8** Look at the Listening skill box. Try to complete the notes and the pie chart on page 89. Then listen again to check.

LISTENING SKILL
Identifying supporting information

When a speaker makes a claim, pay attention to how it is supported. Listen for details and examples, such as:
• Facts or statistics: *Fifty per cent of the people …*
• Common sense: *It's clear that …*
• Examples: *For example/instance, …*
• Informed opinion: *According to …*

7 Work in pairs. Do you think the podcast gives good advice? Why? / Why not?

A street artist performs in Trafalgar Square, London, UK.

Credit cards: Germans 50%, South Koreans 60%, Canadians more than ¹_____

First step in balancing budget = have a ²_____

Money you ³_____ = salary

Living expenses = rent, mortgage, ⁴_____ (electricity, water, gas), petrol, ⁵_____

Luxuries: ⁶_____, ⁷_____

Savings: Money for ⁸_____ or when you stop working

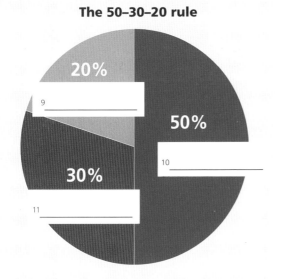

The 50–30–20 rule

20%

9 _____

50%

10 _____

30%

11 _____

GRAMMAR

8 Read the Grammar box. Then complete the notes about balancing your budget.

> **GRAMMAR** Verb patterns with infinitive or *-ing*
>
> Some common verbs are followed by an infinitive with *to*:
> *A lot of people don't **seem to have** a balanced budget.*
> Some common verbs are followed by an *-ing* form:
> *How can we **avoid getting** into trouble with money?*

Go to page 147 for the Grammar reference.

How I'm going to balance my budget

* Start ¹_____ (save) a little money every month.
* Avoid ²_____ (use) my credit card for daily expenses.
* Try ³_____ (find) ways to cut spending on needs.
* Before buying new clothes, ask: 'Do I really need ⁴_____ (buy) this?'
* Stop ⁵_____ (take) taxis to work and try ⁶_____ (use) the bus instead.
* Before going to a restaurant, ask: 'Can I really afford ⁷_____ (pay) for this?'
* Remember ⁸_____ (follow) my budget!

SPEAKING

9 Choose eight of these ideas and write sentences. Use infinitives or *-ing* forms.

My needs

I need …   I can't avoid …
I expect …

My luxuries

I love …   I spend time …
I can't afford …   I hope …

Tips for saving money

You should avoid …   Decide …
I recommend …   Plan …

10 Work in pairs. Tell your partner about some of your ideas in Exercise 9.

EXPLORE MORE!

Search online for 'ways to save money' and find more ideas for living on a budget.

Understanding ways of processing information

LESSON GOALS

• Learn about how culture influences how we process information
• Understand different ways of processing information
• Practise talking to people who process information in different ways

SPEAKING

1 Work in pairs. Discuss the questions.

1 Have you ever spoken to someone who didn't answer your questions directly? How did you feel? Why do you think they did that?

2 Have you ever spoken to someone who was too focused on specific details and missed the big picture? How did you feel? Why do you think they did that?

2 Do the quiz below. Then compare your answers with a partner before checking your scores on page 154.

MY VOICE ▶

3 ▶ 7.2 Watch the video about two ways of processing information. Would sentences 1–2 be said by a Whole-to-Part (W) thinker or a Part-to-Whole (P) thinker?

1 There were more than five fish swimming around in the tank.

2 There was a frog next to a big rock and lots of plants in the tank. It looked like a comfortable home for the fish.

Quiz

1 When you write your name, your surname comes ...
a first.   **b** last.

2 When you write your address, your street name comes ...
a before the name of your town/city.
b after the name of your town/city.

3 Think about a profile picture that you use online. Which is it more like?

a Mostly your face   **b** Mostly the place you're in

4 When you have a headache or a stomach ache, the first thing you think of is …
a making it stop.
b improving your general health.

5 Look at this photo for five seconds. Then cover it and make notes for one minute about what you saw in the photo.

a You made notes about the fields below, the trees, the green grass and the relationships between the people.

b In your notes, you started by describing the people, the colours of their clothes and the food they're eating.

4 ▶ 7.2 Watch again. Then in pairs, say what the video tells us about:

1 The way we write our address
2 The order of our name
3 Looking for the cause of a problem
4 How a Part-to-Whole thinker might feel when talking to a Whole-to-Part thinker
5 How a Whole-to-Part thinker might feel when talking to a Part-to-Whole thinker

5 Look at the Communication skill box. Work in pairs. How can these tips help us when speaking to someone with a different way of processing information from our own?

COMMUNICATION SKILL
Understanding ways of processing information

Sometimes, you may find yourself talking to someone who processes information in a different way to you. For example, they might use a Whole-to-Part way of thinking, while you might use a Part-to-Whole way of thinking.

Try to notice how they might be processing information and consider these tips:

• Be patient.
• Listen and ask questions.
• Try to see things from their point of view.
• If they're Whole-to-Part thinkers, make connections between what they're saying and the main topic.
• If they're Part-to-Whole thinkers, help them see the connections you notice by discussing them.

SPEAKING

6 **OWN IT!** Work in pairs. Look at what Akira and Mikayla said. What do you think are the reasons behind these problems? What advice could you give Akira and Mikayla?

'I can't understand the instructions that my teacher gives sometimes. Yesterday, she said she wanted my help. She asked me to find out what devices my classmates have at home, but I don't know why she's asking me to do this. What does she want to do with this information? Is this something I'm doing for the class or for her? None of this makes sense to me.'

Akira

'Karima really annoys me sometimes! I told her about the argument I had with Jay. I was talking to Jay about maybe going back to university and he just kept looking at his phone. It's like he wasn't interested. So I got angry and Jay walked out of the house. I told Karima he's a selfish person, but Karima kept saying 'maybe Jay was tired because he'd just come home from work' and 'maybe Jay was looking at something important on his phone' … Why is she taking his side?!'

Mikayla

7 Look at the Useful language box. In pairs, say which of these phrases might be useful …

a when a Whole-to-Part thinker is talking to a Part-to-Whole thinker.
b when a Part-to-Whole thinker is talking to a Whole-to-Part thinker.

Useful language Talking to people with different ways of processing information

Asking about connections between things
I'm afraid I don't get the connection between (your grandfather) and (Japanese food).
I'm a bit confused. What has (your grandfather) got to do with (Japanese food)?
I'm not sure I understand how this relates to everything else / what we're talking about.

Looking at the big picture
On the whole, we can see …
What do you think might be the impact on everything else?
I'm not sure if it's that simple. Have you considered the possibility that …

Clarifying what you're saying
I think there are some things we need to consider before we can talk about that.
Before I come to that, let me first talk about the background to this.
I think it'd be good for me to explain the situation to you first.

8 Work in pairs. Roleplay the two situations in Exercise 6, taking turns to be Student A. Use the Communication skill and the Useful language to improve the communication for Akira/Mikayla.
Student A: Akira / Mikayla
Student B: Akira's teacher / Karima

Pros and cons

LESSON GOALS
- Learn to use an essay outline to write a pros and cons essay
- Practise thinking about a topic from different points of view
- Write a pros and cons essay

SPEAKING

1 Work in pairs. Read the text. How different are Jonah's and Naomi's ways of presenting their opinions?

Zaina tells Jonah and Naomi that more and more people are exercising to YouTube videos instead of going to the gym. Jonah thinks that exercising at home to a video would never be as good as going to the gym and tells his friends exactly why he feels strongly about this. Naomi, on the other hand, starts to talk about the advantages and disadvantages of home exercise videos, and the advantages and disadvantages of going to a gym, before coming to a conclusion of her own.

2 Work in pairs. Read essay outlines A and B. Then answer these questions.
1 Which of these two outlines is similar to the way Jonah presented his opinion?
2 Which one is similar to how Naomi presented her opinion?
3 Which essay might be a more balanced presentation of both sides of the argument?

Essay outline A
- Introduction – Introduce the topic and explain how you'll be looking at the pros and cons of this issue.
- Positive Point 1
  Positive Point 2
- Negative Point 1
  Negative Point 2
- Conclusion – Summarize what you've written. State your opinion on the topic.

Essay outline B
- Introduction – Introduce the topic and state your opinion on it.
- Point 1 to support your opinion
  Point 2 to support your opinion
- Something other people might say and why you disagree
  Another thing other people might say and why you disagree
- Conclusion – Summarize what you've written. Restate your opinion and why you believe it's true.

READING FOR WRITING

3 Read the essay about exercise videos on page 93. Choose the correct option (a–d) to answer the questions.
1 The essay topic is probably …
   a Gyms should be free for everyone. Do you agree?
   b Everyone should have their own gyms at home. Do you agree?
   c Online exercise videos should come with personal advice. Do you agree?
   d Using online exercise videos to keep fit is better than going to the gym. Do you agree?
2 The author …
   a doesn't have an opinion on this subject.
   b thinks that the equipment in a gym is better.
   c believes that online exercise videos are useful.
   d feels that no one should exercise at home without proper advice from an expert.

Exercise videos have been around for a long time. However, since exercise videos have started appearing online, most people can now access them easily to get fit. Even so, some people say exercise videos should not replace proper instruction at a gym.

One advantage of online exercise videos is that they are free and convenient. You do not have to pay for a gym membership or expensive exercise equipment. You just need a WiFi connection and you can start exercising anywhere and anytime you like. Also, there are plenty of choices of exercise videos online. You might decide on a more relaxing yoga or Pilates class or go for a more high-energy Zumba workout. You can choose to strengthen your arms, your legs or your stomach muscles.

However, some people might find this wide range of choices confusing. They might not know how to choose the right video to suit their needs. In a gym, you could get advice on what exercises you need to do and how to do it correctly. But at home, it is possible for you to keep doing an exercise incorrectly because you don't have an expert around to correct you.

There are many pros and cons to online exercise videos, but I strongly believe that the pros outweigh the cons. People who are unable to go to the gym now have the option of getting fit at home whenever they want, and some exercise is definitely better than no exercise at all.

4 Look at the Writing skill box. Then answer questions 1–5 using the model essay above and the essay outlines in Exercise 2.

WRITING SKILL
Using an outline for a pros and cons essay

After brainstorming, an essay outline can help you organize your thoughts. When writing your outline, you can choose the main points that you'll be including in your essay and develop your paragraphs in a way that makes sense.

1 Does the model essay follow the structure of outline A or outline B?
2 What information does the introduction contain?
3 What are two advantages of online exercise videos?
4 What are two disadvantages of online exercise videos?
5 What information does the conclusion contain?

5 Look at the Useful language box. Find examples of some of this language in the model essay.

Useful language   Writing a pros and cons essay

Introducing a point
One advantage of (exercise videos) is …
First of all, (exercise videos are popular) because …
Some people say/believe that …

Showing contrast
However, …
On the other hand, …
People who disagree may say/believe that …

Considering both points of view
There are many pros and cons to (exercise videos).
While (exercise videos may be convenient), (there are also some disadvantages).
I (strongly) believe the cons outweigh the pros.

WRITING TASK

6 Work in pairs. Choose two of the three essay topics and note different points of view for each topic.
1 Now that we can shop online, we never need to go to the shops again. Do you agree?
2 Everyone should work from home if they can. Do you agree?
3 Every child should have their own mobile device. Do you agree?

7 Choose one of your two essay topics and write your essay outline. Pick two pros and two cons and use an outline from Exercise 2 to help you.

8 **WRITE** Write a pros and cons essay of about 250 words. Use your essay outline from Exercise 7 and the Useful language to help you.

9 **CHECK** Use the checklist. You …
☐ used an essay outline to help your writing.
☐ included an introduction paragraph.
☐ described different points of view.
☐ summarized both points of view in the conclusion.
☐ stated/restated your opinion in the conclusion.

10 **REVIEW** Work in pairs. Read your partner's essay. Is their essay a balanced presentation of both sides of the argument? Why? / Why not?

Go to page 133 for the Reflect and review.

A woman sits on her adventure touring bike at Salinas Grandes, Susques, Argentina.

Essentials

GOALS

- Recognize ellipsis in an article
- Discuss the environmental impact of clothes shopping
- Describe different types of food
- Activate vocabulary before listening
- Understand different ways of giving and receiving feedback
- Write a blog post about essential skills

1 Work in pairs. Discuss the questions.

1 Look at the photo. What do you think the woman is carrying in the luggage on the back of her motorbike?

2 Have you ever travelled and had to fit a few possessions into a suitcase or backpack? Where did you go? What did you take with you?

WATCH ▶

2 ▶ 8.1 Watch the video. Answer the questions.

NATIONAL GEOGRAPHIC EXPLORERS

RUBÉN SALGADO ESCUDERO

MARY GAGEN

1 What is Rubén's most important item?

2 What two things does he mention that have a lot of different uses?

3 What's important for Mary to do when she travels?

4 What three things is Mary talking about when she says 'practical things'?

3 Make connections. Discuss the questions.

1 If you were packing for a year away, would you take any of the items Rubén and Mary talked about?

2 What other items would you take?

I really missed good coffee

LESSON GOALS

* Understand an article about life on the International Space Station
* Recognize ellipsis
* Personalize the ideas in an article

READING

1 Work in pairs. Discuss the questions.

1 What foods or drinks would you really miss if you couldn't have them?
2 What favourite things do you use often that you wouldn't want to stop using?

2 Read the article on page 97. Which paragraph (1–5) describes each of the following?

a special things that astronauts only occasionally receive in space
b things that can only be found on Earth, not on the ISS
c things that make life on the ISS challenging
d what astronauts want when their mission is over
e a machine that was added to the ISS to make astronauts more comfortable

3 Read the article again. Are these sentences true (T) or false (F)?

1 Astronauts are often hungry because of limited food on the ISS.
2 Families usually include fresh fruit in the 'care packages' they send.
3 Before 2015, astronauts only had instant coffee on the ISS.
4 Scott Kelly says that parts of the ISS are painted green to make astronauts more comfortable.
5 Astronauts rarely have pizza on the ISS.

4 Work in pairs. Would you like to live for a month on the ISS? Why? / Why not?

5 Look at the Reading skill box. Then complete sentences 1–5 with the words that the writer has left out.

READING SKILL
Recognizing ellipsis

Writers sometimes leave out certain words to improve the flow of the text. This is called ellipsis. For example:

There's plenty of healthy food on the ISS, but it's mostly not fresh – [the food is] prepared on Earth, packaged and sent into space.

1 Clothing is limited and _____ can't be washed, so _____ must be worn for several days.
2 It's hard, but _____ an amazing experience.
3 These 'care packages' measure 23 x 42 x 25 centimetres and _____ have a maximum weight of 5 kilograms.
4 While _____ there, he said, the only thing from Earth he really missed was espresso.
5 Scott Kelly missed nature and _____ being able to go outside.

SPEAKING

6 Look at the Critical thinking skill box. Astronaut 'care packages' measure 23 x 42 x 25 centimetres and have a maximum weight of 5 kilograms. What would you ask for in a care package? Make a list.

CRITICAL THINKING SKILL
Personalizing

It's sometimes possible to understand information more deeply by thinking specifically about how ideas might relate to you and your life. Ask:
* What would I do in this situation?
* Are my own ideas the same as those in the text or are they different?
* Why might my ideas be different or the same?

7 Answer the questions. Write notes.

1 Are the things you would want in your care package the same as those mentioned in the article?
2 Why are your ideas of things to include in the package the same or different?

8 Work in pairs or small groups. Explain your answers to Exercise 7.

I like chocolate, so I'd probably ask for that, but paper books are too big. Instead, I'd choose …

EXPLORE MORE!

Search online for 'International Space Station + images' for more amazing photos.

Hot showers and good coffee

What astronauts miss when working in space

European Space Agency astronaut Samantha Cristoforetti enjoys her first drink from the ISSpresso machine.

[1] Life on the International Space Station (ISS) isn't comfortable. There are no showers, so astronauts must wash with very little water using a small cloth. Clothing is limited and can't be washed, so must be worn for several days. There's plenty of healthy food on the ISS, but it's mostly not fresh – prepared on Earth, packaged and sent into space, heated if necessary, then opened and eaten. Even so, the astronauts love living on the ISS. It's hard, but an amazing experience. But it also makes them very aware of simple needs and pleasures.

[2] About four times a year, astronauts on the ISS receive a bag containing a few items sent from Earth by their families, delivered by spaceship. These 'care packages' measure 23 x 42 x 25 centimetres and have a maximum weight of 5 kilograms. Astronauts ask for items such as chocolate, sweets, cheese and traditional books made of paper, which provide a rest from looking at electronic screens. In addition to the care packages, the spaceship deliveries to the ISS also include fresh fruit and vegetables sent by the space-station support teams on the ground, which the astronauts are always delighted to receive.

[3] Italian astronaut Luca Parmitano spent 166 days working on the ISS. While there, he said, the only thing from Earth he really missed was espresso – strong, dark coffee. He wasn't the first space traveller to wish for better hot drinks. Astronauts forced to drink instant coffee had dreamed for years of something better. It finally became a reality on 3rd May 2015, when another Italian astronaut – Samantha Cristoforetti – made the first cup of espresso in space. The espresso machine was provided by the Italian Space Agency, who worked closely with the Lavazza coffee company and an aerospace engineering company to design and build it.

[4] But there are some things that can't be sent to the ISS. Scott Kelly spent a total of 520 days in space, with one mission lasting a whole year. He said he missed nature and being able to go outside, 'the colour green, the smell of fresh dirt, and the feel of warm sun on my face.' He adds, 'My colleagues liked to play a recording of Earth sounds, like birds and rustling trees, and even mosquitoes, over and over. It brought me back to Earth.'

[5] Steven Vander Ark is responsible for helping astronauts prepare for long missions on the ISS. He says that when in space, they spend a lot of time thinking about the first meal they'll have when they return home. 'We often hear that pizza, ice cream and fizzy drinks are what astronauts miss most. But beyond food, what we hear most is that as soon as they get back on the ground, astronauts want a hot shower and hugs from their families.'

Clothes that we don't need

LESSON GOALS
- Understand someone talking about an infographic
- Learn to use defining and non-defining relative clauses
- Notice elision in words with *th*
- Talk about the impact of clothing waste

LISTENING AND GRAMMAR

1 Work in pairs. Discuss the questions.

1 How many pieces of clothing do you think you own?

2 *Fast fashion* refers to inexpensive fashionable clothes that are designed and made very quickly. How much of the clothing you buy is fast fashion?

2 Work in pairs. Look at the infographic below. What do these numbers represent?

a 80,000,000,000   d 50%
b 10   e 7
c 5, 1980   f 2,100,000,000,000

80 billion pieces
of clothing are produced each year. That's about 10 pieces for every person on this planet!

Fast fashion is cheap, so people are buying

5x more clothes
than they did in 1980.

On average, clothes are

only worn 7 times
before they're thrown away.

50% of fast fashion is thrown away
in less than a year.

2.1 billion tonnes
(about 2.1 trillion kg) of clothes are thrown away every year. Most of it ends up in landfills.

NATIONAL GEOGRAPHIC EXPLORER

3 🎧 **8.1** Listen to Mary Gagen talking about the infographic. Answer the questions.

1 How does Mary feel about fast fashion?
2 What did she do a few years ago?
3 What was her reaction to the fact that we currently produce ten new pieces of clothing a year for every person on this planet?
4 What happens when fast fashion goes to landfills?
5 What are the two things Mary says we can do?

4 Read the Grammar box. In pairs, find the relative pronouns in the example sentences and say what they refer to.

> **GRAMMAR** Defining and non-defining relative clauses
>
> Use relative clauses to give more information about a person, thing or place. Use the relative pronoun *who* for people, *which* for things and *where* for places. Use *whose* to mean *of who / of which*.
>
> - Use defining relative clauses to give information that is essential for understanding the person, thing or place you're talking about.
>
> *The plastic in the materials **which make these cheap clothes** ends up in our seas and oceans.*
>
> In defining relative clauses, you can replace *which* or *who* with *that*.
>
> *We throw away clothes **which/that** only have been worn about seven times.*
>
> *There are people out there **who/that** are buying hundreds of pieces of clothing every year!*
>
> - Use non-defining relative clauses to give extra information that is not necessary for understanding the person, thing or place you're talking about.
>
> *All these clothes usually end up in landfills, **which are areas of land where rubbish is buried.***
>
> In non-defining relative clauses, you can't replace *which/who* with *that*.
>
> *People are buying more clothes because of fast fashion, **which is cheap and fashionable.***
>
> Go to page 148 for the Grammar reference.

5 Work in pairs. Underline the relative clauses in sentences 1–5. Which of them are defining (D) and which are non-defining (N)?

1 Fast fashion, which started in the early 2000s, has changed the way we buy clothes.
2 Fast fashion brings styles which are seen in this season's fashion shows to the high-street stores at cheap prices.
3 Fast-fashion companies pay celebrities, whose fashion styles are often copied by their millions of followers, to wear their clothes.
4 There's a growing number of shoppers who are happy to buy second-hand clothes.
5 Many people are using websites like eBay and Vinted, where users can buy and sell second-hand goods, to make money from selling their old clothes.

6 Work in pairs. Look at the sentences in Exercise 5 again. Circle the relative pronouns and say what they refer to.

7 Complete the sentences with *which, who, where, whose* or *that*. Some sentences might have two possible answers.

1 Many of us throw away clothes _____ we don't want instead of recycling them.
2 The tidying-up expert Marie Kondo, _____ popular show encourages people to own less, tells people they should clear out their wardrobes.
3 The clothes _____ the world throws away each year are worth about $460 billion.
4 There is an environmental cost to producing even one t-shirt, _____ takes about 2,700 litres of water to make.
5 A person _____ drinks 8 cups of water a day would take 2.5 years to drink 2,700 litres of water.
6 In Germany, _____ three quarters of all used clothing is collected for reuse or recycling, there are many processes in place to reduce the environmental effects of clothing waste.

8 Combine the sentences using relative clauses.

1 Many people now think that vintage clothes are fashionable. Vintage clothes are clothes from the past of a different style.
2 I'm trying to convince my cousin to buy more second-hand clothes. My cousin's idea of fun is shopping for new clothes.
3 We should resell clothes. We haven't worn these clothes in a year.
4 Clothes shops should not throw away clothes. These clothes have been returned to them by customers.

PRONUNCIATION

9 🎧 8.2 Look at the Clear voice box and listen to the examples. Notice how the *th* sounds aren't pronounced.

CLEAR VOICE
Understanding elision in words with *th*

When people speak quickly, they sometimes don't pronounce the *th* in some words. This can make it hard to understand what the speaker is saying.
*I have some clo**th**es **th**at I don't want.*
*Plastic from materials **th**at are used in cheap clo**th**es goes into our oceans.*

10 🎧 8.3 Listen and complete the sentences.

1 I believe people should sell _____ clothes _____ they don't use.
2 I can't understand _____ people who throw away clothes after wearing _____ once or twice.
3 It's better to give away clothes _____ to throw _____ away.

SPEAKING

11 Work in small groups. Answer the questions.

1 How many of your clothes do you think never really get worn? Why?
2 What do you usually do with clothes that you don't want? Why?
3 Have you ever bought second-hand clothes? If so, what did you buy?
4 Is there anything else you buy second-hand or that you regularly give away? What? Who to?

EXPLORE MORE!

Find out more about solutions for clothing waste and how we can reduce it. Search online for 'solutions for clothing waste'.

8C
Food that you can't live without

LESSON GOALS
- Learn adjectives to describe food
- Activate vocabulary before listening to a conversation about food
- Practise the sounds /ɪ/ and /iː/
- Learn different ways of using comparatives

SPEAKING

1 Work in pairs. Discuss the questions.
1 What food can't you live without? How would you describe it?
2 What is a typical dish from your country/region? How would you describe it?

LISTENING

2 Look at the Listening skill box. In pairs, answer questions 1–4.

> **LISTENING SKILL**
> **Activating vocabulary**
>
> Before listening, it can be helpful to think about the topic and predict the kinds of words you're likely to hear. This activates the vocabulary that is stored in our brain and we are more prepared when we hear these types of words used.

You're going to listen to three people describing food that they can't live without. Can you think of …
1 three verbs to describe how we cook food?
2 four adjectives to describe different tastes?
3 five types of meat?
4 six vegetables?

3 🎧 **8.4** Listen to Chati, Jamie and Desirée talking about the food they can't live without. Who can't live without these foods – Chati (C), Jamie (J) or Desirée (D)?
1 sticky rice   2 arepas   3 Cullen skink

4 🎧 **8.4** Listen again. Complete the sentences.
1 Arepa is like a thick pancake made from corn _____.
2 You can put different _____ in an arepa – beans, meat or avocado.
3 Cullen skink is a fish soup cooked in butter, milk and _____.
4 Cranachan is a Scottish _____ made with strawberries, raspberries and oats.
5 Larb is like a minced meat _____.
6 Larb tastes hot, _____, sweet and sour at the same time.
7 Larb is often eaten in Laos and _____.

VOCABULARY

5 🎧 **8.5** Work in pairs. Answer the questions. Then listen to check.
1 We sometimes add -y to form an adjective, e.g. something that sticks = *sticky*. How can we describe the taste of food that …
   a has a lot of cheese?
   b has a lot of cream?
   c has a lot of butter?
   d has a lot of salt?
2 What are the adjective forms of these nouns?
   a milk   e fruit
   b oil   f meat
   c water   g spice (like hot chillies)
   d chocolate

Go to page 138 for the Vocabulary reference.

Arepa

Larb

6 Work in pairs. Can you think of a food item for each of the adjectives in Exercise 5?

7 Complete these sentences with the adjectives from Exercise 5.

1 She's put extra strawberries in the cake, so it's nice and _____.
2 He's vegetarian, so don't prepare anything _____ for him.
3 Eating _____ food makes me very thirsty.
4 You might want to thicken the sauce because it's really _____.
5 The curry is very _____. He's put too many chillies in.
6 I like my coffee and tea black. I'm not a fan of _____ drinks.
7 I don't like deep frying vegetables because they get very _____.
8 Don't put too much parmesan cheese on my pasta. I don't like it when it's too _____.

PRONUNCIATION

8 🎧 8.6 Look at the Clear voice box. Listen and repeat.

CLEAR VOICE
Saying /ɪ/ and /iː/

/iː/ is a longer sound than /ɪ/.

When we say /ɪ/, our mouth is relaxed.

/ɪ/ f*i*sh, ch*i*ck*e*n, st*i*cky

When we say /iː/, our mouth spreads wider, like we're smiling.

/iː/ m*ea*t, b*ee*f, cr*ea*m

9 🎧 8.7 Look at these words. Tick (✓) the sound each word contains. Listen to check and repeat.

	/ɪ/	/iː/
1 eat	☐	☐
2 drink	☐	☐
3 milk	☐	☐
4 cheesy	☐	☐
5 sweet	☐	☐
6 this	☐	☐
7 women	☐	☐
8 piece	☐	☐

GRAMMAR

10 Read the Grammar box. Then choose the correct answers for sentences 1–4.

GRAMMAR Comparatives

With adverbs ending with -ly e.g. *slowly, quietly,* we form comparatives with *more/less* + adverb.
*Pierre can get it **more easily** in France.*
We can use *much / a lot / a little / slightly* + comparative adjective to show how big the difference is.
*It makes it **slightly less bitter**.*
*Making arepas with arepa flour is **much better**.*
We use *more or less the same* to say that something is almost the same.
*I think the larb in north-east Thailand is **more or less the same** as the larb in Laos.*
We use *not as* + adjective + *as* to show that two things are not equal.
*I guess the cheese in France is **not as expensive as** the cheese in Thailand.*

Go to page 148 for the Grammar reference.

1 I don't mind eating either chicken or duck. They are *not as / more or less / a lot* the same to me.
2 There's less chilli in this, so it shouldn't be *as / more / less* spicy as the other dish.
3 People say I always eat like I'm in a rush. I'm trying to eat *much / more / a lot* slowly.
4 I have chocolatey treats *quite / not as / a lot* more frequently than I should.

11 Work in pairs. Write sentences using *not as … as.*
1 Restaurants are bigger than cafés.
   Cafés aren't as big as restaurants.
2 Chips are oilier than boiled potatoes.
   Boiled potatoes …
3 My mother's cooking is better than mine.
   My cooking …
4 Fruit juices are healthier than soft drinks.
5 Sauces that are made with butter are thicker than sauces that are made with oil.

SPEAKING

12 Work in small groups. Tell your group about one dish you love and one you really dislike. Describe how they look and taste and why you like/dislike them.

EXPLORE MORE!

Have you ever had chocolate on a pizza? Or chips in a sandwich? Or noodles with cheese? Would you try them? Find out more about interesting food combinations by searching online for 'interesting food combinations'.

Giving and receiving feedback

LESSON GOALS

- Learn about different types of 'feedback sandwiches'
- Consider tips on giving and receiving feedback
- Practise offering developmental feedback

SPEAKING

1 Work in pairs. Discuss the questions.

1 Think of a situation where someone said they wanted to give you feedback on something you did. How did they do it? How did you feel?

2 Do you think feedback is important? Why?

2 Work in pairs. Look at what Rudi and Kabir are saying and answer the questions (1–2).

'I met Kabir for lunch and he started talking to me about the party I had at my house last weekend. He said he had a really good time at the party and loved the music and the atmosphere. He also said it was interesting to see so many meat dishes at the table. We had Spanish chicken paella, Turkish lamb köfte, German beef rouladen and Chinese Peking duck, so I just thought he was really impressed by the variety of food we had. Later that week, I spoke to Kabir's best friend Ezan. Ezan told me that Kabir's recently become vegetarian and was really hungry during my party. I was quite shocked by this information. I had no idea and if Ezan hadn't told me, I'd still have the impression that Kabir loved the party food! I wish Kabir had told me. We're all friends and I'd appreciate some openness.'

Rudi

'I feel that I was very open and clear in the feedback I gave Rudi about his party food. I'm pleased that I dealt with the situation in a way that didn't offend Rudi.'

Kabir

1 Why do you think that Rudi felt Kabir wasn't being honest and yet Kabir felt he was?

2 What would you do if you were Rudi?

MY VOICE ▶

3 ▶ 8.2 Watch the video about giving feedback. Answer the questions.

1 What are the three layers of the feedback sandwich? What is the purpose of the bread?

2 What parts of the feedback sandwich did Kabir prefer to use?

3 What parts of the feedback sandwich did Rudi prefer to use?

4 What should we do when communicating with people from other cultures?

4 Work in pairs. Match the situations (1–4) with the type of feedback sandwich (a–d).

1 'I just wanted you to know that you left the tap running the other day. I know you didn't mean to, but I thought I should mention it. It might be worth checking before you leave the room next time because it's a waste of water.'

2 'Have you brought two suitcases with you on holiday? It's good to have all your essentials with you. You're very prepared.'

3 'Thanks for organizing that virtual call. It was nice to see everyone. How do you feel it went? I enjoyed the games you suggested, but do you think maybe some of the people weren't so keen on playing games? I think the games really gave us something to focus on, but I wonder if some people just wanted to chat and catch up instead?'

4 'That's a beautiful dress. The blue really suits you. I'm not sure if those shoes go well with that dress though. But that necklace is really lovely. You look amazing.'

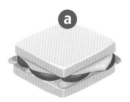

The feedback sandwich

All filling, no bread

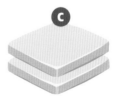

All bread, no filling

Filling and bread combined

5 Work in pairs. Look at the Communication skill box. Discuss which of these you might find the most difficult to do and why.

Giving and receiving feedback

When receiving feedback

• If someone gives you all-bread-no-filling feedback, think about what the developmental feedback might be.

• If someone gives you all-filling-no-bread feedback, focus on how the feedback can help you develop and improve.

When giving feedback

• Use the bread part of the feedback sandwich to soften the developmental feedback. Make the positive feedback specific and genuine.

• Be clear and specific about how your feedback can help them develop.

• Show you have positive intentions.

SPEAKING

6 OWN IT! Read situations A–C. In pairs, answer the questions.

A Yuen invited Tomaž to his house for a home-cooked meal. When Yuen asked Tomaž what he thought of the food, Tomaž said Yuen's cooking is always very salty. Yuen felt unappreciated.

B When Jo introduced Beng to her friends, he spoke all the time and no one else had the chance to speak. Later, Jo told Beng she wanted to talk about his conversation style. She then talked about how lively and chatty Beng was and how others are not as confident as he is. Beng went away feeling pleased that Jo's friends admired him so much.

C When Pensri asked her friend Alba what she thought of her painting, Alba said that it was lovely and that Pensri was very talented. Alba then said that the colours were very dark and suggested that Pensri should try brighter colours. Pensri felt that Alba's positive feedback about her talent wasn't genuine and that Alba didn't really like her painting.

1 How was feedback given?
2 What advice could you give the feedback givers and receivers in each scenario?

7 Look at the Useful language box. In pairs, say how you normally signal positive intention when giving someone feedback in your first language.

Useful language Giving feedback

Giving positive feedback (the bread)
I really like the way you (drew those mountains).
I must say you're so good at (cooking so many different dishes).
I've heard so many people saying such good things about (your artwork).

Showing positive intention
I have some thoughts that might be useful.
I've got some ideas that might help if you'd like to hear them.
I'm saying this because I'd like to support you.

Giving clear developmental feedback (the filling)
It seems to me that (the others didn't really get a chance to speak).
Maybe you could (include some vegetarian dishes)?
Have you thought about (using some bright colours)?

8 Work in pairs. Roleplay the three situations in Exercise 6, taking turns to be the person giving clear feedback. Use the Communication skill tips and the Useful language to give feedback in a way that doesn't damage the relationship.

9 Work in small groups. Discuss the questions.

1 Think about a time when you had to give someone feedback. What happened? How did you tell them about it?
2 What factors do you think might affect the feedback style you choose? Can you give some examples?
3 How do you normally prefer to receive feedback? How does the way feedback is given affect your response to it?
4 How do you think you can improve the way you receive feedback?

8E
Smiling is essential

LESSON GOAL
- Choose an appropriate topic for a blog post
- Learn useful language for saying what's important
- Write a blog post about essential skills

SPEAKING

1 Work in pairs. Look at the list of jobs and activities (1–6) and the list of skills, abilities and qualities (a–g). Which items from each list do you think go together? Why?

1 planning a party
2 playing online games
3 gardening
4 playing the violin
5 teaching
6 photographing people around the world for *National Geographic*

a ability to think and act quickly
b an understanding of weather and seasons
c good communication skills
d good listening skills
e good organizational skills
f patience
g problem-solving ability

A: For playing online games, you need the ability to think and act quickly.

B: You may need patience too. Some games take a lot of practice!

READING FOR WRITING

NATIONAL GEOGRAPHIC EXPLORER

2 Read the blog post by Rubén Salgado Escudero on page 105. Match the headings (a–c) with a section of the blog post (1–3).

a Basic language
b Body language
c Research

3 Work in pairs. Answer the questions.

1 What word does Rubén define in the introduction? Why do you think he gives the definition?
2 What is the danger if Rubén doesn't know a bit about his subjects' culture?
3 What are the benefits of speaking a few words of someone else's language?
4 What type of body language does Rubén use to make his subjects feel comfortable?

WRITING TASK

4 Look at the Writing skill box. Then answer the questions (1–3) to help you decide what to write about.

WRITING SKILL
Choosing a topic for a blog post

When you're writing a blog post about a personal interest, choose a topic that might also be interesting to others and that you can explain well. Ask:
1 What are my interests and activities?
2 Which of these might be interesting to others?
3 What parts of it can I explain in a way that will be clear to others?

5 Now think of some skills, abilities and qualities that are essential for your chosen activity or interest. Make a list.

Climbing: good organizational skills, control fear, physical fitness, …

6 Look at the Useful language box. Write one of each type of sentence about your topic.

Useful language Saying what's important

It's essential to (speak some basic words of their language).
You have to be / It's important to be (friendly).
You have to / It's important to (smile).
(Photographers) need to be able to (understand people).
Don't forget to / Remember to (use body language).
(Communication) is an essential skill for (a photographer).

You have to be fit.

Climbers need to be able to control fear.

Organization is an essential skill for climbing.

7 **WRITE** Write a blog post about your topic. Use the blog post on page 105 as a model and the sentences you wrote in Exercise 6.

Rubén photographs a subject in Chin State, Myanmar.

Three essential skills for photographing someone whose language you don't speak

By Rubén Salgado Escudero

When I travel and take photographs for *National Geographic*, I often don't share a language with my subjects (the people I take photos of). Here are three essential skills for working successfully in that situation.

1 _____

It's essential to study the culture of the person you will photograph. It's important to learn about their way of life and style of communication and what is acceptable or not OK when working with people in that place. You don't want to make someone feel upset or angry, so you have to understand a bit about where that person comes from.

2 _____

Speaking some basic words in your subject's language is an essential skill for a photographer. This helps you break the ice when you first meet them. Being able to say words such as *yes, no, thank you*, or even *you are doing great* really help you when you're photographing people. Also, they usually find it charming that you made the effort, and this makes them feel more comfortable. And if they're comfortable, you'll get better pictures.

3 _____

A photographer needs to know the one language that most of us can understand and connect with. Smiling from the beginning is the key to making friends with your subject and making them feel at ease before and during a photo session. Also, don't be afraid to use your hands and feet to explain things like where to stand or how to position your body. And remember to keep smiling through a session. It changes the energy and feeling between you and your subject and creates a more enjoyable experience for everyone.

---

8 CHECK Use the checklist. The blog post …

- ☐ is about one of your activities or interests.
- ☐ lists 3–5 essential skills/abilities.
- ☐ includes phrases from the Useful language box.
- ☐ explains the importance of each skill/ability.
- ☐ would be clear to someone who doesn't know anything about this activity.

9 REVIEW Work in pairs. Read your partner's blog post. Answer the questions.

1 Does it do all of the things on the checklist in Exercise 8?
2 What did you learn?
3 What would you like to know more about?

Go to page 133 for the Reflect and review.

A father and son practise golf swings on the roof of their apartment building in Nairobi, Kenya.

Taking a break

GOALS

- Understand contrast in an article
- Talk about imagined past situations
- Talk about holidays
- Listen for specific information in a conversation
- Learn to deal with unexpected behaviours
- Write a formal email of complaint

---

1 Work in pairs. Discuss the questions.

  1 Look at the photo. Where was the photo taken?

  2 What are the people doing?

  3 What do you do to take a break at home?

WATCH ▶

2 ▶ 9.1 Watch the video. Answer the questions.

NATIONAL GEOGRAPHIC EXPLORER

GABBY SALAZAR

  1 What did Gabby do when she was a child?

  2 Where does Gabby go when she doesn't want to go far for a holiday?

  3 How was her holiday in Sulawesi different from her other holidays?

  4 What does she like trying when she's on holiday?

3 Make connections. Discuss the questions.

  1 Where do you go when you want a holiday near home?

  2 Do you like planning your holidays in advance? Why? / Why not?

  3 What do you like doing when you're on holiday?

9A
Days off work

LESSON GOALS
- Understand an article about time off from work
- Understand contrast
- Interpret a bar chart

READING

1 Work in pairs. Discuss the questions.

1 Some companies have no limit on the number of paid days off that their employees can take. Why do you think some companies allow unlimited paid holiday?
2 What are the benefits for employees?
3 Can you think of any problems this might cause?

2 Read the article on page 109. Complete the sentences using these words to give the main idea of each paragraph.

---

allowed   bad   employees   good   less   more   rules

---

1 In many countries, employees are legally _____ to take paid time off from work.
2 Companies with unlimited holiday expect employees to make _____ decisions.
3 CharlieHR found that unlimited holiday made people take _____ time off.
4 Rules for time off need to consider all _____ equally.
5 Without _____, people may feel anxious asking for time off.
6 Limiting paid holiday may make workers take _____ time off.
7 Unlimited paid holiday may be _____ for workers.

3 Look at the Reading skill box. Find and circle the contrast expressions in the article.

READING SKILL
Understanding contrast (2): reading for contrast

Writers use certain words and phrases to introduce a contrasting idea in a text. For example: *However, … , Even though … , Despite the fact that …* and *Although ….*

It's important to recognize these phrases in order to fully understand how the ideas they refer to are connected.

4 Work in pairs. Match 1–4 with a–d to give contrasting ideas from the article. Which contrast expressions are used?

1 Most companies limit paid holidays.
2 Unlimited paid holiday sometimes works well.
3 CharlieHR wanted to make employees happy.
4 Unlimited paid holiday may sound like a dream.

a Sometimes it has caused problems.
b In reality, it can cause people to work too much.
c Some companies don't.
d Things didn't turn out that way.

5 Look at the Critical thinking skill box and the bar chart on page 109. Work in pairs. Answer the questions in the box.

CRITICAL THINKING SKILL
Interpreting bar charts

A bar chart is a simple way to compare information in different categories. In a vertical bar chart, the left side gives the values and the bottom shows the categories. The bars show the value for each category. Interpret the chart correctly to understand the information. Ask:
- What categories of information does it show?
- What are the values that are measured?
- Why is a bar chart useful for showing this information?

6 Look at the bar chart again. Complete the sentences.

1 More than half of the companies offer _____ days off per year.
2 Slightly fewer than 20% of companies offer _____ days off per year.
3 Nearly 15% of companies offer more than _____ days off or have no limit.

SPEAKING

7 Work in small groups. Discuss the questions.

1 What do you think is the best way to give employees paid time off? Why?
2 Would you prefer to take time off whenever you want or for your company to close for a month?

Unlimited paid holiday?

It sounds like the best job benefit possible – but do you really want it?

An Emirati family spend time off together, Abu Dhabi, the UAE.

1 In much of the world, the law requires employers to give workers a minimum number of paid days off work each year, often between 20 and 40, including both personal and public holidays. In many places, the law says employees *have to* take time off. Most companies say exactly how many paid days off are available and encourage staff to use them.

2 However, some companies allow employees to take as many days off as they like, including a lot of well-known companies such as Facebook, Dropbox and LinkedIn. Craig Malloy, CEO of an IT company called Bloomfire, says that when you treat people like adults, they act like adults. His employees love it and don't take too much – or too little – paid holiday. The idea is that happy employees work hard for the company.

3 Even though unlimited holiday has been a big success for some companies, others have found that it causes problems. When software company CharlieHR was set up in 2015, the owners decided to offer unlimited paid holiday because they assumed their team would deliver great work and they trusted them to manage their lives in a responsible way. Despite the fact that CharlieHR's intention was to make their employees feel happy and well rested, it didn't turn out that way. The problem wasn't that people took too much time off, but that they took too little. According to CEO Ben Gately, quite a few people took only 21–22 days off per year. 'Personally,' Gately says, 'I don't think that's enough to keep you fresh and at the top of your game.'

4 Gately also points out that the people who aren't on holiday have to do the work of those who are away. So, if you feel you need 30 days off, you give your colleagues more work than the person who takes 20 days off – and this isn't completely fair.

5 The final problem, according to Gately, is that not knowing the limits can make people worry. An employee survey at CharlieHR showed that workers felt nervous asking for time off because they didn't know if they were asking for too much.

6 After three years of offering unlimited paid holiday, CharlieHR decided to give employees 25 days of holiday they can choose to take at any time – on top of national holidays. Gately says that giving employees a certain number of paid days off per year makes them want to take those days. 'When something belongs to you,' he says, 'you immediately value it more highly.' In addition, CharlieHR set a rule that everyone has to take at least 22 days off per year and they strongly encourage everyone to take at least five days off every three months.

7 Although unlimited paid holiday from work may sound like a dream, in reality it seems that it can increase stress at work and cause people to work harder with fewer breaks.

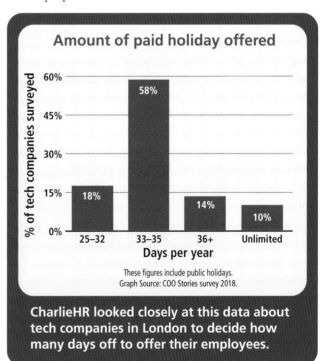

CharlieHR looked closely at this data about tech companies in London to decide how many days off to offer their employees.

EXPLORE MORE!

Search online for 'unlimited holiday' and find out more.

9B
If I had known …

LESSON GOALS
- Understand a text about holiday regrets
- Practise using the third conditional
- Practise saying aspirated consonants

READING AND GRAMMAR

1 Work in pairs. Complete the sentences with your own ideas and explain your answers.

1 If I had some time off next week, I would …
2 If I could go to any country in the world, I would go to …
3 If travel was no longer allowed, I would spend my holidays …
4 I would feel like I'm on holiday if I were …
5 If I were an explorer, I would …

NATIONAL GEOGRAPHIC EXPLORER

2 Read about Gabby Salazar's holiday regrets below. Then answer questions 1–4.

1 What was Gabby not able to do on Réunion? Why?
2 What did Gabby not take enough of to Costa Rica? What happened as a result?
3 What lesson did Gabby learn when she was in Russia?
4 What would you say to Gabby if she told you about these regrets?

3 Choose the correct words to complete the sentences.

1 When Gabby is talking about Costa Rica, she is talking about the *past / present / future*.
2 In reality, Gabby *did / didn't* take enough cash to Costa Rica.
3 Gabby wishes that she *had taken / hadn't taken* more cash.

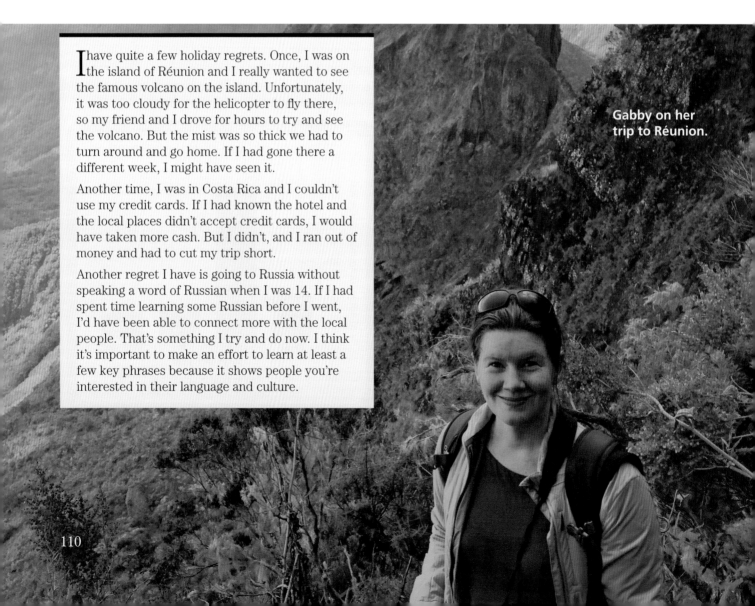

I have quite a few holiday regrets. Once, I was on the island of Réunion and I really wanted to see the famous volcano on the island. Unfortunately, it was too cloudy for the helicopter to fly there, so my friend and I drove for hours to try and see the volcano. But the mist was so thick we had to turn around and go home. If I had gone there a different week, I might have seen it.

Another time, I was in Costa Rica and I couldn't use my credit cards. If I had known the hotel and the local places didn't accept credit cards, I would have taken more cash. But I didn't, and I ran out of money and had to cut my trip short.

Another regret I have is going to Russia without speaking a word of Russian when I was 14. If I had spent time learning some Russian before I went, I'd have been able to connect more with the local people. That's something I try and do now. I think it's important to make an effort to learn at least a few key phrases because it shows people you're interested in their language and culture.

Gabby on her trip to Réunion.

110

4 Read the Grammar box. In pairs, say what the differences are between sentences 1–3.

GRAMMAR Third conditional

Use the third conditional (*if* + past perfect, *would have* + past participle) to express an imaginary past result of an imaginary past action.

*If I **had known** the hotel and the local places didn't accept credit cards, I **would have taken** more cash.*

Use *could* or *might* instead of *would* to reduce the certainty of the result.

*If I had gone there a different week, I **might** have seen it.*

Go to page 149 for the Grammar reference.

1 If I go on a beach holiday, I'll read my book all day.
2 If I went on a beach holiday, I'd read my book all day.
3 If I had been on a beach holiday, I would have read my book all day.

5 Complete Lim's sentences. Use the third conditional.

1 'If I _____ (be) on time for my flight, I _____ (go) on holiday with my friends.'
2 'If I _____ (not take) the train, I _____ (not stop) in that beautiful small Italian town called Otranto.'
3 'If Rosa _____ (check) her phone, she _____ (see) that her friends had changed their meeting place.'
4 'If it _____ (not be) raining, we _____ (not share) an umbrella.'
5 'If I _____ (speak) Italian, I _____ (ask) for her name.'
6 'If we _____ (not be) on holiday in Madrid at the same time, we _____ (not meet) again.'

6 Work in pairs. Use the sentences in Exercise 5 (in any order) to write a story about how Lim met his wife Rosa.

7 In pairs, look at these holiday regrets (1–5). Change the sentences into the third conditional.

1 When I was a teenager, my parents didn't let me travel, so I didn't join my friends on their trips.
If my parents had let me travel, I would have joined my friends on their trips.

2 I wasn't adventurous, so I went to the same places every year.
3 I was afraid of trying new things, so I didn't try the local food.
4 I didn't talk to any of the local people, so I didn't get to know the local culture.
5 I didn't research the local culture in advance, so I made many mistakes.

8 Think about the last holiday you had. In pairs, complete these sentences and make them true for you.

1 If I'd had more money, I …
2 If I'd had more time, I …
3 If I'd gone with someone different, I …
4 If I'd been ten years younger, I …
5 If I'd done more research, I …

PRONUNCIATION AND SPEAKING

9 🎧 **9.1** Look at the Clear voice box. Listen and repeat.

CLEAR VOICE
Saying aspirated /p/, /t/ and /k/

Put your hand in front of your mouth and say *holiday*. Notice how we push out a puff of air when we say /h/ in *holiday*. This is called aspiration.

When the consonants /p/, /t/ and /k/ are at the beginning of a word and are followed by a vowel, we say them with the same puff of air: /pʰ/, /tʰ/ and /kʰ/.
/pʰ/   **p**ast, **p**ool
/tʰ/   **t**ime, **t**alk
/kʰ/   **k**eep, **c**amp

But when these consonants are grouped with other consonants or when they are at the end of a word, we don't say them with the same puff of air.
/p/   **p**lace, tri**p**
/t/   **t**ry, spo**t**
/k/   **c**razy, ba**ck**

10 🎧 **9.2** Work in pairs. Decide if the consonants /p/, /t/ and /k/ are aspirated (A) or non-aspirated (N). Then listen to check and repeat.

1 **p**lane   4 **t**rain
2 **p**ark   5 **c**ar
3 **t**icket   6 wor**k**

11 Work in small groups. Do you have any holiday regrets? What are they? What do you wish you had done differently?

EXPLORE MORE!

What kind of holiday regrets do people often have? Search online for 'holiday regrets'. Are any of them similar to your holiday regrets? Do any of them surprise you?

9C
I would just go camping

LESSON GOALS
• Listen for specific information in a conversation about holiday advice
• Practise giving advice
• Learn holiday vocabulary
• Practise saying consonant groups

SPEAKING

1 Work in pairs. Think of somewhere that you've been on holiday. Now, imagine your partner wants to go to the same place on their holiday. Give them advice using these questions.

1 What do you think they should take with them?
2 What do you think they should do in advance?
3 What do you think they should be careful not to do?

LISTENING

2 Work in pairs. Look at the Listening skill box. Which of the phrases (a–f) might you expect to hear when listening for holiday advice?

LISTENING SKILL
Listening for specific information

When we listen, we often listen with a purpose. Perhaps we might be looking for the answers to certain questions, or getting specific information about something.

It can help to:
• have a clear idea of what we're listening for.
• predict the type of words/phrases that might signal where that specific information can be found.
• listen out for those words/phrases or variations of them.

a I'd advise you to …
b If I were you, …
c I must remember to …
d I'm fed up with …
e I wouldn't do …
f Can I suggest that …?

3 🎧 **9.3** Listen to Bogdan and Alessia's conversation. Discuss these questions with a partner.

1 Why is Alessia giving Bogdan advice?
2 What advice does she give about …
   a deciding on a destination?
   b accommodation?
   c sleeping?
   d knowing what places to visit?
3 Which pieces of Alessia's advice do you think Bogdan will take? Why?

GRAMMAR

4 Read the Grammar box. How do you give advice and recommendations in your first language?

GRAMMAR Giving advice

Use *should / ought to* + infinitive to give advice.
*You **ought to try** it!*
*You **should** just **take** a tent.*
Use (*If I were you,*) *I would/wouldn't* + infinitive to say what we think someone should/shouldn't do.
*(**If I were you,**) **I'd pack** my bags, **jump** into my car and **go** on a road trip.*
Use *suggest/recommend* + *-ing* to give suggestions and recommendations.
*I **suggest getting** an air mattress.*
You can also use *suggest/recommend (that).*
*I'd definitely **recommend (that) you take** a sleeping bag.*

Go to page 150 for the Grammar reference.

5 Rewrite these sentences using the words in brackets. Then in pairs, say if you agree with this holiday advice.

1 It's a good idea to check if you can use your phone in that country. (should)
2 Take your phone charger with you! (ought to)
3 Don't forget to check the visa requirements. (would)
4 I think it's a good idea to get travel insurance. (suggest)
5 I don't think it's a good idea to post your holiday dates on social media. (wouldn't)
6 My advice is to book a package holiday. It's much more convenient. (recommend).

6 Rewrite these sentences using *suggest/ recommend + -ing.*

1 I suggest that you weigh your suitcase before you go to the airport.
2 I recommend that you call your bank before you use your bank cards abroad.
3 He recommended that I travel by train.
4 She suggested that I don't bring too many clothes.

VOCABULARY

7 🎧 **9.4** Complete the text with these words. Then listen to check.

---
abroad   accommodation   check   deposits
destination   insurance   luggage
making   reservations   unpacking   up

I enjoy [1] _____ **holiday plans**. I like **booking my** [2] _____ six months in advance. I [3] _____ **out the travel advice** about my **holiday** [4] _____ before my trip. And I always **make** [5] _____ at the best restaurants. But the last time I **went** [6] _____, all my plans went wrong. I was [7] _____ **my suitcase** when I realized I'd forgotten to bring my phone charger. This meant I couldn't **look** [8] _____ **any maps on my phone** and I couldn't find the restaurant addresses. So I ended up **losing the** [9] _____ I'd paid. And when the airline **lost my** [10] _____ on the flight back, I couldn't give them my **travel** [11] _____ details because all the information was on my phone! I wish we weren't so dependent on our phones!

Go to page 139 for the Vocabulary reference.

8 Work in pairs. Discuss the questions.

1 Do many people you know go abroad for their holidays? Where do they often go to?
2 What are some popular holiday destinations in your country?
3 How many different types of holiday accommodation can you name?
4 When you go away, do you normally unpack your suitcase as soon as you get there? Why? / Why not?
5 Do you usually make reservations when you go to a restaurant? Why? / Why not?
6 Have you ever lost anything while on holiday? What happened?

PRONUNCIATION

9 🎧 **9.5** Look at the Clear voice box and listen to the examples. How do you normally say words like 'plans' and 'advice'?

CLEAR VOICE
Saying consonant groups (2): inserting a short vowel

Some students might find words with two or three consonants together difficult to pronounce.

Instead of not pronouncing a consonant, it's easier for people to understand you if you try inserting a short vowel between the consonants.

For example, when saying 'plans', instead of saying /pænz/ or /lænz/, try saying /pᵊlænz/.

*pl*ans = /plænz/, /pᵊlænz/

When saying 'advice', instead of saying /əvaɪs/, try saying /ədᵘvaɪs/.

*adv*ice = /ədvaɪs/, /ədᵘvaɪs/

10 Work in pairs. How would you say these words? Where are the consonant groups?

1 travel   3 block
2 special   4 smartphone

SPEAKING

11 In small groups, create a list of top ten travel tips. Then compare your tips with those of the other groups. Which of the other groups' tips do you agree with? Which do you not agree with? Why?

EXPLORE MORE!

Search online for 'top travel tips'. Are there any that you hadn't thought of before? Which of these tips are the most useful for the holidays you go on?

9D
Dealing with unexpected behaviours

LESSON GOALS
- Reflect on how we tend to deal with unexpected behaviours
- Practise considering different interpretations of unexpected behaviours
- Discuss different interpretations of unexpected behaviours

SPEAKING

1 Work in pairs. Think of a time when you were introduced to a new group of people, e.g. colleagues at a new workplace, a new group of friends, a friend's family, and they did things differently from you. Discuss the questions.

1 What did they do that surprised you?
2 How did you feel about what they did?
3 How did you react?

2 🎧 9.6 Peter is on holiday and starts chatting to Lee in a café. Listen to the conversation between Peter and Lee. In pairs, answer the questions.

1 What impression would Lee make on you?
2 What might Peter think of Lee?

3 🎧 9.7 Peter later told his friend about his meeting with Lee. Listen to what Peter says. In pairs, answer the questions.

1 How did Lee make Peter feel uncomfortable?
2 How might Lee's conversation style be different from what Peter expected?

MY VOICE ▶

4 ▶ 9.2 Watch the video about dealing with unexpected behaviours. Answer the questions.

1 When we meet someone who does things differently from us, how do we often interpret their behaviour?
2 The video suggests going through the three steps of Describe, Analyse, Evaluate. Which steps did Peter take instead?
3 When describing what happened, what should we be careful <u>not</u> to do?
4 The video suggests three interpretations of Lee's behaviour. Can you think of other possible interpretations?
5 By practising using these three steps, what are we training ourselves to do?

5 Look at the Communication skill box. Work in pairs. Answer questions 1–2.

COMMUNICATION SKILL
Dealing with unexpected behaviours

When you encounter a behaviour that is different to what you expect, use the D-A-E steps to better understand what you're experiencing.

Describe – Say what's happening without any judgement.

Analyse – Reflect on why this is happening. Try to give at least three different possible reasons or interpretations for the behaviour.

Evaluate – Consider how each interpretation in the *Analyse* step makes you feel.

Why do you think it is important …
1 <u>not</u> to jump from *Describe* to *Evaluate*?
2 to give at least three different possible interpretations for the behaviour?

6 Look at the Useful language box. Notice the use of *might* and *would*. Why do you think these are good verbs to use when dealing with different behaviours?

Useful language Considering unexpected behaviours

Describe
What happened was (he asked too many personal questions).

Analyse
Maybe (he) did that because (he was trying to show interest).
It might be due to (his style of questioning).
Perhaps he was (nervous).

Evaluate
That would make me feel (uncomfortable).
I would find that behaviour (aggressive).
I would (be happy to give him more information).

A tourist shops at a craft fair in Olinda, Brazil.

7 Work in pairs. Put steps 1–3 about a holiday situation in the correct order: Describe (D), Analyse (A) and Evaluate (E).

1
> What happened was I walked into a shop and the shop assistants didn't smile at me or say hello. I asked one of them, 'Do you have any postcards?' and they simply said 'No' and didn't give me any other information. In my country, I'm used to shop assistants smiling and offering a lot more help.

2
> a It's good to know they weren't being unfriendly. It makes me realize how much I depend on smiles to know if someone is friendly and being polite. I can see why some cultures might not assume the same thing.
>
> b If that was the case, then I would feel really bad about walking in at this moment. I'd actually be glad they weren't trying to smile and make small talk with me.
>
> c I would understand that because sometimes I find it scary when I suddenly have to speak English to people I don't know.

3
> a Perhaps people don't show friendliness through smiles and constant interaction here.
>
> b Maybe they did that because one of them just told the other some very bad news.
>
> c I think maybe they were nervous about their English.

SPEAKING

8 **OWN IT!** Work in pairs. Use the D-A-E steps shown in Exercise 5 and the Useful language to discuss the different behaviours in each of these holiday situations.

1 You paid in advance to see a tourist attraction but when you arrive, you realize half the attraction is closed. You complain to the staff and you were expecting them to give you an explanation and suggest some solutions. Instead, they simply smile and say, 'We're sorry.'

2 While waiting for the bus, you get into a conversation with someone. You tell them you work in information technology. They ask you, 'How much money do you make every month?' You don't think asking about someone's salary is polite.

3 You meet some locals at a café and you get into a discussion with them about the recent news. One of them makes a comment which you openly disagree with. The locals all smile at you and they say, 'That's very interesting' and 'You're very knowledgeable'. You think they admire your confidence.

9 Work in small groups. Discuss the questions.

1 After considering at least three different interpretations, we might want to find out which interpretation is the most accurate one. How can we do this?

2 Have you ever felt confused or upset by someone's behaviour because it wasn't what you were expecting? How did you deal with it? How might you apply these three steps to the experience?

9E
My stay was very unpleasant

LESSON GOALS
- Learn about what you can include in an email of complaint
- Practise useful language for complaining
- Write an email of complaint

New Message

To: A.Weber@Hotel789.com

From: Caleb.G@Gerger.com

Subject: Complaint about my stay in Bielefeld in March

Dear Ms Weber,

I'm writing about my recent stay at your hotel. I've stayed at other hotels in your chain many times before and have always been satisfied with my experience.

However, when I stayed in Bielefeld from the 15–17th March this year, the experience was very different. These are some of the issues I had:

- I had booked a double room but was given a room with two single beds.

- The room hadn't been cleaned well.

- When I tried to take a shower, there was no hot water.

- The hotel WiFi was not working and I wasn't able to get online with my phone or my laptop.

I mentioned all of this to the receptionist at that time and asked for a change of room, but unfortunately nothing was done about it.

My stay was very unpleasant and, as a result, I wasn't able to enjoy my holiday.

I would like to request a fifty per cent refund for my stay, to be transferred back to me within fourteen days, please.

Best regards,

Caleb G.

SPEAKING

1 Work in pairs. Discuss the questions.

1. Have you ever been dissatisfied with a product or service? What happened?
2. Do you ever complain about the products or services you receive? What are the pros and cons of complaining by phone, by email or in person?

READING FOR WRITING

2 Read the email on the left. In pairs, answer the questions.

1. What is Caleb writing to Ms Weber about?
2. Why was Caleb dissatisfied with his stay on the 15–17th March?
3. What did he try to do about it at the time?
4. What does he hope to achieve by writing this email?

3 Look at the Writing skill box. Find examples of 1–5 in the email on page 116.

WRITING SKILL
How to write an email of complaint

When writing an email of complaint, it can be helpful to:

1 Start with something positive.
2 Keep the details of your complaint short and clear. Use bullet points if you have multiple points to make.
3 Make references to any previous communication, e.g. phone calls, emails.
4 Be clear about the impact of the problem.
5 Specify what you want them to do, e.g. offer a refund or apology.

4 Work in pairs. Answer the questions.

1 Why might it be a good idea to start the email with something positive? Do you agree with this suggestion? Why? / Why not?
2 Why might using bullet points make the email more effective?
3 When making references to previous communication, what details might you include?

WRITING TASK

5 Work in pairs. Using tips 1–5 in the Writing skill box, say what you might include when writing an email of complaint in these situations.

1 You ordered some large t-shirts online for your holiday. When they arrived, you packed them straight into your suitcase. When you took them out during your holiday, you realized they were the extra-small size.
2 The airline changed the flight time without telling you. You arrived at the airport five hours early. The airline staff said they had sent you an email, but you know you never got that email.
3 You booked to go on a one-day sightseeing tour, but the tour bus took you to a jewellery store and then a carpet store and you ended up spending four hours shopping and only three hours sightseeing.

6 Look at the Useful language box. In pairs, consider the situations in Exercise 5 and replace the words in brackets with words that suit each of those situations.

Useful language Writing an email of complaint

Starting with something positive
I've (been a customer) for a long time and have always been (happy) with (your service/products).
Your (product/company) came highly recommended by my friends.

Making references to previous communication
I tried to (call your company three times in the last week) but (was unable to get a response).
I spoke to (the manager) about this, but (I haven't heard back from him).
I mentioned this to (the receptionist) but (nothing was done about it).

Specifying what you want them to do now
I would like to request a refund.
This is (not what I ordered), so please (give me a full refund).
I hope that you can/will (deal with this quickly).

7 **WRITE** Write an email of complaint. Use the Useful language to help you. Choose an option (a or b).

a Choose a situation from Exercise 5. Describe and include details about what happened. Then state the impact on you and what you want them to do about it.
b Think of a time when you were unhappy with a product or service that you received. Say what happened, what the impact was on you, and what you want them to do about it.

8 **CHECK** Use the checklist. The email …

☐ uses appropriate greetings at the start and at the end.
☐ starts with something positive.
☐ gives details about the complaint in a short and clear way.
☐ makes references to previous communication.
☐ is clear about the impact of the problem.
☐ specifies what you want to be done.

9 **REVIEW** Work in pairs. Read your partner's email. How many of the points in the checklist does it include?

Go to page 134 for the Reflect and review.

A woman reacts to the strong smell of a 'corpse flower' at the University of California, Berkeley, US.

10

The senses

GOALS

- Paraphrase ideas in an article
- Learn about language and colour
- Use the passive voice
- Make predictions
- Listen to people's problems
- Write about a memory

1 Work in pairs. Discuss the questions.

1 Look at the photo. What sense is causing the woman to react?
2 How do you think she feels?
3 Do you know any plants that have a strong smell – either good or bad?

WATCH ▶

2 ▶ **10.1** Watch the video. Answer the questions.

NATIONAL GEOGRAPHIC EXPLORER

PRASENJEET YADAV

1 What does Prasenjeet find interesting about the calls of the frogs?
2 What causes the spotted deer to make its call?
3 What does the call of the Malabar Whistling Thrush sound like?

3 Make connections. Discuss the questions.

1 What interesting animal sounds have you heard?
2 Do you hear or see birds or other animals in your daily life?

10A
Most tastes of toast

LESSON GOALS
- Understand an article about senses
- Practise paraphrasing
- Interpret a diagram

READING

1 Work in pairs. Answer the questions.

1 What are some things around you that you can see, hear or smell and some things you might feel or taste?

2 Do you think one of your senses is especially strong or especially weak?

2 Read the article on page 121. Tick (✓) the three ideas it discusses.

a Interesting writing describes the senses in detail.

b Some people experience a mixing of the senses – 'tasting' words, 'feeling' flavours.

c Mixing of the senses is caused by brain damage.

d It's normal for very small babies to have mixed senses, but unusual for adults.

e Mixing of the senses has many benefits and could be useful for everyone.

3 Look at the Reading skill box. Find the original sentences in the article for paraphrases 1–3.

READING SKILL
Paraphrasing

One way to show that you've understood a text or part of a text is to explain the ideas in your own words. To paraphrase:

- Note the main ideas in the sentence or sentences you want to paraphrase.
- Write your own version, changing the word order and using different words with similar meanings where possible.
- Check to make sure your version isn't a copy of the original.

1 For James Wannerton, the word *most* tastes like toast, *college* has the flavour of sausage and the name *Karen* tastes of yoghurt.

2 James and others experience words as flavours, but some people 'taste' with their hands, using their sense of touch.

3 Children may get synaesthesia from their parents, but experts don't know what causes the condition.

4 Work in pairs. Write one sentence to paraphrase lines 27–32 from the article.

5 Look at the Critical thinking skill box and the diagram on page 121. Answer the questions in the box.

CRITICAL THINKING SKILL
Interpreting a diagram

A diagram is a drawing or plan that shows what something looks like or how it works. Understanding how a diagram is connected to a text can help you understand a writer's ideas. Ask:

- What does the diagram show?
- Which part of the text is it related to?
- What ideas does it help explain?

6 Which of the following conclusions can we draw from the article?

a People with synaesthesia realize they're different when they begin talking about it.

b Most people with synaesthesia learn from their parents how to use it.

c People with synaesthesia have stronger senses than people without it.

d Senses are connected with how we learn and how we make memories.

e A cure for synaesthesia is unlikely because most people who have it wouldn't want one.

SPEAKING

7 Look at the text and the shapes below. In pairs, answer the questions.

> This experiment shows how the brain makes connections between words and shapes. It may give you some idea of what it's like to have synaesthesia.

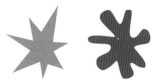

1 One of these shapes is called Bouba and the other is called Kiki. Which do you think is Bouba and which is Kiki?

2 Compare your answers with the rest of the class.

3 What do you think the result shows?

The flavour of words

¹ James Wannerton doesn't like the word *most*. Why? Because it tastes of 'cold toast with hardly any butter on it,' he says. 'I would never write it. I'd find an alternative. It distracts me, and all I can think of is toast.' *College*, for
⁵ James, tastes of sausage. The woman's name *Karen* has the flavour of yoghurt. The scientific name for this mixing of senses is synaesthesia, and two to five per cent of people experience it. Most of them consider it a gift, not a problem.

¹⁰ While some people like James 'taste' words, others connect letters, words or sounds with colours or 'feel' flavours with their hands, as though they're touching something. Almost all of them have a story of the day they realized that their experience of the world is rare. Holly Baxter asked a friend
¹⁵ at university, 'What colour is Monday?' The friend had no idea what she meant. Charlene Soraia, aged eleven, tried to imagine what her next school would be like. While most kids would think about classrooms, teachers and new friends, Charlene pictured
²⁰ 'yellow lines, with green bits'. When she told a friend, the response was 'What are you talking about?' She then understood that others didn't think in colours.

The cause of synaesthesia isn't known,
²⁵ though some researchers believe it may be passed from parents to children. We know that at birth, the senses in the brain are not completely separate. This means that a sound may cause
³⁰ activity in the 'vision' part of the brain. As a result, very young babies 'see' a colour in addition to hearing the sound. However, for most people, by the age of eight months, the connections between
³⁵ senses are broken and each sense is processed in a separate part of the brain. But in some people, the connections remain and two or more senses continue to work together – like the baby who both hears and
⁴⁰ 'sees' a sound.

Benefits of this connection between senses include good memory, artistic ability and strong creativity. Psychologists also believe that synaesthesia helps people see patterns of information, so they may have an
⁴⁵ advantage in areas such as language learning, where patterns like grammar forms and word combinations are extremely important. When learners associate both meaning and, for example, colour with words and phrases, they remember them better.

⁵⁰ Because of the potential benefits of synaesthesia, experts are trying to find out if it can be learned and developed by people who don't naturally have it. Synaesthesia researcher Dr Clare Jonas trained a group of young adults to connect letters with colours and found that their
⁵⁵ ability to remember words improved. Other researchers, however, have discovered that for synaesthesia 'learners', the effect doesn't last because people forget which colours and letters go together. Research continues. Dr Jonas told the *Guardian* newspaper, 'It would be really
⁶⁰ nice if we could find a way to give the useful bits of synaesthesia to people who don't have it.'

SENSES AND THE BRAIN

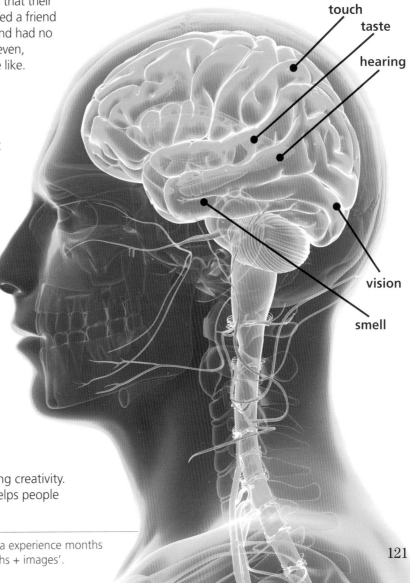

touch
taste
hearing
vision
smell

EXPLORE MORE!

Find out more about how people with synaesthesia experience months as colours. Search online for 'synaesthesia + months + images'.

Seeing blue

LISTENING AND GRAMMAR

1 Look at the photo above. Answer the questions.

1 What colour is the sea?
2 What colour is the sky?
3 What are the names of these colours in other languages you know?

2 🎧 **10.1** Look at the colours in the box and listen to the information. Then choose the best way to complete the sentence (a, b or c).

Two colours or one?

The conclusion of the research is that:

a it's impossible to know if other people see colours the way we do.
b the language you speak affects the way you see and think about the world.
c English is simpler than Greek or Russian.

3 Complete the facts with these phrases.

---

are seen   is given   is remembered   is used   was noticed

Colours, seeing and the brain: Five facts

- Colours [1]_____ with the brain, not the eyes.
- More than a third of the brain [2]_____ for seeing.
- A picture [3]_____ more easily than words.
- When something [4]_____ a name, we are able to see it more easily.
- The colour blue [5]_____ and named by the Ancient Egyptians.

4 Choose the correct option to complete the statements about the sentences in Exercise 3.

1 The focus of each sentence is the *action or object of / person or thing doing* the action.
2 The word *by* in the final sentence introduces who *saw / did* the action.
3 The verbs are formed using *be* and *an infinitive / a past participle*.

5 Read the Grammar box. Check your answers to Exercise 4.

GRAMMAR   Passives

Use the passive voice (*be* + past participle) when the agent (the person or thing that did the action) is obvious, is not known or is not important. The passive focuses attention on the action or the object of the action.

*When researchers **show** English speakers these two colours, they identify both as blue.* (active)

*When English speakers **are shown** these two colours, they identify both as blue.* (passive)

Sometimes the agent is added after the passive verb using *by* + noun.

*When English speakers **are shown** these two colours **by researchers**, they identify both as blue.*

Go to page 150 for the Grammar reference.

6 Complete the description with passive forms.
The Water Cube in Beijing [1]_____ (build) for the 2008 Summer Olympic Games. It [2]_____ (design) by a group of architects in China and Australia. It [3]_____ (make) of steel and very strong blue plastic. It [4]_____ (use) for the swimming and diving competitions. Twenty-five world records [5]_____ (break) there in the 2008 Games. Since the Olympics, the building [6]_____ (use) as a water park and art [7]_____ (display) there.

7 Complete the passive and active sentences in each pair (a–b). Use these verbs.

choose   paint   produce   see   ~~use~~

1 a The colour blue __has been used__ in logos by hundreds of tech companies including Samsung, Nokia and Twitter.
  b Hundreds of tech companies including Samsung, Nokia and Twitter ___have used___ the colour blue in their logos.
2 a The first blue paint _____ more than 3,000 years ago by the Ancient Egyptians.
  b More than 3,000 years ago, the Ancient Egyptians _____ the first blue paint.
3 a Blue is the colour that _____ the most often by both women and men as their favourite.
  b Both women and men most often _____ blue as their favourite colour.
4 a When Earth _____ from space by astronauts, it looks like a bright blue ball.
  b When astronauts _____ Earth from space, it looks like a bright blue ball.
5 a A picture called *The Blue Room* _____ by the famous artist Pablo Picasso in 1901.
  b The famous artist Pablo Picasso _____ a picture called *The Blue Room* in 1901.

8 Work in pairs. Which passive sentences in Exercise 7 need the *by* phrase to make sense? Which ones can you delete the *by* phrase from?

PRONUNCIATION AND SPEAKING

9 Look at the Clear voice box. Work in small groups. Discuss the questions in the box.

CLEAR VOICE
Noticing challenging sounds

Most learners of English find that some words or sounds are difficult to pronounce. Being aware of the sounds that cause you difficulty is an important part of making sure that other people can understand you.

• What sounds are difficult for me?
• Do these sounds cause communication problems? Do people *not* understand me because of my pronunciation in these areas?
• If people don't understand me, how can I change my pronunciation to make it clearer?

I find the bl *in* blue *difficult to pronounce.*

10 Work in pairs.
   Student A: Turn to page 154.
   Student B: Use the Useful language to ask Student A questions about these buildings.

Júzcar, a village in Spain.

Useful language   Asking questions about famous buildings

When was it built? / When were they built?
What's it made of? / What are they made of?
Why was it built? / Why were they built?
How has it been used? / How have they been used?
What interesting things have been done there?
Can the building(s) be visited by the public?

11 Work in pairs.
   Student A: Use the Useful language to ask Student B questions about this building.
   Student B: Turn to page 154.

The Blue House, South Korea.

12 Work in pairs. Discuss the questions.
   1 Do you know any other buildings that are famous for their colour?
   2 Colours are sometimes associated with feelings. For you, what is blue associated with?
   3 What colours are considered lucky? Happy? Sad?

EXPLORE MORE!

Find out more about famous blue buildings. Search online for 'famous blue buildings + images'. What other examples can you find?

10C

The internet of senses

LESSON GOALS
- Talk about technology and the senses
- Practise collaborative listening
- Practise making predictions
- Reflect on ways of correcting pronunciation mistakes

SPEAKING

1 Work in pairs. If you could improve one sense, which one would you choose? Why?

VOCABULARY

2 🎧 **10.2** Read 'Technology and the senses'. Match the words in bold (1–10) with these definitions (a–j). Then listen to check.

a relating to or involving technology
b tube-shaped pieces of equipment that allow us to see things that are far away
c make something go further
d small devices that are worn inside the ear to make sounds louder
e spoken language
f the ability to see
g pleasant smells
h a new way of doing things that changes a situation
i an environment produced by a computer
j feelings

Go to page 139 for the Vocabulary reference.

3 Which of the technological solutions in the infographic have you used?

LISTENING AND GRAMMAR

4 🎧 **10.3** Look at the Listening skill box. Listen to the first part of a talk about 'the internet of senses' and make notes about topics 1–2. Then compare your notes with a partner. Did you hear the same information?

LISTENING SKILL
Collaborative listening

Often when we listen, we don't hear or understand everything. Different people may hear and understand different things. Sharing information can help you understand more about the topic. When you listen collaboratively:
- Focus on the things you think you understand.
- Make brief notes.
- Compare notes with a partner to confirm or add to your own notes.

1 Technology we use now
2 Technology we will use in the future

TECHNOLOGY AND THE SENSES

Technology has been used for hundreds of years to make life easier and to improve or ¹**extend** our senses. This timeline shows the history of several specialized sense-extending ²**technological** solutions – some that many of us use every day.

late 1200s
Eyeglasses improve problems with ³**eyesight**.

late 1800s
The telephone sends ⁵**speech** over long distances.

early 2000s
⁷**Scents** can be sent over the internet.

2020s
The 'internet of senses' is the latest ⁹**development** in the effort to make our senses reach further.

early 1600s
⁴**Telescopes** allow us to begin looking into space.

Electronic ⁶**hearing aids** improve life for deaf people.

1950s

2010s
Apps are made that can recognize faces and read ⁸**emotions**.

¹⁰**Virtual reality** can make the brain believe we're in a different world.

5 [🔊 10.4] Now listen to a conversation about some of the ideas from the talk. Answer the questions. Then compare your answers with a partner.

1 What do the speakers think about the predictions from the talk in Exercise 4?

2 What idea related to shopping do they talk about?

6 Which sentence is more certain: a or b? How do you know? Read the Grammar box to check your answer.

a We will be able to use our senses online.

b You might be able to taste a meal.

GRAMMAR Making predictions

Use the modal verbs *will (not) / could / may (not) / might (not)* + infinitive to make predictions about the future.

Use *will* to talk about something likely. Use *could, may* or *might* to talk about something possible. Use *will not* to talk about something impossible.

*What developments **will** we **see** in the future?*

*This **could allow** us to use our sense of touch by wearing a glove.*

*Of course, we **won't be** able to do things like try clothes on.*

You can also use *that* clauses to show that you aren't 100% sure about a prediction.

*It's also **possible that** we'll taste things online.*

*It's **unlikely that** everyone **will** be able to use it.*

Go to page 151 for the Grammar reference.

---

7 Complete the predictions (1–6) with these words.

It's possible that   It's unlikely that   might
probably won't   will   won't

How likely?
100%

1 We _____ be able to smell a flower over the internet.

2 _____ a shopper will be able to feel products online.

3 You _____ be able to taste cake online.

4 _____ we'll be able to try clothes on online.

5 Virtual reality _____ be in everyone's home soon.

6 We _____ be able to travel back in time using the internet.

0%

PRONUNCIATION AND SPEAKING

8 Look at the Clear voice box. Answer questions 1–2.

CLEAR VOICE
Correcting pronunciation mistakes

When we communicate, sometimes we make a pronunciation error and need to repeat information or change our pronunciation to help other people understand.

*A: I like the idea of **d**rying clothes online.*

B: Drying clothes … ?

*A: **T**rying – t – **t**rying on clothes online. But I think it's unlikely.*

When you correct a mistake:

• Don't worry too much. Mistakes are a natural part of communication.

• Notice the word or sound that causes confusion.

• Try saying it again in a different way.

• Try emphasizing the sound you're trying to correct.

• Remember: Mistakes can help you identify areas where you need to improve.

---

1 Can you think of a time when someone didn't understand you because of your pronunciation?

2 What happened? Did you correct the mistake? If so, how?

9 Look at the information. Choose three of the predictions and say how likely you think they are.

Researchers at Ericsson, the mobile phone company, asked 7,600 people around the world what they believe technology will be like in the near future. Here's what people said.

In the near future, we may be able to …

• think of where we want to go to and immediately see a map using special glasses – 59%

• see through walls with special glasses – 56%

• wear a device that sends sound directly to the brain without using our ears – 51%

• go on digital adventure holidays using virtual reality – 43%

I think it's unlikely that we'll be able to see through walls in the near future. We might be able to do that in fifty years' time.

10D
Listening to people's problems

LESSON GOALS
• Learn about different ways of listening
• Consider ways of listening to people's problems
• Practise asking questions that develop thinking

SPEAKING

1 Work in pairs. Look at the old English nursery rhyme *A wise old owl*. Answer the questions.

1 Why do you think the owl spoke less when he heard more?

2 Do you know of any sayings in your language that describe the importance of listening?

2 ∩ 10.5 Fabio is listening to Beyza's problem. Listen to their conversation. In pairs, answer the questions.

1 How well do you think Fabio is listening? Why do you think that?

2 Do you think Fabio could listen in a different way?

3 ∩ 10.6 Listen to this alternative conversation between Fabio and Beyza. In pairs, answer the questions.

1 What did Fabio do differently in this version?

2 How does Beyza respond to Fabio in this version?

3 In which version do you think Fabio demonstrates active listening skills? Why?

4 Work in pairs. Discuss the questions.

1 Have you ever had conversations with people who don't listen the way you want them to? What did they do? How did it make you feel?

2 What do you think people should do in order to be better listeners?

A wise old owl

A wise old owl lived in an oak.
The more he heard, the less he spoke.
The less he spoke, the more he heard.
Why aren't we all like that wise old bird?

5 ▶10.2 Watch the video about listening. Answer the questions.

1 In what ways can listening well help people?
2 What are we really saying when we give advice without truly listening?
3 What are two ways we can help the other person develop their thinking?

6 Work in pairs. Look at the Communication skill box. Which of these do you think are more difficult for you to do? Why?

COMMUNICATION SKILL
Listening to people's problems

When people come to us to talk about their problems, we should:

• listen with our full attention and without judgement.
• avoid interrupting and jumping in with advice.
• allow them the silence to think and develop their thoughts.
• ask questions that allow them to explore the problem and their feelings.

7 Work in pairs. Look at situations 1–4. Which of the Communication skill tips are Klaus, Shilpa, Faruq and Tasya not following? What do you think might be the impact of what these 'listeners' are saying?

1 Diego is telling Klaus about his relationship problems. Klaus regularly jumps in to agree with Diego, saying 'Yes you're right, I've always thought that she was a difficult person.'

By constantly agreeing with Diego, Klaus is showing his support. But he's also blocking Diego from seeing things from a different perspective.

2 Gloria is talking about her money problems. Shilpa has never had money problems before and says, 'I don't know why you don't try and save more. I think we're all responsible for managing our own finances properly.'

3 Meili is upset and starts crying as she talks to Faruq about her difficulties with her colleagues. Faruq says, 'Don't be upset. They're not worth getting upset over.'

4 Eryk is worried about his new job and tries to talk about his worries with Tasya. Tasya keeps saying things like 'You need to believe in yourself more' and 'You're better than you think you are.'

SPEAKING

8 Work in pairs. Look at the Useful language box. What kind of questions do you often ask when you're listening? Which of these questions have you asked before?

Useful language Asking questions when listening to people's problems

Is it always (urgent / difficult / like this)? Can you think of a time when it wasn't?
What makes you think that?
What's stopping you from (doing those things)?
What do you need to do to make that happen?
What haven't you tried yet?
Who can help you?
What do you need to change for things to work?
What's the worst thing that could happen?

9 **OWN IT!** Work in pairs. Take turns to choose an option (a or b). When someone is talking, try not to interrupt or give advice. When appropriate, use the Communication skill tips and the Useful language to help the speaker develop their thinking.

a Roleplay a situation from Exercise 7 or invent a different problem that you might have. Include your own details about this imaginary problem.

b Use this opportunity to reflect on your English learning journey. Answer the following questions:

• What's going well with your English learning journey? What successes have you had recently?
• What difficulties do you have with learning English?
• What would increase your motivation for learning English?

10 Work in small groups. Discuss the questions.

1 When doing Exercise 9, what did you find the most difficult to do when you were listening? How did the use of silence work for the speakers?
2 When listening to people's problems, when should you give advice? When do you think it's better to hold back advice?

EXPLORE MORE!

Search online for 'how to listen to other people's problems'. Can you summarize the top five tips that you find?

That's when I saw the leopard

LESSON GOAL

* Practise bringing a story to life using the senses
* Practise using time expressions
* Write an anecdote

SPEAKING

1 Work in pairs. Discuss the questions.

1 What memories do you have connected with a taste – the first time you tasted a certain food or a flavour that is connected with a special time or place for you?

2 Are there any smells that remind you of your childhood or some other special time or place?

3 Do you have any favourite sounds – waves on the ocean? Birds singing? A certain type of music?

READING FOR WRITING

NATIONAL GEOGRAPHIC EXPLORER

2 Read Prasenjeet Yadav's anecdote below. Answer the questions.

1 What did Prasenjeet see?

2 Why didn't he take many photos?

3 How did the experience end?

3 What expressions does Prasenjeet use to indicate the order that things happened in?

That's when …,

4 Look at the Writing skill box. Find an example of 'showing' in Prasenjeet's anecdote for each 'telling' sentence (1–5).

WRITING SKILL
Showing instead of telling

When we write about an experience, we can use the five senses to show our readers what we're talking about rather than just telling them.
For example:

Telling | **Showing**
I felt cold. | *The cold had started to bite my skin.*

1 I was tired from walking.
2 I felt cold.
3 The leopard and I both relaxed.
4 A noisy car came.
5 The leopard ran away.

A favourite memory

It was a morning in February 2018 in India's Spiti Valley. I'd walked for more than an hour, alone in the snow with my heavy gear on my back. The -20°C air had started to bite my skin. That's when I saw the beautiful snow leopard resting very close to the road, a little below me. I could smell his wild animal scent when the breeze blew in my direction. He kept his eye on me but didn't seem bothered. As I sat down, the leopard rested his chin on his front legs. He was comfortable and that gave me confidence.

I wanted to take photos, but every time I did the leopard heard the click of the camera and looked at me. I didn't want to disturb him, so I didn't take many. After a while, I heard the complaining sound of a car's engine as it drove through the snow. The leopard heard it, immediately got up and disappeared silently down into the valley. Then the driver stopped and asked me why I was sitting in the snow in the middle of nowhere. I couldn't feel my legs because of the cold and asked for help getting up. I told the driver my story and he was kind enough to give me a lift back to my camp, where I sat peacefully enjoying the fact that I'd finally seen a snow leopard up close.

– Prasenjeet Yadav

WRITING TASK

5 Think of a memory you'd like to write about. Make notes in at least three categories.

Things I could …

see: _bright sunshine_

hear: _____

smell: _____

taste: _____

feel: _____

6 Choose three things that you noted in Exercise 5. For each one, write a sentence that shows rather than tells your experience.

bright sunshine: The hot sun cooked the land and made me almost close my eyes to protect them.

7 Work in pairs. Explain your memory and share your sentences from Exercise 6.

8 **WRITE** Write about a memory of your own. Use Prasenjeet's anecdote as a model and the sentences you wrote in Exercise 6. Use the Useful language to help you.

Useful language Time expressions

That's when …
As …
Every time …
After a while, …
Immediately, …
Then, …
Finally, …

9 **CHECK** Use the checklist. Your anecdote …

☐ says where and when the experience happened.

☐ includes details about the experience.

☐ uses the senses to 'show' the memory.

☐ uses time expressions to say when things happened.

10 **REVIEW** Work in pairs. Read your partner's anecdote. Discuss the questions.

1 What does your partner's anecdote 'show' you?

2 What senses does it describe?

3 What questions does it make you want to ask?

Go to page 134 for the Reflect and review.

A snow leopard in Spiti Valley, India. Photo by Prasenjeet Yadav.

EXPLORE MORE!

Learn more about how to tell a story. Search online for 'how to tell a story'.

Reflect and review

1 Identity

1. Look at the goals from Unit 1. How confident do you feel about them? Write the letters (a–f) in the table.
   a Preview an article before reading
   b Describe photos and different identities
   c Practise using adjectives to describe character
   d Understand sequence
   e Understand different communication styles
   f Write an online self-introduction

I feel confident	I need to improve

2. Write down …
   - five adjectives to describe someone's character.
   - three expressions to describe a photograph.
   - three things to think about when you proofread your own writing.

   Now compare your notes with a partner. Did you think of the same ideas?

3. Choose three ways you can improve the Unit 1 goals. Then share your ideas with a partner.
   - [ ] Find three articles and identify the topic of them before reading
   - [ ] Introduce myself in an online group
   - [ ] Describe a photo to a friend
   - [ ] Write a paragraph about my personality then proofread it
   - [ ] Start a discussion about different communication styles with a friend
   - [ ] Watch a video or listen to a podcast and write the phrases used to sequence events

2 Success
Pages 22–33

1. Look at the goals from Unit 2. Tick (✓) three that you feel you have achieved. Tell a partner your choices and how you think you achieved them.
   - [ ] Read fluently by noticing chunks in an article
   - [ ] Talk about past actions with present consequences
   - [ ] Practise describing jobs
   - [ ] Summarize with bullet points while listening
   - [ ] Learn ways to build trust
   - [ ] Decide what information to include in a *how-to* article

2. Write a list of words and phrases related to work you have learned in this unit. Then write questions using the words and phrases. When you have finished, ask a partner your questions.

   work part-time ➔ *Have you ever worked part-time?*

   run a company ➔ *Would you like to run your own company?*

3. Read the ideas for working on the Unit 2 goals. Choose two ideas, then look for useful apps or websites you can use to practise. Make a note of them.
   - [ ] Read an article on success and note down chunks of language
   - [ ] Listen to a podcast or a talk about someone's road to success
   - [ ] Watch a video and note down the main ideas with bullet points
   - [ ] Learn one new word or phrase per day to describe jobs
   - [ ] Research and write my own *how-to* article

3 Working together *Pages 34–45*

1 Look at the goals from Unit 3. How confident do you feel about them? Write the letters (a–f) on the scale.
   a Identify supporting examples in an online forum
   b Talk about an important relationship
   c Think about what you already know before listening to a news report
   d Talk about teamwork
   e Learn about managing conflict
   f Write an email of apology

Not confident   Very confident

◀━━━━━━━━━━━━━━━━━━━━▶

2 Complete the sentences with your own ideas. Then share with a partner.
   1 Some phrases I can use to identify supporting examples are …
   2 One way of managing conflict is …
   3 If I want to apologize, I can say …

3 Choose two ways you can work on the Unit 3 goals. Add one more idea, then share with a partner.
   Read an online text and make a note of any signal words or ways examples are given
   Write a short paragraph about someone who has helped me
   Find exercises online to practise the present perfect and past simple
   Make notes on what I already know before listening to a news report
   Write an apology email for another option from Exercise 5 in lesson 3E
   My idea: _____

4 Routines *Pages 46–57*

1 Look at the goals from Unit 4. How confident do you feel about them? Rank them from 1 (very confident) to 6 (not confident at all).
   Understand new vocabulary in an article using affixes
   Describe routines when greeting people
   Deal with unknown words while listening
   Practise using phrases with dependent prepositions
   Deal with uncertainty
   Write about household routines

2 Work in pairs. Discuss the questions.
   1 What do you think you did well in the unit? Why?
   2 What goals do you want to improve on? Why?
   3 Which goals are the most important to you for outside the class? Why?

3 Write three ways to improve one of the goals from Exercise 2. Use some of these phrases or your own ideas.

> keep a vocabulary diary
> listen to online videos and talks
> look for affixes practice online
> speak about my daily routine with a friend
> read more about greetings around the world
> write conditional sentences
> read the unit again
> write questions using language from the unit
> use an online dictionary

Three ways to improve my goal are …

   • _____
   • _____
   • _____

Reflect and review

5 Art Pages 58–69

1 Look at the goals from Unit 5. Tick (✓) two goals you feel you've achieved. In your notebook, make notes about how you can use these two skills outside of the classroom.

Analyse quotations in an article

Talk about images and unlikely or imaginary situations

Describe a piece of art

Learn about how intonation can affect what we understand

Write a description of an event

I can listen to a person's intonation to help me understand how they are feeling.

2 Choose a topic and write a short paragraph.
- what you think of when you hear the word *art*
- a performance you've seen and what you thought of it
- a song you've heard that made you feel a certain way
- a misunderstanding you've experienced
- an event you're going to in the next few months

3 Think about the goals in Exercise 1. Choose two goals you need more practice on. Make a plan for how you will achieve this.

For each goal:
- Write two things you will do to work on this goal.
- List the resources you will use to help you, e.g. websites, apps, this unit.
- Set yourself a deadline for achieving the goal, e.g. by next week, by next month.

6 Where I'm from Pages 70–81

1 Look at the goals from Unit 6. Work in pairs. Use these words and phrases or your own to say how you feel about each goal. You can use the words and phrases more than once.

important	improve	more practice
not so confident	OK	very confident

- Interpret a bubble chart in an article
- Talk about moving to a new place
- Practise describing a neighbourhood
- Listen for signposts in a story
- Manage group conversations
- Write a travel plan

2 Work in pairs. Discuss the questions.
1 What do you think you did well in the unit?
2 What are three useful things you learned? Why?
3 Which goals do you want to improve on? Why?

3 Think about your answer to question 3, Exercise 2. Complete the sentences with your own ideas.
1 I want to improve …
2 To improve this I can … and …
3 I can practise this goal outside of my classes by …

7 Balance *Pages 82–93*

1 Look at the goals from Unit 7. Tick (✓) the three you feel the most confident about.

Identify supporting reasons in an advice column
Talk about the future
Talk about managing money
Identify supporting information in a podcast
Deal with different ways of processing information
Write a pros and cons essay

2 Complete the sentences with your own ideas. Then share your answers with a partner.

1 One of the goals I feel confident about is … because …
2 In this unit, I improved my *reading/writing/speaking/listening* skills by …
3 A goal I want to improve is …

3 Write three ways to improve the goal from Exercise 2. Use some of these phrases or your own ideas.

---

do online grammar practice exercises
review the unit again
highlight supporting ideas in a text
keep a vocabulary diary   make vocabulary flashcards
watch online videos about money and budgeting
listen for signposts in podcast discussions
make a plan before writing
find a topic and write a pros and cons essay

To improve my goal, I will …

1 _____
2 _____
3 _____

8 Essentials *Pages 94–105*

1 Look at the goals from Unit 8. How confident do you feel about them? Write the letters a–f in the table.

a Recognize ellipsis in an article
b Discuss the environmental impact of clothes shopping
c Describe different types of food
d Activate vocabulary before listening
e Understand different ways of giving and receiving feedback
f Write a blog post about essential skills

I feel confident	I need to improve

2 Tell a partner …

1 if the relative clause in this sentence is defining or non-defining, and how you know.
*I have so many clothes **which** I haven't worn, so I'm giving them to my sister.*
2 five adjectives to describe food.
3 how a sandwich is related to giving and receiving feedback.

3 Think about the goals you said you need to improve in Exercise 1. Work in pairs. Discuss one way to practise and improve each goal.

To activate vocabulary before listening, I can look at the topic and predict the kind of words I might hear.

Reflect and review

9 Taking a break Pages 106–117

1 Look at the goals from Unit 9. How confident do you feel about them? (1 = very confident, 4 = not confident at all)

- Understand contrast in an article
- Talk about imagined past situations
- Talk about holidays
- Listen for specific information in a conversation
- Learn to deal with unexpected behaviours
- Write a formal email of complaint

2 Work in pairs. Discuss the questions.

1 What are some words or phrases to indicate contrast?
2 What are three words or phrases for giving advice?
3 What tips would you give someone to help them write a formal email of complaint?

3 Think about one of the goals you want to improve from Exercise 1. Complete sentences 1–3 with your own ideas. Then ask a partner to suggest other ways to improve the goal and complete sentence 4.

1 The goal I want to improve is …
2 To improve this goal, I can …
3 Some online resources I can use to improve this goal are …
4 My partner's advice to improve this goal is … and …

10 The senses Pages 118–129

1 Look at the goals from Unit 10. Work in pairs. Tell your partner how confident you feel about each goal. Where possible, give examples of how you can use this goal outside of the classroom.

- Paraphrase ideas in an article
- Learn about language and colour
- Use the passive voice
- Make predictions
- Listen to people's problems
- Write about a memory

2 Write one true sentence about yourself and one false sentence. Choose from these topics.

- A prediction you have about your own future
- A problem someone has shared with you
- A memory you have from your childhood

Then share your sentences with a partner. Can they guess which sentence is true and which is false?

3 Think about the goals in Exercise 1. Choose one goal you need to improve. Draw a mind map with things you will do to achieve this. Then share your mind map with a partner.

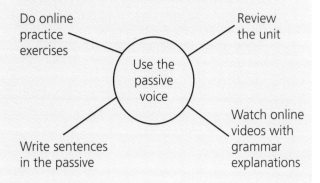

Do online practice exercises

Review the unit

Use the passive voice

Write sentences in the passive

Watch online videos with grammar explanations

Vocabulary reference

UNIT 1

academic (adj) /ˌækəˈdɛmɪk/   *Kemi's very academic. She loves learning and studying.*

adventurous (adj) /ədˈvɛntʃərəs/   *I'm quite adventurous with food – I'll try anything!*

ambitious (adj) /æmˈbɪʃəs/   *Are you ambitious?*

competitive (adj) /kəmˈpɛtɪtɪv/   *My brother's so competitive and will do anything to win.*

independent (adj) /ˌɪndɪˈpɛndənt/   *By 19, I was independent and living on my own.*

messy (adj) /ˈmɛsi/   *My roommate is so messy.*

organized (adj) /ˈɔːɡənaɪzd/   *Koldo's so organized! He always knows where everything is.*

sensible (adj) /ˈsɛnsəbl/   *I wish I was as sensible as you!*

shy (adj) /ʃaɪ/   *I used to be shy when I was younger.*

sociable (adj) /ˈsəʊʃəbl/   *She's more sociable nowadays!*

1   Complete the email with the correct words from the word list.

Hi Pilar!

University is quite difficult. I usually choose a class I know a lot about, but this year I wanted to be ¹_____ and try something new. It's much harder than I expected.

My new roommate is very ²_____. She just throws her things on the floor! It's hard for me because I'm so ³_____. She's also quite ⁴_____, so she doesn't speak much. When I ask her to come out with me, she doesn't want to. I guess she isn't very ⁵_____, as she doesn't like spending time with other people. But maybe it's a good thing she's ⁶_____ and is happy being by herself. She might just be really ⁷_____ and enjoy studying.

My part-time job is good, and I'm doing really well. But you know me, I'm ⁸_____, so I want to be in charge already! I work harder than everyone in my team, and it needs to stay that way so my boss notices, then makes me manager when I graduate. You probably think I'm too ⁹_____! I know I don't always have to be better than everyone else … But you've always been the ¹⁰_____ one out of the two of us!

How's everything with you?

Marta

2   Write a paragraph describing someone you know. Try to use at least five adjectives from the word list.

UNIT 2

apply for a job (phr) /əˈplaɪ fɔːr ə dʒɒb/   *I applied for the job a while ago, but I haven't heard back yet.*

call in sick (phr) /kɔːl ɪn sɪk/   *Have you called in sick?*

do overtime (phr) /duː ˈəʊvətaɪm/   *I need you to do some overtime this weekend – Joanna's sick.*

go freelance (phr) /ɡəʊ ˈfriːˌlɑːns/   *I decided to go freelance when I had my daughter.*

meet deadlines (phr) /miːt ˈdɛdlaɪnz/   *Do you think you'll be able to meet the deadline?*

run a company (phr) /rʌn ə ˈkʌmpəni/   *Who runs the company day-to-day?*

take on responsibilities (phr) /teɪk ɒn rɪˌspɒnsəˈbɪlətiz/   *I've taken on some new responsibilities at work.*

work for a company (phr) /wɜːk fɔːr ə ˈkʌmpəni/   *I've been working for this company for ten years.*

work part-time/full-time (phr) /wɜːk pɑːt taɪm/ / wɜːk fʊl taɪm/   *My partner works part-time.*

work shifts (phr) /wɜːk ʃɪfts/   *Doctors often work shifts.*

1   Match the beginning of the sentences (1–10) with the endings (a–j).

1   I applied for
2   As a manager, I now have to take on
3   Do you work for
4   I'm a police officer, so I often work
5   We've still got a lot to do, so it'll be hard to meet
6   Someone has called
7   I've always wanted to go
8   I love my job. I work
9   Would you like to run
10   I need to do

a   a company or for yourself?
b   the deadline for this project.
c   a job at the supermarket down the road.
d   overtime to save some extra money for my trip.
e   responsibilities that I didn't have before.
f   12-hour shifts.
g   in sick today, so I need you to work late.
h   full-time as a secretary, so forty hours a week.
i   freelance, but I know it can be quite difficult.
j   your own company one day?

2   Work in pairs. Discuss the questions.
1   What information do you need to give when you apply for a job?
2   What are some jobs that require a person to work shifts?
3   Do you know anyone who runs their own company? What do they do?

Vocabulary reference

UNIT 3

belong to (phr v) /bɪˈlɒŋ tuː/ *I belonged to a chess club when I was younger.*

carry out (phr v) /ˈkæri aʊt/ *They're going to carry out a survey.*

come up with (phr v) /kʌm ʌp wɪð/ *I came up with an idea for a new business.*

consist of (phr v) /kənˈsɪst ɒv/ *The tournament consists of five teams from around Europe.*

deal with (phr v) /diːl wɪð/ *I'm not very good at dealing with problems.*

give up (phr v) /gɪv ʌp/ *Don't give up – you're the best player on the team!*

keep on (phr v) /kiːp ɒn/ *You need to keep on training, so you get faster.*

sign up (phr v) /saɪn ʌp/ *Does anyone want to sign up for the basketball team?*

work on (phr v) /wɜːk ɒn/ *I need to work on my fitness.*

1 Complete the sentences with the correct form of the verbs from the word list.
1 I've _____ a new strategy for our match on Saturday.
2 Can you _____ Anya's problem please, Sam? I'm busy and don't really have time.
3 As a freelancer, it's a good idea to _____ different professional organizations so you can meet people and find work.
4 You'll need to _____ online first if you want to hear when tickets go on sale.
5 Hanka's ballet technique is good, but she needs to _____ her balance.
6 Come on, team – you have to _____ moving, even if you're tired!
7 A football team _____ eleven players.
8 Have you ever _____ doing something because you thought you weren't good at it?
9 The company _____ an investigation into the problem last year.

2 Work in pairs. Discuss the questions.
1 Do you belong to any clubs or professional organizations? Which?
2 Have you ever encouraged anyone to keep on doing something, even if they wanted to give up?
3 Which English skill would you like to work on more – speaking, listening, reading or writing? Why?
4 What would your perfect day consist of?

UNIT 4

Verb + preposition

believe in (phr v) /bɪˈliːv ɪn/ *I believe in you!*

commit to (phr) /kəˈmɪt tuː/ *Louis committed to making a difference.*

feel guilty about (phr) /fiːl ˈgɪlti əˈbaʊt/ *I feel guilty about not remembering your birthday.*

feel proud of (phr) /fiːl praʊd ɒv/ *You should feel proud of yourself for passing your driving test first time.*

look forward to (phr v) /lʊk ˈfɔːwəd tuː/ *We're looking forward to seeing you this weekend.*

reward myself with (phr) /rɪˈwɔːd maɪˈsɛlf wɪð/ *I've worked hard this week, so I'm going to reward myself with a meal out!*

spend time on (phr) /spɛnd taɪm ɒn/ *Saadia spends a lot of time on her homework.*

Adjective + preposition

enthusiastic about (phr) /ɪnˌθjuːziˈæstɪk əˈbaʊt/ *The students are really enthusiastic about learning English.*

fed up with (phr) /fɛd ʌp wɪð/ *I'm fed up with my job.*

worried about (phr) /ˈwʌrid əˈbaʊt/ *I'm worried about saying the wrong thing in the meeting.*

1 Choose the correct option to complete the sentences.
1 This weekend, *spend time on / believe in* planning your research projects.
2 I'm *worried about / enthusiastic about* Ken. I haven't heard from him for two weeks.
3 My friend *felt guilty about / felt proud of* forgetting our dinner plans.
4 I'm *fed up with / worried about* you telling me what to do all the time!
5 Do you *believe in / feel guilty about* yourself?
6 We're really *fed up with / looking forward to* going camping next month.
7 I *feel proud of / reward myself with* my hard work.
8 You need to sound more *enthusiastic about / worried about* the job if you want to get it.
9 I've *looked forward to / committed to* my goals.
10 Once I've finished the project, I'm going to *reward myself with / feel guilty about* a weekend away.

2 Work in pairs. Discuss the questions.
1 When was the last time you felt proud of someone? What happened?
2 What do you spend a lot of time on?
3 What are you looking forward to?

UNIT 5

annoyed (adj) /əˈnɔɪd/   *I'm so annoyed she forgot my birthday!*

annoying (adj) /əˈnɔɪɪŋ/   *It was annoying that the museum was closed by the time we got there.*

confused (adj) /kənˈfjuːzd/   *I didn't enjoy that series at all. I was so confused.*

confusing (adj) /kənˈfjuːzɪŋ/   *That was such a confusing story.*

disappointed (adj) /dɪsəˈpɔɪntɪd/   *Farah was disappointed with her results.*

disappointing (adj) /ˌdɪsəˈpɔɪntɪŋ/   *Liz found the performance disappointing.*

embarrassed (adj) /ɪmˈbærəst/   *I get embarrassed when I forget someone's name.*

embarrassing (adj) /ɪmˈbærəsɪŋ/   *I fell over and it was so embarrassing!*

frightened (adj) /ˈfraɪtnd/   *Are you frightened of snakes?*

frightening (adj) /ˈfraɪtnɪŋ/   *That film looks frightening.*

inspired (adj) /ɪnˈspaɪəd/   *I felt so inspired after I saw that documentary.*

inspiring (adj) /ɪnˈspaɪərɪŋ/   *My mum is so inspiring.*

relaxed (adj) /rɪˈlækst/   *I feel relaxed after a bath.*

relaxing (adj) /rɪˈlæksɪŋ/   *Yoga is so relaxing.*

shocked (adj) /ʃɒkt/   *I was shocked when you told me.*

shocking (adj) /ˈʃɒkɪŋ/   *She made a shocking discovery.*

1 Complete the sentences with the correct form of the words.
1 Can you stop asking me so many questions? It's really _____ (annoy)!
2 I dropped my coffee all over the floor. It was so _____ (embarrass).
3 I find jazz music really _____ (relax).
4 I was _____ (shock) when I saw him. He looked so different to how I remember.
5 Your essay is quite _____ (confuse). You mention a lot of points but don't explain them.
6 Mikhail was _____ (disappoint) with the view. The website said you could see the sea.
7 He was a great musician. People often left his concerts feeling _____ (inspire).
8 My car broke down last night. It was a _____ (frighten) experience.

2 Complete the sentences with your own ideas. Then compare with a partner.
1 An inspiring person I know is … because …
2 I get annoyed when …
3 I feel relaxed when …

UNIT 6

chain store (n) /tʃeɪn stɔː/   *There aren't many chain stores here; most shops are independently owned.*

district (n) /ˈdɪstrɪkt/   *I work in the business district.*

harbour (n) /ˈhɑːbə/   *We stayed in a pretty fishing village next to the harbour.*

hostel (n) /ˈhɒstəl/   *I went backpacking and stayed in hostels and shared a room with other travellers.*

monument (n) /ˈmɒnjʊmənt/   *Chichén Itzá is a famous monument in Mexico.*

neighbourhood (n) /ˈneɪbəhʊd/   *We moved to a new neighbourhood, just outside the city.*

office block (n) /ˈɒfɪs blɒk/   *The flats have now been replaced by three new office blocks.*

shopping mall (n) /ˈʃɒpɪŋ mɔːl/   *That new shopping mall is open now. Shall we go and have a look?*

stall (n) /stɔːl/   *At the night market, there are lots of stalls selling different street food.*

suburbs (n) /ˈsʌbɜːbz/   *Let's buy a house in the suburbs, where there's more space for the children to play.*

1 Write the correct word or phrase to match each description.
1 An area outside a city where people live. _____
2 One of a group of shops that belong to one company. _____
3 A place where travellers stay, often very cheap and with shared rooms. _____
4 An area with ships and boats. _____
5 Something to remember a special person, place or event. _____
6 A temporary shop where food, clothes or other items are sold. _____
7 A large building with many floors where people work. _____
8 A place where you can buy things, eat, watch a film and walk around. _____
9 An area of a town or city that has a certain characteristic. _____
10 The community and area that surrounds someone's home. _____

2 Work in pairs. Take turns to talk about …
Student A
1 a shopping mall you've visited that you enjoyed
2 a famous monument you'd like to visit
3 some of the different districts in your town or city
Student B
1 the neighbourhood you live in
2 a popular chain store you've been to
3 where you'd prefer to live: the city or the suburbs

Vocabulary reference

UNIT 7

afford (v) /əˈfɔːd/ *I can't afford a new car with the amount I earn.*

be worth (phr) /bi wɜːθ/ *How much do you think this jacket is worth if I sell it?*

budget (n) /ˈbʌdʒɪt/ *We will have to have a daily budget when we go travelling.*

expenses (n) /ɪksˈpɛnsɪz/ *We need to reduce our monthly expenses.*

financial (adj) /faɪˈnænʃəl/ *The government provides financial assistance for unemployed people.*

loan (n) /ləʊn/ *I'm going to get a loan from the bank so I can buy a better car.*

luxuries (n) /ˈlʌkʃəriz/ *Booking weekends away and eating in nice restaurants are my luxuries.*

mortgage (n) /ˈmɔːgɪdʒ/ *I pay the mortgage every month and my partner pays the bills.*

salary (n) /ˈsæləri/ *That job has a much higher salary than you get now. You should apply for it.*

waste (v) /weɪst/ *Don't waste your money on that shirt if you already have something similar.*

1 Choose the correct option to complete the sentences.
1 I'm so happy I got the job! With my new *salary / loan,* I'll be able to *waste / afford* to go out more.
2 I've been doing some *luxuries / financial* planning. If we put down a 10% deposit on the house, our monthly *mortgage / budget* payments will be much cheaper than the rent we pay now.
3 We're going to get a business *mortgage / loan* to start the company.
4 What *budget / expenses* do you have to buy a car?
5 We need to cut down our living *expenses / salary* if we're going to save. That means you need to stop spending on all your *budgets / luxuries.*
6 Our trip wasn't *worth / financial* the price we paid for it. We *afforded / wasted* a lot of money.

2 Work in pairs. What would you do in these situations?
1 You get offered two jobs: one you don't like with a high salary, or one you love with a low salary.
2 You want to go travelling but can't afford it. You could get a loan and go now, or you could save money for a year then go.
3 Your friend tells you you can't stay at her house anymore. You could move to your parents' house and try to get a mortgage which will take time, or you could rent a place on your own immediately.

UNIT 8

buttery (adj) /ˈbʌtəri/ *What smells better than freshly baked, buttery bread?*

cheesy (adj) /ˈtʃiːzi/ *I love everything cheesy – sandwiches, pizzas … I have cheese on everything!*

chocolatey (adj) /ˈtʃɒkləti/ *I only eat chocolatey desserts like chocolate cake or ice cream.*

creamy (adj) /ˈkriːmi/ *Sandra has thick, creamy yoghurt with fresh fruit for breakfast every morning.*

fruity (adj) /ˈfruːti/ *My favourite tea is called 'Red Berry Burst'. It's quite fruity and has a strawberry flavour to it.*

meaty (adj) /ˈmiːti/ *My mum made these delicious, meaty empanadas. Do you want to try one?*

milky (adj) /ˈmɪlki/ *I like my coffee milky, so it's not too strong.*

oily (adj) /ˈɔɪli/ *Salmon is an oily fish.*

salty (adj) /ˈsɔːlti/ *The salty flavour of the fish tastes really nice with these sweet potatoes.*

spicy (adj) /ˈspaɪsi/ *How spicy do you like your curries?*

watery (adj) /ˈwɔːtəri/ *Pho is a Vietnamese dish, with meat and vegetables in a watery soup.*

1 Choose the correct option to complete the sentences.
1 Excuse me, my noodles are supposed to be in soup, and instead they're fried and really *oily / milky.*
2 I can't eat this dish. There are so many chillies, it's too *spicy / milky.*
3 Can you get me one of those *buttery / fruity* drinks from the supermarket? I like the apple and mango one.
4 Mum, remember Se-Ri is coming for dinner tonight and she's vegetarian. She doesn't eat anything *salty / meaty.*
5 What shall we have for dinner tonight? I fancy something *cheesy / creamy* like a pizza.
6 Elif, why is this cake mixture so *fruity / watery?* I thought it was supposed to be thicker than this.
7 I don't like *salty / chocolatey* desserts. They're too sweet for me.
8 I love a milkshake, especially when it's made with thick and *creamy / buttery* ice cream.

2 Write a short blog post using the prompt or your own idea. Try to use at least five words from the word list.
Last night, my friends and I had a terrible experience at the new restaurant in town. First of all, …

UNIT 9

book accommodation (phr) /bʊk əkɒməˈdeɪʃ(ə)n/ *We must book our accommodation for our trip to Paris.*

check out travel advice (phr) /tʃɛk aʊt ˈtrævl ədˈvaɪs/ *We should check out travel advice for places to stay.*

go abroad (phr) /gəʊ əˈbrɔːd/ *My family and I usually go abroad together once a year.*

holiday destination (phr) /ˈhɒlədeɪ ˌdɛstɪˈneɪʃən/ *My favourite holiday destination is Greece. I love it!*

look up (phr v) /lʊk ʌp/ *We should look up directions to the museum before we leave the hotel.*

lose a deposit (phr) /luːz ə dɪˈpɒzɪt/ *If we don't get to the hotel soon, we might lose our deposit and the room!*

lose my luggage (phr) /luːz maɪ ˈlʌgɪdʒ/ *The airline lost my luggage the last time I went abroad.*

make holiday plans (phr) /meɪk ˈhɒlədeɪ plænz/ *Shall we start making our holiday plans for the summer?*

make a reservation (phr) /meɪk ə ˌrɛzəˈveɪʃən/ *Don't forget to make a reservation for dinner tonight.*

travel insurance (phr) /ˈtrævl ɪnˈʃʊərəns/ *You always need travel insurance for a holiday.*

unpack my suitcase (phr) /ʌnˈpæk maɪ ˈsuːtkeɪs/ *The worst part of any trip is unpacking my suitcase at the end.*

1 Match the beginning of the sentences (1–8) with the endings (a–h).

1 We should have made a reservation because
2 If you're going skiing,
3 I've never been abroad,
4 Alima, you must unpack your suitcase because
5 I can't believe the airline lost my luggage,
6 We should try and make some holiday plans
7 If you don't bring the rental car back on time,
8 I can't believe we're lost and

a it's Saturday night and the restaurant will be busy.
b before places start getting booked up.
c but I would love to go to Seoul one day.
d and I'm not even sure they know where it went!
e get travel insurance that covers winter sports.
f we can't even use your phone to look up directions!
g you will lose your deposit.
h it's been a month since you got back!

2 Complete the sentences with your own ideas. Then share your sentences with a partner.

1 My dream holiday destination is … because …
2 If an airline lost my luggage, I would …
3 If you unpacked my suitcase, you would find …
4 You should get travel insurance if …

UNIT 10

development (n) /dɪˈvɛləpmənt/ *The development of technology allows us to communicate faster than ever.*

emotions (n) /ɪˈməʊʃənz/ *I feel a lot of different emotions when I hear this song.*

extend (v) /ɪksˈtɛnd/ *Technology may extend beyond our understanding.*

eyesight (n) /ˈaɪsaɪt/ *My eyesight has got worse since I started working in front of a computer all day.*

hearing aid (n) /ˈhɪərɪŋ eɪd/ *My grandad wears a hearing aid to help him hear things more clearly.*

scent (n) /sɛnt/ *Dogs are able to smell scents that humans can't.*

speech (n) /spiːtʃ/ *Some informal expressions are used more in speech than in writing.*

technological (adj) /ˌtɛknəˈlɒdʒɪk(ə)l/ *There has been more technological change over the last forty years than at any time before.*

telescope (n) /ˈtɛlɪskəʊp/ *I got a telescope for my birthday so I can look at the moon and stars.*

virtual reality (n) /ˈvɜːtjʊəl ri(ː)ˈælɪti/ *Virtual reality is being used in some school classes now.*

1 Write the correct word from the word list to match each sentence.

1 This is an experience that is different from a real-world situation. _____
2 I once saw the International Space Station through it. _____
3 I need it to be able to listen to conversations more clearly. _____
4 I think I need to get some glasses. Things aren't as clear as they used to be. _____
5 I'm so angry. I can't believe he said that about me. _____
6 There have been a lot of new changes in the technology of electric cars. _____
7 My brother has just baked fresh bread. It smells wonderful. _____
8 The course is now six months, not three. _____

2 Work in pairs. Discuss the questions.

1 Have you ever used virtual reality? What did you think? / Would you like to?
2 Is there a particular scent which reminds you of something or someone?
3 What technological changes do you think there will be in the next ten years?

Grammar reference

UNIT 1

1B Present simple and present continuous

Present simple

- Use the present simple to talk about permanent situations and regular activities or habits that are unlikely to change.
  *She **lives** with her husband and two children.*
  *I **travel** a lot for work.*

- You can also use the present simple to give background details about a person, a thing or a situation in a photo.
  *In this photo, we**'re** in Malta. We **go** there every year.*

Present continuous

- Use the present continuous to talk about temporary or changing states.
  *I**'m living** with my sister at the moment while I look for my own flat.*
  *Emine**'s working** from home until the new office is ready.*

- You can also use the present continuous to describe something happening at the moment of speaking, or around the present time.
  *I**'m learning** to play the guitar. (= around this time in the present)*
  *Mustafa**'s reading** a book. (= now, as I speak)*

- You can also use it to describe what can be seen or what's happening in a photo.
  *Here, you can see we**'re waiting** to get on the flight to Portugal.*
  *I**'m** a father of three children. In this photo, I**'m helping** them surf for the first time!*

- Form the present continuous with *be + -ing* form.
  *I**'m working** here until I find something better.*
  *Elise **is deciding** what to study at university.*

> **Remember!**
>
> | I am | He/She/It is | You are |
> |------|--------------|---------|
> | You are | We are | They are |

State verbs

- State verbs describe states rather than actions. Some common state verbs are *agree, appear, believe, know, like, love, need, prefer, seem* and *remember*.
  *That **smells** good! What are you cooking?*
  *Jakob **seems** happier than usual.*

- State verbs aren't usually used in continuous tenses, so use the present simple with state verbs, not the present continuous.
  *I **prefer** snowboarding to skiing.*
  NOT ~~I'm preferring snowboarding to skiing.~~

- Some verbs can be both a state verb or an action verb, depending on how they are used, for example *have* and *think*.
  *I **have** a new laptop. (= possession)*
  *In this photo, we**'re having** dinner in my favourite restaurant. (= action, describing an activity)*
  *I **think** it's a great option. (= state, giving an opinion)*
  *Bao**'s thinking** about the different options. (= action, actively considering something)*

1 Choose the correct options to complete the sentences.

1 In this photo, I *win / am winning* the 100-metre race.

2 I *'m thinking / think* about what to wear to the party tonight.

3 I *work / am working* as a cartographer, which means I create maps.

4 At the moment, Jung-hoon *lives / is living* with his brother until he can afford his own place.

5 This is my friend Alba. She *speaks / is speaking* Spanish and Italian.

6 Please be quiet! I *'m watching / watch* a great film.

7 I *know / 'm knowing* you from somewhere. Did we go to the same school?

8 My dad *comes / is coming* from Oman. He was born there, but he's lived in Athens for 25 years.

1C Used to and would

Used to

- Use *used to* + infinitive and *didn't use to* + infinitive to talk about things in the past that are not true anymore.
  *We **used to live** in Australia when I was younger.*
  *I **didn't use to like** eating sweets, but I love them now!*

- Use *used to* to talk about past states, past habits and repeated past actions.
  *He **used to play** tennis every weekend. (= repeated past action)*
  *She **didn't use to be** very friendly, but we've got to know each other more now. (= past state)*

- Form questions using *did* + subject + *use to* + infinitive.
  ***Did you use to go** to school together?*

Would

- Use *would* + infinitive or *wouldn't* + infinitive to talk about past repeated actions that no longer happen.
  *When we were young, we **would go** fishing with our grandad once a month.*
  *When I was teaching, I**'d spend** all weekend planning lessons.*

- Don't use *would* for past states.
  I used to have red hair.
  NOT ~~I would have red hair.~~

Remember!

Would can be shortened to *'d.*
When he was young, he'd play tennis every weekend.

2 Complete the sentences with the correct form of *used to* or *would*. Use the negative (–) where necessary. Sometimes, both *used to* and *would* are possible.

1   My family and I _____ go to the same hotel every year when I was young.
2   Jonah _____ like maths, but he's enjoying it more now he's improved. (–)
3   _____ you _____ have a pet?
4   My grandpa _____ paint the most beautiful landscapes.
5   Sara _____ wear glasses, but now she wears contact lenses.
6   I didn't like reading when I was younger, so I _____ read a lot of books. (–)

UNIT 2

2B   Present perfect and past simple

Present perfect

- Use the present perfect to connect something in the past to the present. You can use it to talk about unfinished actions that started in the past and continue to the present.
  I've studied English for over twenty years. (= started twenty years ago, still studies now)
- You can also use it to describe a finished action in the past with a consequence or result in the present or future.
  She's broken her leg! (= she broke it, but the break affects the present and the future, until it heals)
- You can also use the present perfect to talk about life experiences from an unspecified time in the past.
  Leo's been to France before.
- Form the present perfect using *have/has* + past participle.
  I've lost my phone!
  Amira's worked for the same company for fifteen years.
- Use *for* with the present perfect to talk about duration, and *since* to talk about something's starting point.
  I've played the guitar for ten years.
  I've lived here since 2001.
- You can use the present perfect with *never* to mean 'at no time' in a positive sentence, and *ever* to mean 'at any time' in a negative sentence or a question.
  I've never been on a plane / I haven't ever been on a plane.
  Have you ever studied abroad?

Past simple

- Use the past simple for finished actions. Use it to tell a story about things that happened in the past, with no result in the present.
  My first job was as a receptionist.
  I finished university last year.
- You can use the past simple with or without a time word or expression, *e.g. yesterday, ten years ago, when I was twenty, last year*, etc.
  I moved out of my parents' house when I was twenty.
  Yesterday, I flew back from Mumbai.

1 Find and correct one mistake in each sentence.

1   Have you ever took an English course?
2   My daughter has ever learned to swim.
3   He's worked for this company for 2019.
4   I've ever been very good at sports.
5   I think I've seen your parents yesterday.
6   I've did a lot of overtime this month.

2C   *Have to, must, don't have to* and *mustn't*

Have to and *must*

- Use *have to* + infinitive and *must* + infinitive to express obligation.
  We have to wear a uniform to school.
  I must call my mum and tell her the good news.
- Use *have to* to express external or impersonal obligations. These are often rules or laws.
  You have to wear a seatbelt in the car. (= present)
  I had to buy a tie for work. (= past)
- *Must* expresses a personal obligation. It expresses what the speaker thinks is necessary.
  I must hand my essay in by Friday.
  You must try to get here on time.
- Don't use *to* after *must*.
  I must get a new phone.
  NOT ~~I must to get a new phone.~~
- You can also use *must* for strong recommendations.
  You must watch that documentary I told you about. It's shocking!
  The cakes here are delicious. You must try one.

Don't have to

- Use *don't/doesn't have to* + infinitive to show that there is no obligation to do something. The person can do something if they want to, or not do it.
  You don't have to come to the party if you don't want to.
  He doesn't have to walk; I can pick him up.

Mustn't

- Use *mustn't* + infinitive to talk about prohibition or something a person is not allowed to do.
  You mustn't speak while the exam is in progress.
  You mustn't use your phone in class.

Grammar reference

- Don't use *to* after *mustn't*.
  You **mustn't enter** without permission.
  NOT ~~You mustn't to enter without permission.~~

2 Rewrite the sentences with *have to, must, don't have to* and *mustn't*.

1 You aren't obliged to come for dinner.
  You don't have to come for dinner.

2 Amit isn't obliged to wear a suit to work tomorrow.

3 Haruki is obliged to do his homework tonight.

4 Students aren't allowed to eat or drink in the classroom.

5 You are obliged to drive on the left in Malta.

6 You really should come and watch the film with me.

UNIT 3

3B   Past tenses review

Past simple

- Use the past simple to describe an action that started and finished in the past.
  She **studied** in Italy.
  I **didn't finish** the presentation.
  Did you **hear** what the teacher said?

- You can also use the past simple to tell the main events in a story.
  *Fahad's parents **moved** to Brighton in 1995 and **bought** their first house.*

- To form the past simple of regular verbs, add *-ed* to the infinitive. If a verb ends in *-e*, only add *-d*. If a verb ends in *-y*, remove the *-y* and add *-ied*.
  She **loved** arts and crafts when she was younger.
  *Diego **cried** when he heard the news.*

- For irregular verbs, the past simple form is different. For a full list, see page 152.
  He **broke** his arm when he **fell** off his bike.
  *Agata **spoke** three languages.*

Past continuous

- Use the past continuous to describe an activity that was continuing at a specific time in the past.
  I **was talking** to my mum on the phone after dinner.
  He **wasn't answering** the questions very clearly in his interview.
  Was she **doing** research with you?

- You can also use the past continuous to tell the background of a story.
  The sun **was shining** and I **was feeling** happy.
  When he **was living** abroad, he **was meeting** new people every day.

- Use the past continuous and the past simple together to show that one event was in progress when another event happened.
  We **met** when we **were travelling** around India.
  He **was walking** along the road when he **saw** her across the street.

- Form the past continuous using *be + - ing* form.
  He **was listening** to music.
  The children **were laughing** at the film.

Past perfect simple

- Use the past perfect simple to give background information and provide details of events that happened before the main events in a story.
  Chen **had left** before I got to her house to say goodbye.
  Had you **been** to Dubai before that trip?

- You can also use the past perfect simple and the past simple together to show that one action was completed before another past action.
  He**'d** already **gone** to work by the time I **got up**.
  Amira **hadn't studied** the animals of this area before she **arrived**.

- Form the past perfect simple using *had + past participle*.
  They **had started** the meeting without me.
  I **had signed** up to the site before it became popular.

1 Complete the diary entry using the correct form of the verbs.

I ¹_____ (go) to Singapore with my family last year to see the Grand Prix. What an amazing experience! When we ²_____ (arrive), the first thing I saw was the city skyline. I ³_____ (not / see) anything like it before, and I also ⁴_____ (not / feel) heat like it! It was so hot and humid, and I couldn't wait to get to the hotel to change my clothes. The next day, while we ⁵_____ (walk) to the racetrack, we went past an open-air food market, and it ⁶_____ (smell) so good. We ⁷_____ (decide) to have an early lunch, so we got some Laksa, which I ⁸_____ (try) before. It's a Malaysian noodle soup, and it's usually quite spicy. I didn't tell my parents this, so their faces ⁹_____ (get) redder and redder the more they ate! They couldn't finish it! It was so funny!

3C   *Make* and *let*

- *Make* can mean *cause someone to do something*. This thing can be good or bad. Use *make* + object + infinitive.
  *Finding out about the problem **made him come up with** a solution.*
  *I think this will **make me cry**!*

- *Let* can mean *allow* or *give permission*. Use *let* + object + infinitive.
  I **let them go** without a warning.
  The coach will **let him sign** up to the club if he wants to.

- Don't use *to* before the infinitive with *make* or *let*.
  My sister really makes me laugh.
  NOT ~~My sister really makes me to laugh.~~
  My boss let me leave work early today.
  NOT ~~My boss let me to leave work early today.~~

2 Choose the correct option to complete the sentences.

1 The teacher doesn't *make / let* her students use their phones in class.
2 We will *let / make* new members sign up next season.
3 The advertising campaign *let / made* people notice our organization.
4 If you ask nicely, I might *make / let* you borrow my car.
5 My mum always *makes / lets* me wash the dishes after dinner. I hate it!
6 Knowing she's about to take her final exams has *made / let* her work harder.

UNIT 4

4B   Zero and first conditionals

Zero conditional

- Use the zero conditional (*If/When* + present simple, … present simple) to describe something that is a general truth or fact.
  *If I **drink** a lot of coffee, I **can't** sleep.*
  *When I **greet** people, I **shake** their hand.*
- You can swap the order of the clauses. This doesn't change the meaning.
  If I have a routine, I can make more time for studying. ➔ *I can make more time for studying if I have a routine.*

Remember!
When the *If/When* clause comes first, use a comma before the second clause.
If you need help, call me.

First conditional

- Use the first conditional (*If* + present, … *will/won't* + infinitive) to describe things that might happen in the future.
  *If I **go** travelling, I**'ll go** to Malaysia.*
  *If I **see** him, I **won't tell** him about the surprise party.*
- The first conditional can describe a present situation with a positive or negative future consequence.
  *If I **do** some exercise, it **will give** me more energy.*
  *If I **don't get** this project completed on time, the boss **will think** I'm useless.*
- You can swap the order of the clauses. This doesn't change the meaning.
  If I start reading this book, I'll never stop! ➔ *I'll never stop if I start reading this book!*

Alternatives to *if*
Most conditionals use *if*, but sometimes other words are used, e.g. *as soon as, unless, as long as* and *in case*.

- *As soon as* means *immediately*, or at the very moment another action is completed.
  ***As soon as** you arrive, send me a message.*
  *I'll let you know **as soon as** I hear anything,*
- *Unless* means *if … not*.
  *You have to go to work **unless** you're ill.* (= You have to go to work if you're not ill.)
  *I'll get angry **unless** I eat something soon.* (= I'll get angry if I don't eat something soon.)
- *As long as* means *if and only if*.
  *You can go out **as long as** you come back before it's dark.*
  ***As long as** you pay me back, I'll lend you some money.*
- Use *in case* to talk about preparing for an action or event that might happen in the future.
  *We'll look at the work together **if** there are any mistakes.* (= We will only look at it together if there are mistakes.)
  *We'll look at the work together **in case** there are any mistakes.* (= We will look at it together to check for mistakes.)

1 Match the beginning of the sentences (1–8) with the endings (a–h).

1 Unless the weather gets better,
2 If you go to the party tonight,
3 I'll give you a call
4 Romain will be here soon
5 I'll feel proud of myself for giving the presentation
6 If I go to bed late,
7 If you visit Istanbul,
8 We'll miss the train

a unless there's a lot of traffic.
b as long as it goes well.
c I can pick you up when it finishes.
d if we don't leave soon.
e we won't be able to have a barbecue.
f as soon as I leave the gym.
g I wake up tired.
h I'll be able to show you around.

4C   Quantifiers

- Use a quantifier + noun to talk about a number or amount of something.
- *Too much/many* means more than necessary. Use *too much* with uncountable nouns and *too many* with countable nouns.
  *I spend **too much** time in front of the computer.* (time = uncountable)
  *I've worked **too many** shifts this week.* (shifts = countable)

Grammar reference

- *So much/many* means a very large quantity. Use *so much* with uncountable nouns and *so many* with countable nouns
  *You put **so much** sugar in your tea!* (sugar = uncountable)
  *I've received **so many** emails today.* (emails = countable)

- *A lot of, lots of* and *plenty of* mean a large quantity of something. You can use them with both countable and uncountable nouns.
  *I have **a lot of** work to do this afternoon.*
  *There are **lots of** nice people in my class.*
  *I have **plenty of** books at home.*

- *A (tiny/little) bit of* means a small amount. Use it with uncountable nouns only.
  *I only want **a tiny bit of** chocolate.*

- *Too little* and *not enough* mean less than what is needed. Use *too little* with uncountable nouns. You can use *not enough* with both countable and uncountable nouns.
  *I have **too little** information to answer your question.* (information = uncountable)
  *There are**n't enough** hours in the day.*
  *There's **not enough** time.*

- To ask about amounts, use *much, many, lots of* or *a lot of*.
  *Do you do **much** overtime?*
  *Do you have **many** pairs of trainers?*
  *Did you go on **lots of / a lot of** family holidays when you were younger?*

2 Rewrite the sentences using a quantifier to replace the phrases in bold.
  1 I have **a large quantity** of books to read over the summer.
  2 Do you have **a large number of people** in your English class?
  3 I think I put **more than necessary** perfume on this morning!
  4 There are **less than needed** spaces at the table.
  5 There's **a small amount** of cake left if you want it.

UNIT 5

5B Second conditional

- Use the second conditional (*If* + past simple, … *would/could* (*not*) + infinitive) to describe imaginary situations or events that aren't real now, and are unlikely to happen in the future.
  *If I **was** the boss, I'**d let** you all leave work early on Fridays!*
    (= I'm not the boss, so it's not possible to leave work early on Fridays.)
  *If I **won** some money, I'**d buy** a house by the sea.*
    (= I haven't won any money and it's probable I won't in the future.)

Remember!
Would can be shortened to *'d*.

- You can swap the order of the clauses. This doesn't change the meaning.
  If I had more money, I could buy that car. → *I could buy that car if I had more money.*
  If she had time, she would travel more. → *She would travel more if she had time.*

Remember!
When the *If/When* clause comes first, use a comma before the second clause.

- When *if* is followed by the verb *be*, you can use *were* instead of *was* for *I* and *he/she/it*. It's common to see this in writing and hear it in formal speech.
  *If I **were** taller, I'd like to be a basketball player.*
  *If he **were** younger, he'd know this song.*

1 Write second conditional sentences using the correct form of the words.
  1 It / be / sunny day / I / have a picnic in the park.
    If it was/were a sunny day, I'd have a picnic in the park.
  2 I / win / lots of money / I / travel the world.
  3 It / not / be / raining / I / play football with my friends.
  4 Sarah / be / happy / have more free time.
  5 I / be / your manager / I / give you the promotion.
  6 I / come out for dinner / do / not / feel ill.

5C -ed and -ing adjectives

- Adjectives ending in *-ed* describe how a person feels, or an emotion. It's often a temporary feeling.
  *I'm **bored**. Let's go out and do something!*
  *Zhang is so **disappointed** that he couldn't get tickets to the festival.*

- Adjectives ending in *-ing* describe the characteristic of a person, thing or situation that causes a feeling.
  *Your friend is really **interesting**.*
  *This morning's maths lesson was so **confusing**!*

- Many adjectives can have both an *-ed* and *-ing* form. Some common examples are *tired–tiring, bored–boring, confused–confusing, frightened–frightening, surprised–surprising, worried–worrying*.
  *My day at work was so **tiring**. I'm really **tired**.* (= the day at work caused the emotion of the speaker feeling tired)
  *Your presentation was very **inspiring**. I now feel **inspired** to start my own business!* (= the presentation caused the speaker to feel inspired)

2 Complete the sentences with the correct form of the words.

1 I was _____ (impress) by *The Starry Night*. I loved the use of colour.

2 Petra fell over and everyone laughed. I felt so _____ (embarrass) for her.

3 I don't really understand what my mum does. Her job sounds very _____ (confuse).

4 How _____ (annoy) is it when people talk during a film in the cinema?

5 That cheese smells _____ (disgust). It's so strong!

6 What makes you feel _____ (relax)?

UNIT 6

6B Present perfect continuous

Present perfect continuous

- Use the present perfect continuous to talk about past actions or states which are connected to the present.
  I've been working in the business district for five years.
  He hasn't been living next door for long.
  Have you been waiting for me?

- You can also use the present perfect continuous to talk about an action that started in the past, is still continuing in the present and might continue into the future.
  I've been studying English for two years.
  She's been reading her book all morning.

- Use the present perfect continuous to focus on the duration of an activity and to say *how long*.
  We've been living in Canada for the past ten years.
  Joaquín has been working in the sales department since February.

- Compare this to the present perfect simple, which describes a completed action.
  I think I've read that book too. (= at an unspecified time in the past)

- You can also use the present perfect continuous to talk about a recently completed action you can see evidence of.
  Have you been shopping? You've got loads of bags!
  I've just been running, so I'm really tired.

- Form the present perfect continuous with *have/has + been + -ing* form.
  Tatiana's been watching a film.
  Matt hasn't been working very hard today.

- Form a question by changing the position of the subject and *have/has*.
  Has she been doing her homework?
  Have they been telling people your news?

Time expressions

- Use *for* with the present perfect continuous to talk about duration.
  He's been cooking for hours!

- Use *since* to refer to a starting point.
  She's been playing tennis since midday.

- Use *this week / month / year / today / all day* to talk about an unfinished period of time.
  Sylvie's been studying all day.

- Use *recently* to mean *not long ago*.
  I've been exercising a lot recently.

1 Complete the sentences with the present perfect simple or the present perfect continuous form of the verbs.

1 I _____ (eat) lunch already, thanks.

2 I _____ (wait) for you for twenty minutes! Why are you so late?

3 I _____ (make) some really great friends since moving here.

4 My mother _____ (cook) spicy food for me since I was a child.

5 I'm not feeling well, so I _____ (relax) on the sofa for most of the day.

6 We _____ (see) this film before. We saw it at the cinema last year.

7 My sister has a job interview today. She _____ (prepare) for it for weeks.

8 _____ you _____ (paint)? You've got some paint on your shirt!

6C Describing movement

Verb of movement + adverb

- Use a verb of movement + adverb of manner to say how someone or something is moving. You can use the adverb after the verb, or at the end of the sentence.
  Bara dances beautifully.
  He's trying to drive, but he's doing it very slowly!

- Other verbs of movement are: *catch, carry, climb, dive, drop, follow, go, hit, hold, knock, leave, fetch, jog, jump, lift, move, open, pick up, play, push, put down, run, swim, throw, turn.*
  She opened the box quickly.
  Kris hit the ball hard.

- You can form an adverb by adding *-ly* to the end of an adjective.
  slow → slowly
  bad → badly
  quick → quickly

- If an adjective ends in *-y*, remove it and add *-ily*.
  happy → happily
  noisy → noisily
  easy → easily

Grammar reference

- Some adjectives do not change. The adjective form is the same as the adverb.
  fast → *fast*
  straight → *straight*
  hard → *hard*

Verb of movement + preposition

- Use a verb of movement + preposition to describe the direction something or someone is moving in.

*He **jumped over** the wall.*

*We **went through** the forest to get to the lake.*

*They were **walking by** the river.*

*He **went across** the road.*

*I kept trying to **walk away** from her.*

*They were **walking towards** each other.*

Verb of movement + adverb + preposition

- Use a verb of movement + adverb + preposition to say the way the action happened and in which direction.
  *They **went quickly into** their house.*
  *He **jogged slowly through** the park.*
  *She **kicked** the ball **straight towards** the goal.*

2 Put the words in the correct order.

1 walked / Baris / quickly / the tunnel / through
2 towards / saw / she / her friends / walking / the shopping mall
3 swam / Angelica / very fast / and / won the race
4 he / the wall / jumped / the neighbour's house / to / over
5 Lois / by / the harbour / jogged / every morning
6 must / carefully / drive / in / you / the city centre

UNIT 7

7B Talking about the future

Be going to

- Use *be going to* + infinitive to talk about future intentions and plans that you've already made.
  *I**'m going to go** travelling next year.*
  *He**'s not going to reply** to that email.*
  ***Are** you **going to meet** each other next weekend?*

- You can also use *be going to* + infinitive to make predictions about something that seems likely or certain based on evidence.
  *It**'s going to rain** this afternoon.*
  *She**'s going to pass** this exam; she did really well in the practice test.*

- To form a *yes/no* question, use *be* + subject + *going to* + infinitive.
  ***Is** he **going to meet** us there?*
  ***Are** they **going to send** you their details?*

- To form a *wh*-question, use question word + *be* + subject + *going to* + infinitive.
  ***When are** we **going to pick** up the new car?*
  ***Where is** she **going to take** the exam?*

Present continuous

- Use the present continuous to talk about arrangements and plans in the future which you've already made some preparation for.
  *I**'m meeting** Yasna at the airport tomorrow.* (= the speaker has already arranged this plan with Yasna)
  *Olga**'s taking** the train to Moscow this afternoon.* (= Olga has already bought her ticket)

> **Remember!**
> Form the present continuous with *be* + *-ing* form.

Will

- Use *will* + infinitive to talk about facts in the future.
  *I**'ll be** 40 next month.*
  *We **won't know** our exam results until October.*

> **Remember!**
> The short form of *will not* is *won't*.

- Use *will* + infinitive to make predictions about the future.
  *He**'ll have** a great time camping.*
  *I'm sure you **won't regret** it!*

- Use *will* + infinitive for things you decide to do at the time of speaking.
  *A: Mr Wu is busy at the moment. B: It's fine, **I'll wait**.*
  *Oh! We're running out of bread, so I **won't eat** this slice.*
- You can also use *will* + infinitive to make offers and promises.
  *Gina **will help** you plan the party.*
  *I **won't tell** anyone – I promise!*
- To form a *yes/no* question, change the position of *will* and the subject.
  ***Will you** pick me up from work?*
  ***Will Marek** want to come with us?*
- To form a *wh*-question, use question word + *will* + subject + infinitive.
  ***When will you hear** about the job?*
  ***Where will we meet**?*

1 Find and correct one mistake in each sentence.

1 We're going plan our budget for our trip.
2 I heard it will going to be a full moon tonight.
3 I'm will fly to Beijing next Monday.
4 It looks like it's will be a nice day for a barbecue.
5 You'll having an amazing time in Berlin. It's a great city.
6 Honza will remember to call us when he arrives?
7 We meeting a financial planner next week to discuss our mortgage.
8 Why you're going to accept the job with the lower salary?

7C Verb patterns with infinitive or *-ing*

Verb + infinitive with *to*

- Some verbs are followed by an infinitive with *to*.
  *I **decided to reduce** my hours at work, so I have more time for myself.*
  *I **plan to move** out of my parents' house soon.*
- Common verbs include *afford, agree, appear, arrange, choose, decide, expect, hate, hope, learn, need, offer, plan, prepare, promise, seem* and *want*.
  *Do you **want to meet** for dinner?*
  *You **seem to be** busy. Let's talk later.*

Verb + *-ing* form

- Some verbs are followed by an *-ing* form. When an *-ing* form is used in this way, it's also called a gerund.
  *I **enjoy camping** in the summer.*
  *You should **avoid going** this way. I think the road's closed.*
- Common verbs include *admit, avoid, consider, discuss, dislike, (don't) mind, enjoy, fancy, finish, keep, mention, practise, prefer, recommend, spend time* and *suggest*.
  *I often **spend time sitting** in the garden with a book.*
  *I **suggest working** out your expenses to find out what you can save.*

Verb + infinitive or *-ing*

- Some verbs can be followed by either an infinitive with *to* or an *-ing* form with no change in meaning.
- These verbs include *begin, continue, like, love, prefer* and *start*.
  *Before you **start to sing** / **singing**, you need to warm up your voice.*
  *I **prefer to buy** / **buying** things I need rather than things I want.*
- Some verbs can be followed by either an infinitive with *to* or an *-ing* form, but the meaning changes.
- These verbs include *forget, remember, stop* and *try*.
  *I **tried to bake** you a cake. (= I made an effort but it was difficult.)*
  *I **tried baking** you a cake instead of buying one. (= I did it to see if it would be good or not.)*
  *I **stopped** the car **to check** my email. (= I interrupted the action of driving to read the email.)*
  *I **stopped checking** my email after I left the office. (= I stopped this activity completely.)*

2 Tick (✓) the correct option (a or b) to complete the sentence. Sometimes, both answers are possible.

1 I didn't _____ offered such a high salary! I think I should take the job.
   a expect to be ☐
   b expect being ☐
2 We can't _____ the credit card bill this month. What are we going to do?
   a afford to pay ☐
   b afford paying ☐
3 Do you _____ on the wrong door when you tried to surprise me for my birthday?!
   a remember to knock ☐
   b remember knocking ☐
4 Why don't you _____ some financial planning? Then you'll understand where all your money goes.
   a start to do ☐
   b start doing ☐
5 You _____ some time for yourself. If not, you're going to _____ this tired and stressed.
   a need taking, keep to be ☐
   b need to take, keep being ☐
6 Even when you're working hard, It's important to _____ time for the things you love.
   a continue making ☐
   b continue to make ☐

Grammar reference

8B Defining and non-defining relative clauses

- Relative clauses give information about a person, place or thing.
- Relative pronouns introduce relative clauses. Use *who* for people, *which* for things, *where* for places and *whose* for possessives (to mean *of who/which*).
  *That's the designer **who** made that dress.*
  *Those are the companies **which** make these cheap clothes.*
  *This is the house **where** I grew up.*
  *Do you know the girl **whose** phone was stolen?*

Defining relative clauses

- Use a defining relative clause to give extra information that is essential for understanding the person, place or thing you're talking about.
  *That's the couple **who** bought our old sofa from us.*
  *This is the restaurant **where** we had that horrible meal.*
- You can replace *who* and *which* with *that*.
  *There are many people **who/that** prefer buying second-hand clothes.*
  *Could you pass me that t-shirt **which/that** is hanging behind the door?*
- In a defining relative clause, you can leave out the relative pronoun *who, which* or *that* when it refers to the object of the verb.
  She is someone (who/that) people admire. (subject = people, object = she)
  That's the book (which/that) I bought for my sister. (subject = I, object = the book)
- You can't leave out the relative pronouns *where* or *whose*.
  *This is the stadium **where** my favourite team play.*
  NOT *This is the stadium my favourite team play.*
  *He's an actor **whose** mum was also famous.*
  NOT *He's an actor mum was also famous.*

Non-defining relative clauses

- Use a non-defining relative clause to give extra information in a sentence. The sentence would still make sense if you removed it.
  *That dress, **which** she made herself, is so beautiful.*
  *Mr Ruda, **who** taught maths, has left the school.*
- Use commas to separate a non-defining relative clause from the main part of the sentence.
  Those clothes, which you bought online, are so lovely.
  My sister, who lives in South Africa, works as a chef.
- You can't use *that* in non-defining relative clauses.
  *My friend Khalid, **who** I went to school with, has just moved in next door.*
  NOT *My friend Khalid, that I went to school with, has just moved in next door.*

- In non-defining relative clauses, you can't leave out the relative pronouns.
  My brother, who you met last week, has six children.
  NOT *My brother, you met last week, has six children.*
  My neighbour, whose brother I work with, has sold her house.
  NOT *My neighbour, brother I work with, has sold her house.*

1 Choose the correct option to complete the sentences.
  1 I found a new job *which / where* allows me to work from home.
  2 The fried rice *whose / that* I ordered is very spicy.
  3 The building, *which / who* was built in 1789, is the most beautiful place in the city.
  4 I'm looking for someone *whose / who* surname is Yoon.
  5 This is the shop *where / which* I bought that lovely second-hand dress.
  6 That chef, *who / whose* makes the town's famous buttery pancakes, is well-known.

8C Comparatives

Adverbs

- Use comparative adverbs to make comparisons between two verbs, adjectives or phrases.
- With adverbs ending in *-ly*, use *more/less* + adverb.
  *This fryer cooks food **more quickly** than an oven does.*
  *Can you talk **less loudly** on the phone in a public place, please?*
- With short adverbs that don't end in *-ly*, use adverb + *-er*.
  *Owen runs **faster** than anyone else on the team.*
  *Sit up **straighter**.*
- Use *much, a lot, a little* and *slightly* to make adverbs stronger or weaker. They explain how big the difference between two things is.
  *You drive **much better** than I do!*
  *He explains things **a lot more slowly** than other teachers.*

Adjectives

- Use comparative adjectives to make comparisons between two people or things.

Remember!
To form comparative adjectives:

One syllable → + -er	longer, higher
Ending in -y, remove -y and add -ier	happier, angrier
Two or more syllables → more + adj	more exciting, more interesting
Irregular	good → better, bad → worse, far → further

- Use *much / a lot* + comparative adjective to say there is a big difference.
  *He drives a **much faster** car than I do!*
  *His jacket is **a lot more expensive** than mine.*

- Use *a little / not much / slightly* + comparative adjective to say there is a small difference.
  *Science is **a little more interesting** for me than maths.*
  *The number of sales has been **slightly lower** than we expected.*

More or less the same

- Use *more or less the same (as)* to say something is almost the same or equal.
  *She's **more or less the same** age **as** me.*
  *Pierogi are **more or less the same as** jiaozi.*

(Not) as + adjective + as

- You can use *as* + adjective + *as* to say two things are equal.
  *Today's just **as hot as** yesterday.*
  *This jerk chicken is just **as spicy as** I make it at home.*

- Use *not as* + adjective + *as* to say two things are not equal.
  *The chocolate here **isn't as sweet as** in my country.*
  (= The chocolate in my country is sweeter than the chocolate here.)
  *This cake **isn't as fruity as** I expected.* (= I expected the cake to be fruitier.)

2 Match the beginning of the sentences (1–6) with the endings (a–f).

1 You're a lot more
2 Lara paints more
3 I don't think you're as
4 I think we've spent more
5 Ozlem needs to take things less
6 Amanda works just as

a seriously sometimes.
b beautifully than I ever could.
c old as I am!
d hard as everyone else in the team.
e experienced as a chef than you say on your CV.
f or less the same amount on our shopping trip today.

UNIT 9

9B   Third conditional

- Use the third conditional to talk about the consequences of an unreal or imaginary situation in the past. The situation and the result did not happen so cannot be changed.
  *If I **had gone** on holiday, I **would've been** able to relax.*
  (= I didn't go on holiday, so I couldn't relax.)
  *We **would have shown** you around the city **if** you **had stayed** with us.* (= You didn't stay with us, so I didn't show you around the city.)

- To form the third conditional, use *If* + past perfect, … *would (not) have* + past participle.
  *If I **had taken** the job, I **would've had** to travel a lot for work.*
  *If she **had picked** us up, we **wouldn't have been** late.*

Remember!
The past perfect is *had* + past participle.

- You can swap the order of the clauses. This doesn't change the meaning.
  If you'd told me, I would have come on holiday with you. → *I would have come on holiday with you if you'd told me.*
  If he'd helped me, I would have been able to put the tent up faster! → *I would have been able to put the tent up faster if he'd helped me!*

Remember!
When the *If* clause comes first, use a comma before the second clause.
If we had left earlier, we would have been on time.

- You can use other modal verbs instead of *would* to change the certainty of a result.
- Use *might* to mean *maybe*.
  *If I had known about the party, I **might** have gone.* (= I didn't know about it, so I didn't go.)
  *If I had gone to university, I **might** have had a different job.*
- Use *could* to mean something was a possibility.
  *If I had put more effort in, I **could** have been a professional dancer.* (= I didn't put effort in, so I didn't become a professional dancer.)
  *I **could** have fixed your laptop for you if you had told me it was broken.*

1 Match the beginning of the sentences (1–8) with the endings (a–h).

1 If our first flight had taken off on time,
2 He wouldn't have gone travelling
3 If we'd had more money when we were younger,
4 If I'd been born in the UK,
5 We would have rented a car
6 If we'd bought tickets to the show a few weeks earlier,
7 We could have had a beach picnic
8 If I'd booked the accommodation,

a if we'd known the roads were safe to drive on.
b we might have had a better view of the stage.
c we wouldn't have missed our next one.
d if he'd taken that job.
e I wouldn't have had to learn how to speak English.
f I could have found something more luxurious than this!
g if the weather had been better today.
h we might have tried to see the world a bit more.

Grammar reference

9C   Giving advice

- There are many different ways to give advice in English. You can use *should / shouldn't* + infinitive.
  *You **should go** to the dentist if you have toothache.*
  *He **shouldn't be** at work if he's ill.*

  Remember!
  Modal verbs such as *should* are never followed by *to*.
  You should ~~to~~ do your homework for tomorrow.

- You can also use *ought to* + infinitive. It cannot be used in a negative way.
  You ought to get some travel insurance for your trip.
  NOT ~~You ought to not get some travel insurance for your trip.~~

- You can use a second conditional with *If I were you, I would/ wouldn't* + infinitive. You are imagining yourself in the other person's position or situation and saying what you would or wouldn't do.
  If I were you, I would take that job offer.
  If I were you, I'd tell her the truth.

- You can swap the order of the clauses. This doesn't change the meaning.
  If I were you, I'd book the tickets early. → *I'd book the tickets early if I were you.*

- You can use *suggest / recommend* + *(not) -ing* to give more indirect advice.
  *I **suggest saving** a bit more money for the holiday.*
  *He **recommends booking** that hotel. He says it's lovely.*

- You can also use *suggest/recommend (that)* + person + infinitive.
  *The waiter **recommended I try** the ramen noodles.*
  *He **suggested that we book** a room on the top floor as it has better views.*

1 Complete the sentences with these words.

| eat   if   making   ought   pack   should   that   travelling |

1 You _____ call him to apologize for what you said.
2 You _____ to drive more slowly in this weather.
3 My brother suggested _____ a reservation for dinner tonight.
4 Ciara suggested _____ I email the airline about my lost luggage.
5 I would see a doctor _____ I were you.
6 This blog recommends _____ around Thailand in December.
7 I shouldn't _____ too much now because I'm going out for dinner later.
8 You ought to _____ a sleeping bag if you're going camping.

UNIT 10

10B   Passives

- In active sentences, the focus is on the person or thing that does the action (the agent). Form active sentences with subject + verb (+ object).
  I developed a new technology.
  He left the window open.

- In passive sentences, the focus is on the action and not who or what did it. This is because the action is not important, not obvious or unknown.

- Form passive sentences with *be* + past participle. Only the form of *be* changes to make the tense. The passive can be used in any tense.

present simple	*am/are/is* + past participle	*Flour **is used** for baking.*
present continuous	*am/are/is being* + past participle	*The virtual-reality headset **is being used** by the students.*
past simple	*was/were* + past participle	*The telephone **was created in** the late 1800s.*
past continuous	*was/were being* + past participle	*The kitchen **was being painted**.*
present perfect	*have/has been* + past participle	*Hearing aids **have been used** since the 1950s.*
past perfect	*had been* + past participle	*The key **had been lost**.*
future simple	*will be* + past participle	*A new technology **will be developed**.*

- You can also use modals (*might, could*, etc.) before *be* + past participle.
  *My laptop **couldn't be fixed** easily.*
  *The homework **should be done** by Friday.*

- Use the object of an active sentence as the subject in a passive sentence.
  *He built **a house**. (a house = object)*
  ***A house** was built. (a house = subject)*

- You can use the passive when you don't want to say who or what does the action. Maybe you don't know, or maybe it isn't important.
  Many people identified the colours as the same. → *The colours were identified as the same.*
  Someone robbed the jewellery store. → *The jewellery store was robbed.*

- Sometimes, you can add who or what did the action by using *by* + noun at the end of a passive sentence.
  *The song was being written **by her brother**.*
  *The house will be designed **by a famous architect**.*
- Passives are often used in formal writing.
  *When the hearing aid **was tested**, there was a significant difference in sound.*

1 Rewrite the sentences in the correct tense in the passive. Use *by* where necessary.

1 Somebody fixed the screen on my phone.

   _____

2 Fifty people have read my blog post. (by)

   _____

3 The cleaner is cleaning the house at the moment.

   _____

4 Erdem had already made reservations for dinner. (by)

   _____

5 Regina was playing the piano. (by)

   _____

6 I will send the email this afternoon.

   _____

10C   Making predictions

- You can use the modal verbs *will (not), may (not), might (not)* and *could (not)* + infinitive to make predictions about the future and to express how sure you are about your prediction.

Likely	Possible	Impossible

◀─────────────────────────────────────▶

will   *may (not), might (not), could (not)*   *will not*

*In ten years, there **will be** a lot more electric cars on the road.* (likely)
*In the future, we **may have** to use our face to access things.* (possible)
*Technology **will not develop** enough for people to smell things through a computer.* (impossible)

Remember!
Modal verbs such as *will, may, might* and *could* are never followed by *to*.
*In a few years, planes **might** ~~to~~ **be** quicker than they are today.*

- You can also make predictions about the future using *that* clauses, e.g. *It's likely/unlikely that … , It's possible that … , It's certain that …* and *It's impossible that … .*

It's …

100%   0%

◀─────────────────────────────────────▶

certain that   likely that   possible that   unlikely that   impossible that

It's certain that *technological changes will continue to happen.* (100%)
It's possible that *more people will travel to space.* (50%+)
It's impossible that *people will be able to time travel.* (0%)

2 Choose the best option to complete the sentences.

certain	impossible	likely	might	possible	won't

1 A: I hate traffic. I'd love this taxi to fly over all the other cars!
   B: Well, although it's _____ to do that right now, maybe it will happen in the future.

2 A: We _____ go on holiday this year, but we haven't decided yet. What about you?
   B: No, we _____ be going away because we're moving house and need to save money this year.

3 A: I wish I could control my phone with my mind. That would make everything so much faster!
   B: It's _____ that will be something mobile phones can do one day; they're already developing the technology.

4 A: I met her sister yesterday, so I know what she looks like. I'm _____ that's her.
   B: Yes! It's definitely her! Hi Abi!

5 A: Do you think people will live on the moon one day?
   B: I don't know – it's _____, but I'm not sure.

Irregular verbs

INFINITIVE	PAST SIMPLE	PAST PARTICIPLE
be	was/were	been
become	became	become
begin	began	begun
bite	bit	bitten
break	broke	broken
bring	brought	brought
build	built	built
burn	burned/burnt	burned/burnt
buy	bought	bought
catch	caught	caught
choose	chose	chosen
come	came	come
cost	cost	cost
cut	cut	cut
deal	dealt	dealt
do	did	done
dream	dreamed/dreamt	dreamed/dreamt
drink	drank	drunk
drive	drove	driven
eat	ate	eaten
fall	fell	fallen
feel	felt	felt
fight	fought	fought
find	found	found
fly	flew	flown
forget	forgot	forgotten

INFINITIVE	PAST SIMPLE	PAST PARTICIPLE
forgive	forgave	forgiven
get	got	got
give	gave	given
go	went	gone/been
grow	grew	grown
have	had	had
hear	heard	heard
hide	hid	hidden
hit	hit	hit
hold	held	held
hurt	hurt	hurt
keep	kept	kept
know	knew	known
lead	led	led
leave	left	left
learn	learned/learnt	learned/learnt
lend	lent	lent
let	let	let
lie	lay	lain
lose	lost	lost
make	made	made
mean	meant	meant
meet	met	met
pay	paid	paid
put	put	put
read	read	read

INFINITIVE	PAST SIMPLE	PAST PARTICIPLE
ride	rode	ridden
ring	rang	rung
rise	rose	risen
run	ran	run
say	said	said
see	saw	seen
sell	sold	sold
send	sent	sent
set	set	set
shake	shook	shaken
show	showed	shown
sing	sang	sung
sit	sat	sat
sleep	slept	slept
smell	smelled/ smelt	smelled/ smelt
speak	spoke	spoken
spell	spelled/ spelt	spelled/ spelt

INFINITIVE	PAST SIMPLE	PAST PARTICIPLE
spend	spent	spent
spread	spread	spread
stand	stood	stood
steal	stole	stolen
stick	stuck	stuck
swim	swam	swum
take	took	taken
teach	taught	taught
tell	told	told
think	thought	thought
throw	threw	thrown
understand	understood	understood
wake	woke	woken
wear	wore	worn
win	won	won
write	wrote	written

Extra speaking tasks

PAGE 42, 3D, EXERCISE 3

Mostly As: Giving in

You often put the needs of others before your own. Relationships are important to you and you prefer to give in and let others have their way if it's what makes them happy. Giving in too often can mean that your own needs are not looked after and problems aren't solved.

Mostly Bs: Avoiding

You don't like conflict and you prefer to avoid it completely by walking away from situations, changing the subject of conversations and not sharing your negative thoughts or feelings about things. Problems that aren't solved can cause bigger issues for the relationship in the future.

Mostly Cs: Working together

You believe that by discussing the problem and by listening and understanding the other points of view, you can find a creative solution where everyone, including yourself, is satisfied. However, this takes a lot of time and effort from all the people involved and resolving every conflict this way can be exhausting.

Mostly Ds: Forcing

When there's a conflict, you want people to see your point of view and realize that they actually agree with you. You sometimes feel like people don't listen to you and you need to push your opinions across. This can be tiring for everyone and might damage relationships.

Mostly Es: Compromising

You believe that in life 'you win some, you lose some' and we can never be 100 per cent satisfied. When there's a conflict, everyone needs to give a little so that we can meet halfway. Although this approach takes less time and effort than 'Working together', there's no real understanding of the different sides of the story and some people may still be dissatisfied with the suggested solution.

PAGE 123, 10B, EXERCISE 11

STUDENT B

Answer Student A's questions. Use the passive voice.

Cheong Wa Dae – South Korea's Blue House

- Builders built the new main building between 1989 and 1991.
- They used 150,000 traditional blue Korean tiles for the roofs of all the buildings.
- They built it as a home, office and press centre for the president of South Korea.
- The presidents of South Korea have lived and worked in the building since 1991.
- Leaders from all over the world have visited the Blue House.
- Tourists visit parts of the Blue House on official tours.

PAGE 90, 7D, EXERCISE 2

Count the points your answers got. How many points do you have in total?

1 a – 2; b – 1

2 a – 1; b – 2

3 a – 1; b – 2

4 a – 1; b – 2

5 a – 2; b – 1

If you have eight points or more, you probably have a Whole-to-Part way of looking at things. You usually start by looking at the big picture, the context and the overall idea before focusing on the individual parts. You tend to think that things happen because of situations and things that surround them and people don't always have control over them. You often pay attention to how relationships, e.g. the mother and child, the wheel and the car, affect a situation. You believe that everything is connected and dependent on each other.

If you have seven points or fewer, you probably have a Part-to-Whole way of looking at things. You usually start by looking at the individual parts before thinking about how they work together. You tend to think of things in terms of their categories, e.g. tomatoes and apples are fruit because they have seeds, the wheel and the engine are parts of a car. You often focus on the specifics or the behaviour of a thing, e.g. the function of a wheel or the personality of an individual. You believe that if you can control the individual parts, you can control the whole unit.

PAGE 123, 10B, EXERCISE 10

STUDENT A

Answer Student B's questions. Use the passive voice.

Júzcar – Spain's blue village

- Sony Pictures, a film company, painted the village blue in 2011.
- The company used it as a location for filming *The Smurfs* film.
- The company chose the village because it's famous for mushrooms, which Smurfs love.
- The painters used 4,200 litres of blue paint.
- Sony was going to repaint the village after making the film, but the villagers decided to keep the blue.
- Fans of *The Smurfs* visit the village.

Audioscripts

UNIT 1

1.2

1 Here, my brothers are painting.
2 In this photo, we're singing.
3 I'm working in this photo.
4 My dad is cooking.

1.4

1

Anna: I used to live at home with my parents, so my life was very different. When I was a high-school student, I didn't use to be independent. I also wasn't too interested in school. I would often spend time with friends instead of doing my homework. Then when I was eighteen, I left home to start university, and of course I became a lot more independent. Now, I'm at university. I still have a busy social life, but now I'm also academic. I'm very interested in my studies in a way that I wasn't five years ago.

2

Erik: I'll be honest with you – I'm a messy person. I never clean the living room. I always leave the kitchen untidy. You may not believe it, but I used to be really organized. A few years ago, when I moved in with my two housemates, I would always do the washing up and put things away in the kitchen. I always tidied the living room. But after a few months, I realized that my two housemates wouldn't ever do any housework. I was doing all of it! So, I decided to leave some work for them. And guess what? They never did it. And neither did I!

3

Layla: I'm not so different from five years ago. I've always been ambitious. I used to be a sales rep. I worked hard and was very competitive. You have to be when you're selling things. The sales manager sets sales targets and the rep who sells the most each month gets extra money. A lot of people found it very difficult, but I loved it, because I love winning. The main difference between then and now is that now I'm the sales manager.

4

Wang Wei: I'm a very sociable person. I love talking to people and I love making new friends. So people are surprised when I tell them that I used to be shy. Not so long ago, in fact. For most of my life I would always feel nervous around people. Then about five years ago, I watched a TED Talk by Kare Anderson. She told her story of being shy and then opening her world by becoming interested in other people's talents. I started reading about how to deal with being shy and my world opened up too.

5

Luisa: I'm retired now, but I used to be a top manager in a firm of accountants. Of course I had to be sensible because every day I made important decisions about other people's money. But it's different being retired. After so many years of being sensible, I've decided to try being adventurous. Of course that means different things for different people, but for me it's finding interesting things to do and trying them. I've started a rock band with some people from the office and I've bought a motorcycle – a Harley Davidson. Some of my friends and family are a bit surprised, but I'm really enjoying the 'new me'!

UNIT 2

2.1

Popi: I've worked on penguin conservation for 31 years now. At the beginning, I used to collect penguins covered in the oil from ships. I wanted to help them, but I realized that I didn't have the necessary education and training. So, I decided to study biology at university. I studied for six years to obtain my first degree in Biology and then it took me another extra five years to finish my PhD. It was really hard because I was working as a tour guide at the same time. But it was because of this hard work that I finally got the skills I needed to become a researcher and conservationist. And it was because of this hard work that I can now study penguins and help protect the places where they eat and breed. I love my job. I've put in thousands of hours studying and learning about penguins worldwide and now, I'm able to share my findings with international audiences. I truly believe that if you have a clear goal and you keep working at it, you can achieve your dreams.

Teresa: I've always wanted to be a writer. But, for years, I never had the courage to actually start writing. One day, a friend suggested that I start a blog. At first, I was worried people wouldn't like it, but more and more people started reading it. They wrote to me saying they felt inspired by my writing. At that time, I was a sea captain, but I really wanted to become a full-time writer. So, I decided it was time to stop dreaming and to focus on becoming a writer. I went to school to study science journalism and then I got a job as a science writer for the news on television.

Audioscripts

Now, I'm a science and technology journalist. I've learned that writing is hard. But I believe if you have a goal, you can reach it by taking one small step at a time. I've taken many steps to becoming a full-time writer. It hasn't been easy, but I've managed to achieve that goal. Now, I have a new goal. I've learned that I love writing for radio. I've started suggesting radio stories to different radio stations. And, I've launched a podcast which will soon be on my regional radio station. I'm hoping this will lead to more writing opportunities.

🎧 2.4

E = Elisa, T = Theo

E: So how's life after leaving school?

T: It's not bad … I'm just anxious to get a job.

E: Yes, you said you wanted to talk to me about a job interview?

T: Yeah, I applied for this job and I have an interview this Thursday.

E: That's good news!

T: It's for this customer-service job for a mobile-gaming company.

E: Hmm! Sounds interesting.

T: The job involves working in a call centre and I have to work shifts.

E: Call-centre work can be hard. You have to talk to customers all the time.

T: That's what I like about it. I applied for the job because the job advert says I have to be good at talking to customers.

E: Yeah, I can imagine you'll be very good at that.

T: I like talking to different people.

E: Well, you must say that in your job interview.

T: I'll try. I'm a bit nervous about it. Do you have any tips for me?

E: Did you say your interview is on Thursday?

T: Yeah.

E: So, between now and Thursday, it'll be good for you to spend some time preparing for your interview.

T: Preparing? I've already sent them my CV. What else do I have to do?

E: You can't just go to the interview unprepared. You have to do your research on the company – find out what experience and skills are important for the job. For example, they might say they want someone who's familiar with how mobile games are developed.

T: Then I'll just lie and say I used to develop my own mobile games.

E: Oh Theo, you mustn't lie in a job interview. It'll look so bad if they find out!

T: Come on, I was just joking … So, it says in the job advert that they're looking for someone with good problem-solving skills.

E: Great. So, prepare a good story about a time when you solved a problem.

T: Hmm … I'll have to think about it.

E: And prepare some questions to ask them too.

T: I thought they ask the questions in a job interview?

E: You don't have to ask questions. But by asking smart questions, you can show them you're the right person for the job. For example, if they are talking about your problem-solving skills, you can ask them 'What sort of problems are typical in this job?'

T: That's a good question.

E: And make sure you dress smart for the interview. It's important to make a good first impression. You don't have to wear a suit or anything like that, but do put on a nice shirt.

T: I was thinking maybe a nice t-shirt and jeans? I don't have any nice shirts. Also, I have a basketball game before the interview and I definitely don't want to take an ironed shirt to the game.

E: Do you have to go to this game? You might need some time to prepare yourself before the interview. And you mustn't be late for the interview. I usually arrive ten minutes early for job interviews.

T: You're right. I didn't think about that. I'll call my friends and cancel the game. I must buy myself a new shirt too.

E: I'll take you shopping if you'd like.

T: Amazing, that would be so helpful! Thanks so much, Elisa.

UNIT 3

🎧 3.4

In South Africa's Kruger National Park, a team mostly consisting of women are working to save endangered animals from illegal hunting. They wear army-style uniforms and try to find and stop people who are killing elephants, lions, rhinos and other animals. But they don't use guns or try to arrest the criminals themselves. So what do they do?

The team work for four hours around sunrise and four hours around sunset – the time when the hunters and the animals are active. Travelling in groups of three, they carry out trips into the park either on foot or in vehicles. They watch and listen, and they don't let hunters move freely in the park. They block roads and make vehicles stop so they can search them. Usually there's no problem and they let the vehicles pass. But when they find something that doesn't seem right, they report what they've seen. Officers who can make arrests immediately come to deal with the problem. The simple fact that the Black Mambas are watching makes a lot of hunters stay away. As a result of their work, illegal hunting has fallen by more than seventy-five per cent.

Of course, this type of work requires training. Members work on their fitness by doing exercises and running. They've also learned about how to find and watch hunters, how to protect themselves from the weather in an emergency and how to survive with little food or water. And of course they've learned how to work as a team.

In addition to their work in the park, the Black Mambas also spend a lot of time in schools. They believe in the power of education to change the world and in teaching people from a young age that living animals are worth more than dead animals.

The women signed up to the Black Mambas when the group was formed because they were unemployed and needed a job. But now they know that being a Black Mamba is much more than just a job. The work is hard and sometimes dangerous, but they're not going to give up. As winners of the United Nations Champions of the Earth award, they're proud to belong to a team that's doing important work saving animals and making communities stronger.

UNIT 4

⌂ 4.1

Alison: The way we greet people can be so different in different countries. I travel a lot, so I have to be aware of the appropriate ways of greeting people. If I'm in the US, I usually shake hands. Often, I'll use two hands because it seems more friendly. If I'm in Europe, I give my European friends a kiss on each cheek. I lived in Nepal for many years and if I go back there again, I'll greet my friends there by putting my palms together and saying 'Namaste'. It's a bit like the Wai greeting in Thailand. But at home, I'm a big hugger. As soon as I see my friends and family, I hug them … Usually when I greet people, I hug them, unless I feel they don't want to hug me. I think recently, we've started greeting people without touching them in case they're trying to avoid contact for health reasons.

Andrej: There are many ways that I greet the different people in my life. In the Balkans, where I come from, we're very connected to each other and so we hug and kiss a lot. As soon as I see my grandmother, mother or sister, I kiss them on the cheek or on the head and hug them. And I always hug and high-five my grandpa and my father. I do the same with my colleagues and friends. It's a part of our culture. If they're female, we give them a hug and a kiss on their cheek. With men, as long as they are very close, they will hug each other. Otherwise, they will usually shake hands or give each other a high-five. I think it's also funny how we repeat these habits even if we're seeing someone for the fifth time that day. For example, if I see a colleague later today, I'll shake his hand or kiss her on the cheek again, no matter how many times we already greeted each other today.

⌂ 4.3

K = Kit, T = Thiago, Y = Yulia

Y: Kit, you're looking good!

T: Yeah you are!

Y: Something's different about you … I know what it is! I've never seen you in cycling shorts before!

K: Yeah, I've started cycling … and changing some of my routines. I'm trying to do things … differently, you know.

T: Oh? Like what?

K: Well, I was getting fed up with feeling tired every day. I wasn't getting enough sleep, and I was staying indoors too much and not getting enough exercise. It's hard working from home because I end up not going out at all. I was just spending way too many hours sitting at my desk.

Y: So what did you do?

K: I just decided that I've had enough of being unhealthy. But it's hard to make big changes, you know?

T: Yeah, it's hard to break a habit.

K: I'm not good at sports – I don't go to the gym or anything like that. I was a bit scared of exercise, I think. So I told myself, 'Start small!' And I found this YouTube exercise channel with short ten-minute workouts. So I committed to doing this before breakfast every morning. I put it in my calendar and told my wife about it.

Y: Is ten minutes enough?

T: Oh, ten minutes of high-energy exercises can be really effective. Plus a little exercise every day is better than nothing!

K: Exactly. Then I started to take a thirty-minute walk after lunch every day. And that made me feel good, so I bought a bike and started cycling twice a week.

T: So you're getting plenty of fresh air now! That'll help you sleep at night.

K: I've also started putting less sugar in my tea. I used to have three teaspoons of sugar …

Y: Three teaspoons?! That's a lot of sugar!

K: I know. And I drink so much tea when I'm working! I now put only a tiny bit of sugar in my tea.

Y: How tiny is tiny? Half a teaspoon?

K: No, half a teaspoon is too little for me! But I'm OK with one teaspoon.

Audioscripts

T: You've done well cutting it down to one. Drinking too much tea isn't good for you either – all that caffeine …

Y: I need to cut down on caffeine too. I drink lots of coffee. In fact, I probably need to stop drinking coffee!

K: I wouldn't cut coffee out completely though. I think it's important to have the things you like sometimes.

T: You must feel so proud of yourself, Kit! Do you reward yourself for all this hard work?

K: I do! They say it's important to reward yourself so that you stay motivated. So I reward myself with a book for each week of exercise.

Y: That's great! Books are a much better reward than coffee anyway!

🎧 4.4

K = Kit, T = Thiago

1

K: I wasn't getting enough sleep and I was staying indoors too much and not getting enough exercise. It's hard working from home because I end up not going out at all.

2

K: I don't go to the gym or anything like that. I was a bit scared of exercise, I think. So, I told myself, 'Start small!' And I found this YouTube exercise channel with short ten-minute workouts.

3

K: So I committed to doing this before breakfast every morning. I put it in my calendar and told my wife about it.

4

K: … half a teaspoon is too little for me. But I'm OK with one teaspoon.

T: You've done well cutting it down to one.

UNIT 5

🎧 5.1

Nirupa: When I was in high school in Singapore, I was in the school choir. We sang in a few different languages, including Chinese and Japanese. This really excited me, because I hadn't learned much about those cultures when I was growing up in India. One of my favourite songs was Japanese – *Yoru*, which means night. The tune is unusual and brings out feelings of danger and mystery and makes you think of the night-time. However, near the end of the song it becomes bright and makes you think of the morning. Then all of the parts of the choir sing together like the rising sun. It was incredibly exciting every time we made that final sound!

I personally find a lot of classical art boring, especially classical portraits. The technical skill of the painters is amazing and I love artists like Johannes Vermeer, who paint unusual subjects. But a lot of other portraits all feel very similar. If I see them all together in a museum, I must admit that I feel a little bored. The South Korean film *Parasite* by director Bong Joon-Ho was really interesting. The film is a thriller and dark comedy that discusses issues in society such as class and money. Although the story is entertaining and full of surprises, the final message is serious and strong. I'm interested in the idea of using an entertaining, humorous film to discuss difficult subjects and to make people think.

🎧 5.2

Alyea: I feel excited by contemporary African dance. In Trinidad and Tobago, there are so many performance artists and dancers who are influenced by traditional West African dance, along with Caribbean and European styles. I attended a play called *Ti-Jean and His Brothers.* The dancers moved their legs like the ocean and opened their hands like they were trying to grab the world. The music is filled with drums and shouting and makes you want to jump and move as well. It's so exciting. You can feel each beat in your heart and through your body and it makes everyone want to move.

From when I was a young girl, I've loved different kinds of art and for me, no artwork is boring. However, there are certain types of art that I'm not very interested in, for example, paintings from the 1800s. Despite the fact that these paintings don't really interest me, I still appreciate the story they tell and respect their beauty. The most interesting art I've seen was at the carnival festival in Trinidad. There's a competition for the best costume and people make some amazing clothes for the event. I met a woman who made a dress from things she had at home, in order to help the environment. She recycled old toilet-paper rolls, spoons and tablecloths from a party, and old cereal boxes she painted gold. The dress was amazing!

🎧 5.3

1

Nirupa: The tune is unusual and brings out feelings of danger and mystery and makes you think of the night-time. However, near the end of the song it becomes bright and makes you think of the morning.

2

Nirupa: The technical skill of the painters is amazing, and I love artists like Johannes Vermeer, who paint unusual subjects. But a lot of other portraits all feel very similar. If I see them all together in a museum, I must admit that I feel a little bored.

3

Nirupa: Although the story is entertaining and full of surprises, the final message is serious and strong.

4

Alyea: From when I was a young girl, I've loved different kinds of art and for me, no artwork is boring. However, there are certain types of art that I'm not very interested in, for example, paintings from the 1800s.

5

Alyea: Despite the fact that these paintings don't really interest me, I still appreciate the story they tell and respect their beauty.

🎧 **5.6**

1

  a Good morning?

  b Good morning!

2

  a Art is <u>fun</u>!

  b Art is fun.

3

  a This painting is <u>very</u> interesting …

  b This painting is very … interesting.

4

  a Well, I'm not <u>really</u> into poetry.

  b Well, I'm not really into <u>poetry</u>.

UNIT 6

🎧 **6.1**

Rubén: I was born in Spain. In 2015, I started travelling around the world for two years before moving to Mexico. I immediately felt at home here and decided to stay. I've been living in Mexico for more than three years now and I love it here. The people are very friendly and I've learned so much from them about their history and culture. Because I speak Spanish, it's easy to have conversations, but the Spanish from Spain is very different from Mexican Spanish. I've been practising and I've learned many new words and sayings since I got here. I've been learning a lot about Mexican art too. They have such a variety of art here, from 3,000-year-old pyramids to modern prints. I've also really liked trying the different types of food here. There are so many flavours and colours in every dish! Unlike Spanish food, the food here is very spicy. They have 150 types of chillies! But I'm lucky because my mother has been cooking spicy food for me since I was a child and I love it! I must say, I miss my family and friends back in Europe, but I've been travelling back to visit once a year. That's very important to me.

🎧 **6.2**

Gena: I've been living in Bogotá for about a year and a half, but I've lived in Colombia for more than six years. I'd taken Spanish lessons in school in the US, but when I moved to Ecuador twelve years ago, I needed to put my Spanish into practice. I've been speaking Spanish since then, so I'm quite comfortable speaking in Spanish. I love the feeling of excitement that comes with moving to a new place. I love being surprised by new things – the sights, smells, habits, food, etc. I think one of the difficult things about moving to a new place is that it can be stressful. You have to get to know a new place and it can be easy to get lost. Because I live by myself, it can be lonely sometimes. Occasionally, you wish there was someone to experience all the new things with!

🎧 **6.6**

L = Leonora, Y = Yongsheng

  L: Yongsheng, did you see that kid dressed as a lion?

  Y: Yeah, she looked so cute!

  L: You know, when I was kid, I thought I saw some lions in the woods.

  Y: Really?

  L: Yeah. It's a funny story, actually.

  Y: What happened?

  L: Well, I used to live in a suburb close to a large school. And on special occasions, like festivals, kids used to dress up to go to school.

  Y: Sounds like fun!

  L: On the road going past the school, there were these woods. During the school holidays, I'd cycle into the woods with my friends to play by the river.

  Y: Uh huh.

  L: One day, we were playing hide and seek – you know that game where one person counts and everyone hides?

  Y: Yes! We call it *zhuomicang*.

  L: We call it *nascondino* in Italian. Anyway, I climbed up a tree. No one could find me. Twenty minutes later, I was still there. That was when I saw the lions! There were these boys dressed up as lions. They were coming from the school. At that time, I didn't know this. I thought they were real lions.

  Y: What did you do?

  L: I waited for the lions to go away and then I climbed down really quietly to tell my friends. But they'd got tired of looking for me and they'd all gone home!

  Y: Without you?! That's terrible!

  L: The next day, I tried to tell them I saw three lions and they all just laughed. I was so upset.

  Y: Oh Leonora, you poor thing!

  L: Thinking about it now, it's kind of amazing how our parents let us go everywhere on our own back then.

Audioscripts

Y: Yeah, my parents were the same. I'd walk for thirty minutes to go to my friends' houses. All on my own. Once, I was like eight years old, and one evening, I was walking to my friend's house, when I noticed this cute grey cat behind me. I lived near a market and I thought it was one of the cats that hang around the market stalls … So, there was this cute cat. It looked at me and I smiled at it. Then, I went across the road. And the cat went across the road. I went through a tunnel. The cat went through the tunnel. I jumped over a fence. It also jumped over the fence!

L: Was it following you? Maybe it liked you!

Y: My mother didn't allow me to have any pets, so I didn't want the cat to think I was taking it home with me.

L: So what did you do?

Y: I kept trying to walk away from it and it kept following me. I walked very quickly towards my friend's house and I saw that it was walking towards the house as well, so I started saying 'No, you can't come with me. Go! Go!' At that point, my friend opened the door and said, 'What are you doing to Wang Wang?'

L: Huh?

Y: The cat was her pet! My friend's pet! I'd never seen her cat before! I didn't even know she had a pet!

L: So it wasn't following you?

Y: No! It was just going home!

🎧 6.8

Situation A

My bookclub friends are sharing stories about their neighbours. I keep planning what I want to say, but before I get a chance to share my story, the topic of conversation has already moved on to something else.

Situation B

My group at my weekly dance class are arguing about the Spanish Armada. I have no idea if the Armada is an animal or a type of Spanish food.

Situation C

I have a new group of work colleagues and I want to break the ice. But when I try making jokes, everyone looks at me in surprise and they just smile uncomfortably.

Situation D

I'm listening to my classmates talking about football. I think they all speak amazing English and I feel a bit shy about my own English. I know they're going to ask me what I think in a minute.

UNIT 7

🎧 7.1

Francisco: In order to keep a good balance between work and family obligations I try to work out a realistic calendar and schedule. I try not work on weekends, when I can spend time with my kids – although I usually work on Sunday evenings.

My plans for the next few months include a trip to Guatemala to visit my father for a few weeks. I also hope to complete an article I'm writing. Later in the year, I look forward to taking a vacation to Guatemala with my children.

We will go there over the December holidays. We're going to go scuba diving. This is something we have done once before. We really had the best time together exploring the sea. I hope it will make up for the long time we had to spend apart lately. It's going to be a lot of fun!

🎧 7.2

Rebecca: In the next few months, I'm taking a few camping trips. It will probably be rainy because Vancouver gets very wet during the fall and winter, so most of the camping I do at that time will be in my car. We're going to put the seats of the car down and sleep in the back. We'll also set up a large covering so that we can cook and hang out outside even if it is raining. Bears are a big concern for me when I go camping, so we'll keep all the food in the car.

I'm also doing a backpacking trip with friends up to a lake high in the mountains of British Columbia. Backpacking means we won't use a car, so we're going to carry all of our gear in our backpacks. The trail will be very steep, so it's going to be pretty difficult! However, the views are going to be amazing at the top.

🎧 7.8

D = Dan, E = Elsa

D: What's next?

E: I want to talk about money and give some practical financial advice, Dan. I've been doing some research on credit cards and budgets. The question is: How can we avoid getting into trouble with money?

D: That sounds like information a lot of us could use.

E: I think it is. A growing number of people are using credit cards. Research by the World Bank shows that fifty per cent of Germans, sixty per cent of South Koreans, and more than eighty per cent of Canadians use a credit card and the numbers are increasing. A lot of people don't seem to have a balanced budget.

D: Can you explain what you mean by a balanced budget?

E: It's simple. When you earn more than you spend, your budget is balanced. But it's not always easy to achieve.

D: So what's your advice?

E: Most people would agree that before you begin balancing your budget, you need to have a budget to balance.

D: Makes sense.

E: I recommend starting with a budget for one month. Here's how you do it. First, write down the money you earn – for example your salary. You need to write down the money you spend – in three separate lists.

D: And the three lists are … ?

E: The first list is 'needs'. This is money for your monthly expenses such as your rent or mortgage, bills for electricity, water, gas. It also includes petrol for the car, food and so on.

D: The second list?

E: The second list is 'wants'. These are luxuries – things you enjoy, but don't really need. For instance, meals out in restaurants or going to the cinema.

D: And the final list?

E: The final list is 'savings'. This, of course, is money you don't use each month – money you put in the bank to save for the future. This might be saving for travel in the future, for when you stop working or for other goals. It also includes paying back borrowed money, for example paying off your credit card.

D: So now we have a budget – we know where our money goes. How do we balance it?

E: I did some more research for this. Financial experts Elizabeth Warren and Amelia Warren Tyagi developed the fifty–thirty–twenty budget rule.

D: The fifty–thirty–twenty budget rule.

E: It's simple. According to Warren and Tyagi, you should spend fifty per cent of your money on your needs, thirty per cent on your wants and you should put twenty per cent in your savings.

D: Fifty per cent on needs …

E: Thirty per cent on wants …

D: And twenty per cent in savings.

E: Right.

D: That's clear. I like it. But it could be hard for a lot of people.

E: Definitely. If you spend eighty per cent of your salary on your needs, then you have only twenty per cent left. If you're in this situation, I suggest looking at ways to reduce the money you spend on your needs. After that, you can begin to think about saving and buying luxuries.

D: Good advice!

UNIT 8

🎧 8.1

Mary: I don't buy clothes very often. In fact, a few years ago, I got so concerned about the clothing industry. The plastic in the materials which make these cheap clothes ends up in our seas and oceans. So I decided not to buy any new clothes for a year. I managed it easily. I wear my clothes for a long time. I've worn the shirt that I wear for fieldwork for about twenty years! I really enjoy finding ways to make my clothes last longer.

The infographic shows us that we currently produce ten new pieces of clothing a year for every person on this planet. It's just not possible that we need so many clothes! There are some people who don't buy many new clothes, like me. And most people around the world can't afford to buy ten new pieces of clothing every year. So that means that there are people out there who are buying hundreds of pieces of clothing every year!

Manufacturers say they make more clothes because people are buying more clothes. And people are buying more clothes because of fast fashion, which is cheap and fashionable.

It's terrible to see that we throw away clothes that have only been worn about seven times. All of these clothes usually end up in landfills, which are areas of land where rubbish is buried. And fast fashion is often made of materials which contain plastic. So every year, millions of pieces of plastic are going into our environment through landfills!

I think there are two things that we can do about clothing waste. We can buy second-hand clothes instead of new clothes, or we can start shopping less but buying better quality clothes. If we spent more on clothes, we'd probably take better care of them and use them more instead of throwing them away. We must remember to reuse and recycle our clothes and protect our planet.

🎧 8.3

1 I believe people should sell the clothes that they don't use.

2 I can't understand these people who throw away clothes after wearing them once or twice.

3 It's better to give away clothes than to throw them away.

Audioscripts

🎧 8.4

C = Chati, D = Desirée, J = Jamie

C: Desirée, Jamie, have you heard? Pierre is moving to Thailand and he said he's going to pack a suitcase full of French cheese to take with him. He can probably get it more easily in France too.

J: Is it hard to get cheese in Thailand?

C: You can get cheese here, but I guess the cheese in France is not as expensive as the cheese in Thailand.

D: I know how he feels. When I moved here, I brought a bag full of arepa flour.

J: What's arepa?

D: They're like thick pancakes made from flour that's made from cooked corn.

C: Couldn't you use normal flour?

D: You can use the corn flour they use for Mexican tortillas. If you mix yellow and white corn flour, it makes it slightly less bitter. But it's not the same. Making arepas with arepa flour is much better!

C: So are arepas a typical Venezuelan food?

D: Yes. They're very typical in lots of countries in the region, not just Venezuela. Colombia and Bolivia too … We eat them for breakfast, lunch or dinner. We just put different fillings in it – beans, meat, avocado … I love cheesy arepas. They're sooo good!

J: I love cheesy foods. I'll happily eat anything cheesy or creamy.

D: Like a creamy dessert?

J: I was thinking more like a warm, creamy Cullen skink.

C: What's Cullen skink?

J: It's a Scottish fish soup. You cook the fish in butter, milk and cream. It's amazing.

C: Sounds tasty! I like anything cooked in butter!

D: When I think of a buttery dish, I think of sweet desserts. I don't immediately think of salty or spicy food.

C: What about Indian butter chicken? Or buttery potatoes?

D: You're right. I guess I've just got sweet desserts on my mind. You say buttery, I think desserts. You say creamy, I think desserts …

J: Creamy desserts are nice too – like a cranachan.

C: A what?

J: A cranachan – it's a creamy Scottish dessert made with strawberries, raspberries and oats.

D: Ooh, nice! What about you, Chati? What food can't *you* live without?

C: I think for me it has to be sticky rice. We eat a lot of sticky rice in Thailand.

D: Sticky rice is really yummy! What do you have it with?

C: You can have sticky rice with any meat or vegetable. It goes really well with larb.

J: What's larb?

C: Larb is like a minced meat salad. You can use chicken, beef, whatever you like. After you fry the minced meat, you add lime juice, fish sauce, sweet chilli sauce, mint and lots of nice herbs. It's hot, salty, sweet and sour all at the same time.

J: Is that the one you wrap in lettuce?

C: Yes! Have you had it before?

J: I have! In a Laotian restaurant. I didn't know you have it in Thailand too.

C: Yeah, I think the larb in north-east Thailand is more or less the same as the larb in Laos. Did you like it?

J: I did! All those flavours come together so nicely. I've never had it with sticky rice though.

C: I make larb and sticky rice all the time. You should both come over for dinner one day!

UNIT 9

🎧 9.3

A = Alessia, B = Bogdan

A: So, Bogdan, you've got two weeks off work next week. What are you going to do with this time?

B: I don't know. All the flights to the popular holiday destinations have been booked up. I think I've left it too late to book anything.

A: If I were you, I'd pack my bags, jump into my car and go on a road trip.

B: Go on a road trip? Where to?

A: Anywhere! Just decide on a direction and start driving!

B: You're kidding.

A: No, I'm serious. Unplanned holidays can be really exciting!

B: How will I know where I'm going?

A: My advice is to just look up a map on your phone, pick a city, maybe even in a different country, and drive in that direction.

B: Don't I need to book my accommodation in advance?

A: You should just take a tent. Then all you need to do is find some camping sites along the way and put up your tent there!

B: Don't you have to book the campsites in advance though?

A: Some people do. But lots of people just turn up without a booking. I think you might need to book if it's a campsite with lots of facilities, like those campsites with their own supermarket, swimming pool, restaurants …

B: I didn't know campsites have their own supermarkets, swimming pools and restaurants!

A: There are all sorts of different campsites these days. I'd just find somewhere simple to put up my tent, like in a field or a forest somewhere.

B: I've never really gone camping before.

A: Really? You ought to try it! It's great fun! You get to sleep under the stars, spend time with nature and get lots of fresh air. It's so relaxing.

B: I'm not sure if I'll like sleeping on the hard ground. It'd be really bad for my back.

A: I suggest getting an air mattress – they're really comfortable. You'll feel like you're in your own bed! And I'd definitely recommend you bring a sleeping bag and a warm blanket. It can get cold at night.

B: Sounds like there's going to be a lot of planning that I'll need to do.

A: Not at all. I'll help you. I have lots of camping equipment that you can borrow.

B: Thanks … but I feel like I'd need to know more about where I'm going and what I'm going to do.

A: Not knowing is part of the adventure, isn't it? You can always speak to the locals when you get there. They will tell you all the best places to visit. Or you could check out websites like Tripadvisor or Trivago. They're quite good for travel recommendations.

B: Yeah, I often use these websites to get ideas when I'm planning a holiday. I think I'm more of a planner. I'm not sure if I'm comfortable with just jumping into my car and driving without a plan in mind.

A: You would hate going on holidays with me then!

🎧 9.6

L = Lee, P = Peter

L: So Peter, where are you from?

P: I'm from Haarlem in the Netherlands.

L: I've been to the Netherlands. Do you live there with your family?

P: Yes, I live with my parents.

L: Brothers and sisters?

P: No, I'm an only child.

L: Girlfriend?

P: No, no girlfriend at the moment.

L: What do you do for a living?

P: I'm a nurse.

L: That's a good job. You help people.

P: Yeah, I love my job.

🎧 9.7

I just met this guy called Lee. He was so weird and kind of aggressive. He stood really close to me and kept asking questions that were too personal. He made me feel really uncomfortable. Why did he want to know so much?

UNIT 10

🎧 10.1

When English speakers are shown these two colours, they identify both as blue. The one on the left may be called light blue and the one on the right dark blue, but they're seen as two shades of the same colour – they're both blue. However, researchers found that when users of Greek as a first language were asked to identify the colours, they said the colour on the left was *ghalazio* and the one on the right *ble* – two different colours. And perhaps more interestingly, it was also discovered that Greek speakers who had lived in the UK for several years and used English regularly became less able to separate *ghalazio* and *ble* accurately. The reason? They'd become used to referring to both colours as blue. Their way of seeing had been influenced by using English. Greek isn't the only language with at least two words for blue. The same is true for Russian, Italian, Korean and other languages too.

🎧 10.3

We humans use technology to improve and extend our senses every day. Glasses are simple technology to improve our eyesight. For people who can't see, a smartphone app can recognize faces and even read people's emotions. In addition to hearing aids, deaf people can use apps that listen to speech and turn it into writing so they can read it. The internet also extends our senses, allowing us to see and hear people who may be thousands of kilometres away. The technology of the senses is part of our everyday life.

So what's next? What developments will we see in the future?

It's likely that in the next ten years, in addition to seeing and hearing things online, we will also be able to use our other senses online. This could allow us, for example, to use our sense of touch by wearing a glove or using some other device with our hands. Of course, we won't be able to do things like try clothes on, but we may be able to feel the quality of a shirt before we buy it in an online shop.

It's likely that we'll be able to experience the scent of a flower online, or trees, or cold wind in the mountains using a kind of virtual reality that includes the nose and technology for producing scents.

It's also possible that we'll taste things online – your friend might be able to send you the flavour of a delicious fruit, or when you look at your holiday photos, you might experience the flavour of the delicious meal you had.

The technology is improving every day. Online connections between people are becoming more important and our ability to extend our senses is becoming greater.

Now I'd like to look more closely at …

Audioscripts

A: That was an interesting talk. Do you think all of those predictions will come true?

B: I think it's likely that the technology will be developed, but it's unlikely that everyone will be able to use it.

A: What do you mean?

B: You'll need special devices to use the internet of senses – gloves so you can touch things or a computer that produces scents. That stuff will be expensive.

A: Yeah, I guess you're right. I mean, virtual reality is possible now, but it might be a long time before everyone uses it because it costs a lot.

B: Right. Of course it's likely that it will become cheaper. Then more people might buy it.

A: I like the idea of drying clothes online.

B: Drying clothes … ?

A: Trying – t – trying on clothes online. But I think it's unlikely.

B: Yeah, but it would make shopping easier!

B = Beyza, F = Fabio

F: You said you needed to talk? What's up?

B: I'm just so exhausted. And I feel I need to talk to someone about it.

F: Yeah, I know what you mean. I'm really exhausted too. But, hey you're a strong person, you'll be fine!

B: I haven't been feeling that strong recently. Since I started working from home, I feel like I'm constantly dealing with either the kids or housework or work …

F: Yeah, I'm exactly the same. I think my boss doesn't trust me working from home. He wants reports and meetings every day to check on what I'm doing.

B: My problem is trying to manage work, and kids and housework at the same time. You know, when I had to go to the office …

F: If I were you, I'd prioritize. Consider what's most urgent and do that first.

B: But when you're managing a home, everything is always urgent. There are always dinners to cook, kids' teeth to brush … It's all so stressful.

F: Don't get stressed. You must teach your kids to do things themselves.

B: That's true. I think the problem is I just always put everybody's needs above my own. And then I feel …

F: Exactly! Don't do that!

B: But I don't want to feel like I'm being a selfish person.

F: You're not selfish! You're one of the most generous people I know!

B: Thanks.

F: Listen, I believe in you.

B: Thanks, Fabio.

F: And you can always come to me when you have a problem, OK?

B: OK.

B = Beyza, F = Fabio

F: You said you needed to talk? What's up?

B: I'm just so exhausted. And I feel I need to talk to someone about it.

F: Go on, I'm listening.

B: Since I started working from home, I feel like I'm constantly dealing with either the kids or housework or work. You know, when I had to go to the office, I had the journey on the bus to get ready for work or to think about my day. But now I'm just going straight from work to cooking dinners and dealing with the kids.

F: That sounds tough.

B: When you're managing a home, there's always things to do. It never ends. It's all so stressful.

F: Why exactly is it stressful?

B: It's just stressful, isn't it? Looking after kids and working …

F: Hmm …

B: I guess I just feel like everyone's depending on me to do things for them. Everything's always so urgent.

F: Is it always urgent?

B: Not always … You know what I need? I need some time for myself. That makes me a selfish person, doesn't it?

F: What makes you think that?

B: I don't know. Focusing on myself seems like a selfish thing to do … but I need to help myself before I can help others, right?

F: What do you need to do to make that happen?

B: I want to spend more time doing the things I love. Play the guitar, dance the samba, paint some pictures.

F: What's stopping you from doing those things?

B: Time? I guess I can get some help with the housework and the kids and make more time for myself. You know what, maybe I should start small … I used to take the bus to work, I could use this time to take a walk instead. That would give me some time to myself. Thank you, Fabio. You're such a good listener.

F: No, thank *you* for sharing.

Acknowledgements

The *Voices* publishing team would like to thank all of the explorers for their time and participation on this course – and for their amazing stories and photos.

The team would also like to thank the following teachers, who provided detailed and invaluable feedback on this course.

Asia

SS. Abdurrosyid, University of Muhammadiyah Tangerang, Banten; Hằng Ánh, Hanoi University of Science Technology, Hanoi; Yoko Atsumi, Seirei Christopher University, Hamamatsu; Dr. Nida Boonma, Assumption University, Bangkok; Portia Chang, SEE Education, New Taipei City; Brian Cullen, Nagoya Institute of Technology, Nagoya; David Daniel, Houhai English, Beijing; Professor Doan, Hanoi University, Hanoi; Kim Huong Duong, HCMC University of Technology, Ho Chi Minh; Natalie Ann Gregory, University of Kota Kinabalu, Sabah; Shawn Greynolds, AUA Language Centre, Bangkok; Thi Minh Ly Hoang, University of Economics – Technology for Industries, Hanoi; Mike Honywood, Shinshu University, Nagano; Jessie Huang, National Central University, Taoyuan City; Edward Jones, Nagoya International School, Nagoya; Ajarn Kiangkai, Sirnakarintrawirote University, Bangkok; Zhou Lei, New Oriental Education & Technology Group, Beijing; Louis Liu, METEN, Guangzhou; Jeng-Jia (Caroline) Luo Tunghai University, Taichung City; Thi Ly Luong, Huflit University, Ho Chi Minh City; Michael McCollister, Feng Chia University, Taichung; Robert McLaughlin, Tokoha University, Shizuoka; Hal Miller, Houhai English, Beijing; Jason Moser, Kanto Gakuin University, Yokohama; Hudson Murrell, Baiko Gakuin University, Shimonoseki; Takayuki Nagamine, Nagoya University of Foreign Studies, Nagoya; Sanuch Natalang, Thammasart University, Bangkok; Nguyen Bá Học, Hanoi University of Public Health, Hanoi; Nguyen Cong Tri, Ho Chi Minh City University of Technology, Ho Chi Minh; Nguyen Ngoc Vu, Hoa Sen University, Ho Chi Minh City; Professor Nguyen, Hanoi University, Hanoi; Dr Nguyen, Hao Sen University, Ho Chi Minh City; Nguyễn Quang Vịnh, Hanoi University, Hanoi; Wilaichitra Nilsawaddi, Phranakhon Rajabhat University, Bangkok; Suchada Nimmanit, Rangsit University, Bangkok; Ms. Cao Thien Ai Nuong, Hoa Sen University, Ho Chi Minh City; Donald Patterson, Seirei Christopher University, Shizuoka; Douglas Perkins, Musashino University Junior and Senior High School, Tokyo; Phan The Hung, Van Lang University, Ho Chi Minh City; Fathimah Razman, Northern University, Sintok, Kedah; Bruce Riseley, Holmesglen (Language Centre of University Of Muhammadiyah Tangerang for General English), Jakarta; Anthony Robins, Aichi University of Education, Aichi; Greg Rouault, Hiroshima Shudo University, Hiroshima; Dr Sawaluk, Sirnakarintrawirote University, Bangkok; Dr Supattra, Rangsit University, Lak Hok; Dr Thananchai, Dhurakijbundit University, Bangkok; Thao Le Phuong, Open University, Ho Chi Minh; Thap Doanh Thuong, Thu Dau Mot University, Thu Dau Mot; Kinsella Valies, University of Shizuoka, Shizuoka; Gerrit Van der Westhuizen, Houhai English, Beijing; Dr Viraijitta, Rajjabhat Pranakorn University, Bangkok; Dr Viraijittra, Phranakhon Rajabhat University, Bangkok; Vo Dinh Phuoc, University of Economics, Ho Chi Minh City; Dr Nussara Wajsom, Assumption University, Bangkok; Scott A.Walters, Woosong University, Daejon; Yungkai Weng, PingoSpace & Elite Learning, Beijing; Ray Wu, Wall Street English, Hong Kong.

Europe, Middle East and Africa (EMEA)

Saju Abraham, Sohar University, Sohar; Huda Murad Al Balushi, International Maritime College , Sohar; Salah Al Hanshi, Modern College of Business and Science, Muscat; Victor Alarcón, EOI Badalona, Barcelona; Yana Alaveranova, International House, Kiev; Alexandra Alexandrova, Almaty; Blanca Alvarez, EOI San Sebastian de los Reyes, Madrid; Emma Antolin, EOI San Sebastian de los Reyes, Madrid; Manuela Ayna, Liceo Primo Levi, Bollate, Milan; Elizabeth Beck, British Council, Milan; Charlotte Bentham, Adveti, Sharjah; Carol Butters, Edinburgh College, Edinburgh; Patrizia Cassin, International House, Milan; Elisabet Comelles, EIM - Universitat de Barcelona, Barcelona; Sara De Angeles, Istituto Superiore Giorgi, Milan; Carla Dell'Acqua, Liceo Primo Levi, Bollate, Milan; John Dench, BEET Language Centre, Bournemouth; Angela di Staso, Liceo Banfi, Vimercate, Milan; Sarah Donno, Edinburgh College, Edinburgh, UK; Eugenia Dume, EOI San Sebastian de los Reyes, Madrid; Rory Fergus Duncan; BKC-IH Moscow, Moscow; Ms Evelyn Kandalaft El Moualem, AMIDEAST, Beirut; Raul Pope Farguell, BKC-IH Moscow, Moscow; Chris Farrell, CES, Dublin; Dr Aleksandra, Filipowicz, Warsaw University of Technology, Warsaw; Diana Golovan, Linguist LLC, Kiev, Ukraine; Jaap Gouman, Pieter Zandt, Kampen; Maryam Kamal, British Council, Doha; Galina Kaptug, Moonlight, Minsk; Ms Rebecca Nabil Keedi, College des Peres Antonines, Hadath; Dr. Michael King, Community College of Qatar, Doha; Gabriela Kleckova, University of West Bohemia, Pilsen; Mrs Marija Klečkovska, Pope John Paul II gymnasium, Vilnius; Kate Knight, International Language School, Milan; Natalia Kolina, Moscow; David Koster, P.A.R.K., Brno; Suzanne Littlewood, Zayed University, Dubai; Natalia Lopez, EOI Terrassa, Barcelona; Maria Lopez-Abeijon, EOI Las Rozas, Madrid; Pauline Loriggio, International House London, London; Gabriella Luise, International Language School Milan, Milan; Klara Malowiecka, Lang Ltc, Warsaw; Fernando Martin, EOI Valdemoro, Madrid; Robert Martinez, La Cunza, Gipuzkoa; Mario Martinez, EOI Las Rozas, Madrid; Marina Melnichuk, Financial University, Moscow; Martina Menova, PĚVÁČEK vzdělávací centrum, Prague; Marlene Merkt, Kantonsschule Zurich Nord, Zurich; Iva Meštrović, Učilište Jantar, Zagreb; Silvia Milian, EOI El Prat, Barcelona; Jack Montelatici, British School Milan, Milan; Muntsa Moral, Centre de Formació de Persones Adultes Pere Calders,

Acknowledgements

Barcelona; Julian Oakley, Wimbledon School of English, London; Virginia Pardo, EOI Badalona, Barcelona;

William Phillips, Aga Khan Educational Service; Joe Planas, Centre de Formació de Persones Adultes Pere Calders, Barcelona; Carmen Prieto, EOI Carabanchel, Madrid; Sonya Punch, International House, Milan; Magdalena Rasmus, Cavendish School, Bournemouth; Laura Rodríguez, EOI El Prat, Barcelona; Victoria Samaniego, EOI Pozuelo, Madrid; Beatriz Sanchez, EOI San Sebastian de los Reyes, Madrid; Gigi Saurer, Migros-Genossenschafts-Bund, Zurich; Jonathan Smilow, BKC-IH, Moscow; Prem Sourek, Anderson House, Bergamo; Svitlana Surgai, British Council, Kyiv; Peter Szabo, Libra Books, Budapest; Richard Twigg, International House, Milan; Evgeny Usachev, Moscow International Academy, Moscow; Eric van Luijt, Tilburg University Language Centre, Tilburg; Tanya Varchuk, Fluent English School, Ukraine; Yulia Vershinina, YES Center, Moscow; Małgorzata Witczak, Warsaw University of Technology, Warsaw; Susanna Wright, Stafford House London, London; Chin-Yunn Yang, Padagogische Maturitaetsschule Kreuzlingen, Kreuzlingen; Maria Zarudnaya, Plekhanov Russian University of Economics, Moscow; Michelle Zelenay, KV Winterthur, Winterthur.

Latin America

Jorge Aguilar, Universidad Autónoma de Sinaloa, Culiacán; Carlos Bernardo Anaya, UNIVA Zamora, Zamora; Sergio Balam, Academia Municipal de Inglés, Mérida; Josélia Batista, CCL Centro de Línguas, Fortaleza; Aida Borja, ITESM GDL, Guadalajara; Diego Bruekers Deschamp, Ingles Express, Belo Horizonte; Alejandra Cabrera, Universidad Politécnica de Yucatán, Mérida; Luis Cabrera Rocha, ENNAULT – UNAM, Mexico City; Bruna Caltabiano, Caltabiano Idiomas, Sao Paulo; Hortensia Camacho, FES Iztacala – UNAM, Mexico City; Gustavo Cruz Torres, Instituto Cultural México – Norteamericano, Guadalajara; Maria Jose D'Alessandro Nogueira, FCM Foundation School, Belo Horizonte; Gabriela da Cunha Barbosa Saldanha, FCM Foundation School, Belo Horizonte; Maria Da Graça Gallina Flack, Challenge School, Porto Alegre; Pedro Venicio da Silva Guerra, U-Talk Idiomas, São Bernardo do Campo; Julice Daijo, JD Language Consultant, Rua Oscar Freire; Olívia de Cássia Scorsafava, U-Talk Idiomas, São Bernardo do Campo; Marcia Del Corona, UNISINOS, Porto Alegre; Carlos Alberto Díaz Najera, Colegio Salesiano Anáhuac Revolución, Guadalajara; Antônio César Ferraz Gomes, 4 Flags, São Bernardo do Campo; Brenda Pérez Ferrer, Universidad Politécnica de Querétaro, Querétaro; Sheila Flores, Cetys Universidad, Mexicali; Ángela Gamboa, Universidad Metropolitana, Mérida; Alejandro Garcia, Colegio Ciencias y Letras, Tepic; Carlos Gomora, CILC, Toluca; Kamila Gonçalves, Challenge School, Porto Alegre; Herivelton Gonçalves, Prime English, Vitória; Idalia Gonzales, Británico, Lima; Marisol Gutiérrez Olaiz, LAMAR Universidad, Guadalajara; Arturo Hernandez, ITESM GDL, Guadalajara; Gabriel Cortés Hernandez, BP- Intitute, Morelia; Daniel Vázquez Hernández, Preparatoria 2, Mérida; Erica Jiménez, Centro Escolar, Tepeyac; Leticia Juárez, FES Acatlán – UNAM, Mexico City; Teresa Martínez, Universidad Iberoamericana, Tijuana; Elsa María del Carmen Mejía Franco, CELE Mex, Toluca; José Alejandro Mejía Tello, CELE Mex, Toluca; Óscar León Mendoza Jimenéz, Angloamericano Idiomas, Mexico City; Karla Mera Ubando, Instituto Cultural, Mexico City; Elena Mioto, UNIVA, Guadalajara; Ana Carolina Moreira Paulino, SENAC, Porto Alegre; Paula Mota, 4 Flags, São Bernardo do Campo; Adila Beatriz Naud de Moura, UNISINOS, Porto Alegre; Monica Navarro Morales, Instituto Cultural, Mexico City; Wilma F Neves, Caltabiano Idiomas, Sao Paulo; Marcelo Noronha, Caltabiano Idiomas, Sao Paulo; Enrique Ossio, ITESM Morelia, Morelia; Filipe Pereira Bezerra, U-Talk Idiomas, Sao Bernardo do Campo; Florencia Pesce, Centro Universitario de Idiomas, Buenos Aires, Argentina; Kamila Pimenta, CCBEU, São Bernardo do Campo; Leopoldo Pinzón Escobar, Universidad Santo Tomás, Bogotá; Mary Ruth Popov Hibas, Ingles Express, Belo Horizonte; Alejandra Prado Barrera, UVM, Mexico City; Letícia Puccinelli Redondo, U-Talk Idiomas, São Bernardo do Campo; Leni Puppin, Centro de Línguas de UFES, Vitória; Maria Fernanda Quijano, Universidad Tec Milenio, Culiacan; Jorge Quintal, Colegio Rogers, Mérida; Sabrina Ramos Gomes, FCM Foundation School, Belo Horizonte; Mariana Roberto Billia, 4 Flags, São Bernardo do Campo; Monalisa Sala de Sá 4 Flags, São Bernardo do Campo; Yamel Sánchez Vízcarra, CELE Mex, Toluca; Vagner Serafim, CCBEU, São Bernardo do Campo; Claudia Serna, UNISER, Mexicali; Alejandro Serna, CCL, Morelia; Simone Teruko Nakamura, U-Talk Idiomas, São Bernardo do Campo; Desirée Carla Troyack, FCM Foundation School, Belo Horizonte; Sandra Vargas Boecher Prates, Centro de Línguas da UFES, Vitória; Carlos Villareal, Facultad de Ingenierías Universidad Autónoma de Querétaro, Querétaro; Rosa Zarco Mondragón, Instituto Cultural, Mexico City.

US and Canada

Rachel Bricker, Arizona State University, Tempe; Jonathan Bronson, Approach International Student Center, Boston; Elaine Brookfield, EC Boston, Boston; Linda Hasenfus, Approach International Language Center, Boston; Andrew Haynes, ELS Boston, Boston; Cheryl House, ILSC, Toronto; Rachel Kadish, FLS International, Boston; Mackenzie Kerby, ELS Language Centers, Boston; Rob McCourt FLS Boston; Haviva Parnes, EC English Language Centres, Boston; Shayla Reid, Approach International Student Center, Boston.

Credits

Illustration: All illustrations are owned by © Cengage.

Text: p13 Nicole Lee. (2016, March 04). Having multiple online identities is more normal than you think. Retrieved from https://www.engadget.com/2016-03-04-multiple-online-identities.html; p13 Michael Zimmer. (2010, May 14). Facebook's Zuckerberg: 'Having two identities for yourself is an example of a lack of integrity'. Retrieved from https://www.michaelzimmer.org/2010/05/14/facebooks-zuckerberg-having-two-identities-for-yourself-is-an-example-of-a-lack-of-integrity/; p25 Fu Yuanhui's Greatest Moments (English subs). (2016, August 10). Retrieved from https://www.youtube.com/watch?v=Jn0nPGfH1HI and https://edition.cnn.com/2016/08/18/health/bronze-medal-psychology-olympics/index.html; p30 Covey, S. R. (2020). The 7 habits of highly effective people.; p60 Andy Warhol. (n.d.); p60 I. M. Pei. (n.d.); p60 Elizabeth Murray. (n.d.); p60 Arsène Wenger. (n.d.); p60 What is Hair Art? (n.d.);

Credits

p61 Paul McGuinness. (2020, June 29). Pop Music: The World's Most Important Art Form. Retrieved from https://www.udiscovermusic.com/in-depth-features/pop-the-worlds-most-important-art-form/; p61 Chris Melissinos. (2015, September 22). Video Games Are One of the Most Important Art Forms in History. Retrieved from https://time.com/collection-post/4038820/chris-melissinos-are-video-games-art/; p61 Emily Baillie. (2014, November 08). A Look at the Vibrant Street Art Scene in Buenos Aires, Argentina. Retrieved from https://untappedcities.com/2014/08/11/a-look-at-the-vibrant-street-art-scene-in-buenos-aires-argentina/; p61 Jonathan Bierman. (2009, May 28). Where Some Call Graffiti Art, Not Vandalism. Retrieved from https://abcnews.go.com/Travel/story?id=7697519&page=1; p73 Michael Safi. (January 18, 2019). 'I have lost my wallet and brother': reuniting at Kumbh Mela, the world's largest festival. Retrieved from https://www.theguardian.com/world/2019/jan/18/kumbh-mela-worlds-largest-festival-lost-and-found; p88 Gabriel García Márquez. (n.d.); p88 Margaret Walker. (n.d.); p97 Scott Kelly. (March 21, 2020). I Spent a Year in Space, and I Have Tips on Isolation to Share. Retrieved from https://www.nytimes.com/2020/03/21/opinion/scott-kelly-coronavirus-isolation.html; p97 A Hot Shower and a Hug. (n.d.). Retrieved from https://www.nasa.gov/audience/foreducators/k-4/features/F_Hot_Shower_and_Hug.html; p109 Ben Gateley. (n.d.). We tried unlimited holiday for three years. Here's everything that went wrong. Retrieved from https://www.charliehr.com/blog/we-tried-unlimited-holiday-heres-everything-that-went-wrong/; p121 Veronique Greenwood. (February 20, 2015). In the world of synaesthesia, words can be tasty and tastes can have physical shapes – but neuroscientists aren't quite sure why. Retrieved from https://www.bbc.com/future/article/20150204-the-man-who-tastes-words; p121 Holly Baxter. (June 13, 2016). What It's Like to Live With Synaesthesia. Retrieved from https://www.independent.co.uk/life-style/health-and-families/what-it-s-live-synaesthesia-a7079241.html; p121 Laura Barnett. (December 05, 2011). Synaesthesia: when two senses become one. Retrieved from https://www.theguardian.com/lifeandstyle/2011/dec/05/synaesthesia-hearing-colours-mixing-senses; p121 Helen Massy-Beresford. (April 26, 2014). How we all could benefit from synaesthesia. Retrieved from https://www.theguardian.com/science/2014/apr/27/benefit-synaesthesia-brain-injury-mental-decline